About the author

Barbara Tizard is a psychologist whose research has been concerned with children and adolescents. She has contributed to the study of residential children's homes and the long-term effects of residential care and adoption on development, and also to the study of the language of young children, early education, and adolescent identity. She has authored or co-authored six books on these topics. Her findings have thrown light, sometimes controversially, on issues to do with ethnic and gender differences in IQ, educational success and identity.

She has travelled extensively as consultant in early education and childcare for WHO and Save the Children. For ten years she was Director of the Thomas Coram Research Unit, a multidisciplinary unit concerned with policy relevant research into the education, care and health of young children and their families.

She is an Emeritus Professor of the Institute of Education, London, a Fellow of the British Psychological Society, an Honorary Member of the Association for Child and Adolescent Mental Health, and a Fellow of the British Academy.

Home is Where One Starts From

This is a remarkable book. Barbara Tizard's memoir of her childhood and youth in the 1940s is important for three reasons. First, it is a vivid personal story of a life that moves from West Ham working-class hardship and poverty to that of a distinguished and successful scientist. Second it is the story of a woman, mother of five children, who faced the prejudices, and constraints on their professional lives of women in the period. And third, she faced these prejudices so successfully, with a career of exceptionally creative original research into what makes real differences in children's lives. It is a splendid book.

JUDITH DUNN,
**Professor of Developmental Psychology,
Institute of Psychiatry, London.**

Barbara Tizard is a most distinguished child psychologist who has written a fascinating account of her childhood, adolescence and later career. Her memoir is full of perceptive comments about the world in which she grew up and about the many exceptional people she encountered during her eventful life. A great read!

PHILIP GRAHAM,
**Emeritus Professor of Child Psychiatry,
Institute of Child Health, London.**

The past is another and unknown country – in this case the years around the 1940s. In this memoir of a childhood and youth that took her from the world of West Ham Labour loyalties to Oxford and the life of a distinguished research scientist, Barbara Tizard has written both an exceptional personal story and that of a moment in British history. I know of no better guide to living and growing up in this period than this book, written with remarkable lucidity, economy and above all, honesty.

ERIC HOBSBAWM,
historian and President of Birbeck College, London.

In this candid memoir Barbara Tizard brings the finely honed powers of analysis that have made her one of the foremost psychologists of her generation to the telling of her own story. In doing so, she illuminates the ways in which social class, generation and gender intersected in women's lives in much of the twentieth century. Yet, this is no dry academic tome. It is an engaging story of a fascinating life, populated with vividly-drawn family and friends and contextualised in time and place. I found it hard to put down and thought provoking long after I had finished reading.

ANN PHOENIX,
Professor of Social and Developmental Psychology, Institute of Education, London.

A wonderful, highly engaging book by one of the country's most distinguished developmental psychologists. Barbara Tizard skillfully weaves three overlapping and interconnected stories into a single fascinating tapestry. First, she describes family life in the 1930s and 1940s, bringing the picture to life with telling personal anecdotes. Second, the book presents the ways in which a precociously intelligent, feisty girl from a very left wing family dealt with the complete mixture of support and trouble arising both from her circumstances and her own uncompromising, assertive sticking by her principles. Third, a postscript dealing with the later years describes how her science was shaped by a wish to make it responsive to policy and by her own strongly held values. This very well written, highly readable book is strongly recommended to anyone interested in social history, people, politics or science. Who else is there?

SIR MICHAEL RUTTER,
Professor of of Developmental Psychopathology, Institute of Psychiatry, London.

HOME
IS WHERE
ONE
STARTS
FROM

ONE WOMAN'S MEMOIR

Barbara Tizard

WP
BOOKS

Published by Word Power Books 2010
43–45 West Nicolson Street
Edinburgh, EH8 9DB
www.word-power.co.uk

Printed and bound in Scotland
Designed by Leela Sooben

British Library Cataloguing in Publication Data.
A catalogue record for this book is available from
the British Library.

ISBN 978-0-9549185-8-3

Title from 'East Coker', by T.S.Eliot (Faber & Faber)

Contents

Preface		viii
Chapter 1	Early childhood in the 1920s	1
Chapter 2	Family break-up 1932–33	16
Chapter 3	At boarding school in the 1930s	29
Chapter 4	A socialist family in the 1930s	56
Chapter 5	High days and holidays 1933–39	82
Chapter 6	Day school, the Munich crisis, evacuation and the 'phoney war' 1938–1940	110
Chapter 7	Living in London during the Battle of Britain and the Blitz 1940–42	134
Chapter 8	A London sixth form. Life, love, and political activities, 1942–44	169
Chapter 9	Oxford: Student life and loves 1944–48	196
Chapter 10	Married life, a death, and a birth 1948–51	233
Chapter 11	Postscript 1951–2010	
	A researcher and a working mother	257
	Political activity and the peace movement	280
	Adventures abroad	285
	Retirement and old age	296
Appendix	List of publications	307
Index		308

Preface

I had several reasons for writing this memoir. I felt a need, as many old people do, to review and think about my life. I also wanted to try to capture the details of everyday living before and during the Second World War. Not only everyday life, but also attitudes and values, were so different then that people of my generation sometimes find it difficult to feel part of contemporary society. But also I wanted the challenge of writing in a way that would be new for me. I have written, alone or jointly, six academic books and many journal articles. All were reports and discussions of scientific findings, and inevitably constrained by the convention of writing neutrally, in the third person. I wanted now to write about my own thoughts and feelings, and to try to make events and people from the past come alive to those who read about them. I did not intend initially to publish the memoir, but I knew that I would enjoy both the writing and the research into the past that would be involved.

Joan Didion wrote that she had already lost touch with a couple of the people she used to be. I too feel that I am a survivor of a long line of people I used to be, though I haven't lost touch with them, I can still remember how they felt and thought. But as a psychologist I know that long-term memory is very fallible – it reconstructs, rather than reproduces, past experiences. Since I want to contribute to social history in a small way, I have tried as far as possible to get independent evidence for the factual basis of this memoir. One way in which I did this was to send drafts of each chapter for comment to at least two people, often three or four, who had shared the experiences I describe. The first two chapters, about our early childhood, were read by my brother and cousin. Naturally, my informants' attitude to past experiences often differed from mine, but if they threw convincing doubt on the accuracy of a memory I corrected it or removed it from the script.

I supplemented these sources by the use of archival material. I obtained information from Bedford High School, and the archivists at

St. Paul's Girls' School and Balliol College gave me access to relevant records and Minutes. No letters from my parents and grandparents survive, except a few letters from my mother to me, but I collected basic data about them from birth, marriage and death certificates and obituaries, and I read articles my mother and grandfather had written, and reports about them, in newspapers and union journals in the newspaper section of the British Library at Colindale and the library of the National Union of Teachers. I also contacted the archivist of the *Radio Times* for information about my father. My mother's friends were no longer alive, but I talked to a teacher who had been the youngest member of the staff in the school where she had been headmistress. With some undefined notion that I would one day want them I had fortunately kept many of the letters written to me by relatives, friends, lovers and my husband between the ages of ten and twenty two, and, puzzlingly, I found a number of letters to them written by myself. These helped me to understand how I had felt about the events of my adolescence, or at least how I described my feelings at the time. On most of my travels abroad, other than family holidays, I kept quite detailed diaries.

I wrote this book very intermittently between 2002, when I was seventy-six, and 2009. I deeply regret not having started it earlier, at a time when a few people who had known my parents were still alive. I was also too late to consult a number of my own friends, especially the men, who had died before I started to write. I was unable to show my brother the later chapters of the book, since he died in 2003. My husband, Jack died thirty years ago.

Although it emerged that I remember more of the past than many of my contemporaries, I was surprised by how much the research revealed that I had forgotten. The most spectacular example of this was my failure to recall the bailiffs battering their way into our rooms, which I recount in Chapter 2 from my brother's description. But more disturbing were the false memories, when I was certain of an experience that seems not to have happened. All were trivial, but none the less unsettling. An example involved my recollection, described in Chapter six, of going to lunch at the age of twelve with the grandfather of a friend in a very imposing house near Hyde Park. I vividly remember being impressed by the butler of whom, even now, I retain a clear visual image. My friend has died, but her brother, who read the account, assured me that their grandfather had never had a butler, and his cousin confirmed this. So, despite my best efforts, I cannot guarantee the veracity of everything I describe.

I am very grateful for the time and help of all the informants I have mentioned, and especially those who read and commented on the completed book – my daughter Jenny, my nephew Peter Parker, my friends Judith Dunn, Philip Graham, Eric Hobsbawm, Ann Phoenix and Michael Rutter. It was Jenny who persuaded me to publish the memoir, and arranged for its publication.

Barbara Tizard
London 2009

Chapter 1

Early childhood in the 1920s

I was born in 1926, and so spent my childhood in the aftermath of the First World War and the shadow of the second. For a few it was a time of cocktails and dancing all night, but for many more existence was a struggle. In Britain half a million men under thirty had been killed in the 1914–18 war. Proportionately more of these were officers, who were mown down as they led the charges from the trenches. A quarter of all Oxford and Cambridge male students in the forces under the age of 25 were killed. Many more soldiers, including my father, had been wounded and traumatised. Promised by the Prime Minister 'a land fit for heroes', ex-servicemen often joined the dole queues. The old industries where Britain had led the world, steel, coal and shipbuilding, went into a precipitous decline. In parts of Scotland, the north of England and south Wales unemployment reached nearly seventy per cent, although in parts of the south where light manufacturing industries were expanding it was only three per cent. Hunger marches from the north began in the slump of 1921 and continued throughout the thirties. The poorest workers still lived in slums. The long term unemployed, the sick and the impoverished elderly depended on means tested handouts from the Poor Law Guardians. Nutritionists estimated that nearly a third of the population were malnourished. Ninety per cent of children were educated only in 'elementary' schools, and started work at fourteen.

Two weeks after I was born an unprecedented General Strike of three million workers in support of claims by the miners brought the economy to a halt. Fearing that working people would follow the example of the Russian Bolshevik revolution of 1917, and the post war uprisings in other European countries, the government responded with a show of force. Two infantry battalions marched through Liverpool, tanks patrolled the London streets and troops set up camp in Hyde Park. Middle class volunteers, including many students from Oxford and Cambridge, flocked to break the strike by manning the basic services. But in fact the overwhelming majority of strikers had no revolutionary aims and wanted only to improve their conditions. However, most TUC and Labour Party leaders were almost as worried as the government by what they saw as the revolutionary potential of the situation and after nine days called off the strike.

These events reverberated through my family, who, although all Labour activists and very anti-communist, had opposing attitudes to the strike. My mother's father, a militant member of the N.U.R. (National Union of Railwaymen), led the strike in his area. After the strike ended he was promptly sacked, as were many other local union leaders. He was fifty-five, had worked in the railways for thirty-five years, and he never found another job. But my father, Herbert Parker, a Labour councillor who had stood for parliament in the 1924 election, was opposed on principle to the idea of a general strike, arguing for negotiation rather than strikes. My mother supported the strike but was preoccupied with a new baby and a toddler, and with the violence within her marriage, which after only two and a half years was heading for disaster.

My parents had met in 1917 when my father was a recently commissioned army officer, my mother, Elsie Kirk, still at college. They had much in common. Both came from working- class families, my mother's father was a railway signalman, my father's was a Lancashire mill hand, and both through better education had moved out of the working-class. They had, however, remained active in the Labour Party and trade union movement and very unusually for the time were also militant anti-monarchists and atheists. Neither of my parents had been christened and nor, of course, were my brother and I. But whilst my mother was firmly embedded in the political and trade union life of West Ham (now Newham) where she had always lived and where her father was a local trade union activist, my father had left his roots far behind. His father died while he was a child and he was subsequently supported and his education overseen by his uncle, J.R.Clynes. Clynes was a trade union leader who in 1906 became one of the first Labour M.P.s. He was a minister in the wartime coalition cabinet and subsequently in the Labour cabinets of 1924 and 1929. With his help, my father had received – though not completed – a university education and was launched on a professional career. But my mother had attended only a two-year teacher training college, which qualified her to work as an elementary (i.e. non grammar school) teacher.

At the time of their marriage in 1923 my father had a good job as joint editor of the *Radio Times*. Broadcasting had begun in the previous year, and there was only one programme. The *Radio Times* was started because newspapers, fearing competition, refused to print their listings. From the start the *Radio Times*, priced at two pence, contained much more than a list of programmes. Each issue would include the text of some talks, a correspondence column and photographs. Its first Christmas front cover was a full-page coloured illustration of their ideal audience. Entitled 'Just a song at twilight', a family was depicted gathered round a glowing fire, heads turned towards the loudspeaker of their wireless, as it was then usually called, thoughtful expressions on all their faces. Within three years the circulation of the *Radio Times* reached a million.

The provision of news bulletins was seen as radio's most important function. Initially they were read twice – first rapidly, then slowly, repeating points which listeners might want to note down. The bulletins were very formal in style, the newsreaders, all male, spoke with public school accents and until 1939 had to wear evening dress. As well as the news there were lectures, orchestral concerts, religious talks and opera. Reith, the first Director, was slow to cater for more popular tastes, arguing that the radio was an agent for human improvement and that 'our responsibility is to carry into the greatest possible number of homes everything that is best in every department of human knowledge and endeavour.' Few people, he believed, know what they want and very few what they need. Whilst this high seriousness sounds absurdly patronising today, there was undoubtedly a thirst for education at that time in those who had been ill-served at school. Many middle aged or older listeners would have left school at ten, eleven or twelve. During a newspaper circulation war in 1933, what the *Daily Herald* chose to entice readers with was the complete works of Dickens for eleven shillings (fifty-five pence) and ninety-six newspaper coupons. This was so successful that the *Daily Express* competed with a different edition of Dickens' works for ten shillings and sold 124,000 copies.

My father stayed less than two years at the *Radio Times* – predictably, as his work history showed. At the end of the war he had been awarded a grant to attend Christ's College Cambridge. After only a year he left to work in Burma as assistant manager of the London-

Rangoon Trading Company. Returning to London a year later he held in rapid succession jobs as advertising manager, publicity manager and journalist. I don't know whether he was sacked from these posts, perhaps because of his heavy drinking, or whether he was too restless ever to settle down. It is possible that his war experiences had caused or contributed to this instability and also to his drinking problem, but whatever the cause my grandmother saw him as a highly undesirable husband for her daughter and refused to attend the wedding.

After leaving the *Radio Times* he worked for a number of years as a journalist on the Labour newspaper, the *Daily Herald*, often with assignments overseas. As well as a drink problem he had affairs with other women, lost money gambling at cards and was addicted to an extravagant life style – taxis home from the West End, meals at the Savoy, impulsive gifts of expensive jewellery to my mother at a time when he was heavily in debt and the gas bill was unpaid. My mother was devastated when a few years after her marriage their house was burgled. She lost the jewels and her engagement ring, along with everything else they had that was portable and of value. At that time only the well-to-do were insured.

My brother Michael was born eleven months after the wedding, an unintended pregnancy my mother told me, and I was born seventeen months later. My father's drunkenness, extravagant spending and unreliability led to an atmosphere of violence within our family. Neither Michael nor I could remember any occasion when our parents were together and not shouting at each other. We children did not usually understand what they were quarrelling about but we did understand the regular Sunday rows. On Sundays my mother would explode with anger when my father returned from the local pub too late and too drunk to eat the traditional Sunday lunch that she always cooked. He would insist on taking Michael along, leaving him to wait outside the pub. I don't believe now that there was ever physical violence between my parents but we were frightened by the violence in their anger. I remember vividly an occasion when a heavy blue earthenware fire fender fell on my mother's foot and she screamed terribly. I at once assumed that my father had deliberately dropped it on her, though in retrospect this seems extremely unlikely.

He certainly drank too much to be a reliable parent. Once at the seaside when I was about three our father, who was supposed to be in charge of us, fell asleep on the beach. According to Michael he had drunk too much at lunch. He was woken by Michael screaming that I was in the sea, whereupon he ran in fully clothed to rescue me. I remember the rescue clearly, the shouting, my father dripping, the small crowd gathered on the beach, but I don't think I realised that I had been in danger. After we started at Infant school there were a number of occasions when he was supposed to collect us from school but did not do so, so that eventually we came home on our own and had to wait outside our house in the street till he appeared.

As my father's debts mounted my mother, a determined and independent woman, decided to return to work. When she married at the age of twenty-six she had already taught for six years in what was then called a senior elementary school, for those girls, the great majority, who would leave school at fourteen. There was considerable societal pressure on women at that time to stay at home after marriage and to be financially dependent on their husbands. In many organisations, including most education authorities and the civil service, women had no choice – they were required to leave on marrying.

But there was a long tradition on both sides of my family of married women working, principally because of poverty. In the Lancashire town, Oldham, where my father was born, married women customarily worked in the mills to supplement the exceptionally low wages their husbands earned. My mother's mother worked as a dressmaker because her husband gave her so little of his wages, whilst my great aunt on being widowed became a washerwoman to support her children. Her mother, my great grandmother, worked as an untrained midwife after she was widowed as a young woman, and continued to do so after remarrying. In my mother's case the West Ham education authority required women to leave on marrying, but there was a little known loophole in the regulation that my mother took advantage of – it did not apply to supply (temporary) teachers. So when I was twelve months old she returned with the connivance of the Education Officer, a friend of hers, to full-time teaching in the top class of her old school, nominally as a supply teacher.

My mother needed to work for financial reasons but she was also glad to do so. She was uninterested in most aspects of 'homemaking', and although devoted to her children she did not find babies and young children appealing company. She did, however, love teaching older children and tried very hard to extend their ideas and aspirations. But my mother's ambitions extended well beyond teaching into the public arena. Until 1928 only women over thirty were allowed to vote, but there were no barriers to their involvement in trade unions. As soon as she started to teach my mother become deeply involved in educational politics. At the age of twenty-two she became the youngest person ever to be elected to the West Ham education committee. At the age of thirty, when I was two, she was elected to represent the Greater London branch of the National Union of Teachers on the executive committee of the union, and in the following year she also began to serve on the Burnham Committee on Teachers' Salaries. Later she became president of the National Union of Teachers and a member of numerous government advisory committees, including a Royal Commission on Gambling.

She was happy to leave us in the care of Grace, our nursemaid, who had been one of her pupils. My mother often went straight from school to one meeting or another. Since my father, as a journalist, was liable to keep very late hours and in any case was totally unreliable, she relied on Grace to put us to bed and baby-sit. I have only shadowy, but warm, memories of Grace. According to my aunt she was the oldest in a large family, fond of children, very responsible and undaunted by the task of looking after two very small children whilst also doing the housework. The housework itself must have been a formidable task. Pollution in the atmosphere from coal fires, and coal fires within the house, made a great deal of dirt, and very few families, certainly not ours, owned the machines which ease life today – vacuum cleaners, washing machines, refrigerators. It was not until the mid-fifties that as many as half of all households had a vacuum cleaner. When I was about four Grace left because Michael and I were away from home for months, in hospital and convalescing, and she was later succeeded by a young woman called Florence. Florence was a general purpose maid more than a nursemaid, since Michael and I had both started school by then. I remember not liking her, perhaps because there were terrible rows between my parents about her. Years later my aunt told me that this was because my father was having an affair with her.

When we were ill, or as often happened, my mother had meetings or conferences at weekends, Grace, who was, after all, a teenager, was not expected to cope. Instead my mother's sister Ivy was summoned to take us to her home in our big pram, walking the two miles north to Leyton. At that time, and this was still true when my children were young, there were no buggies that could be taken on buses and few people had cars, so women with young children often pushed prams for long distances. Auntie Ivy, who was several years older than my mother, was a crucial resource for her from the time my brother was born. Ivy had no children herself and was delighted to look after her sister's. Later, after years of accepting her infertility philosophically, she unexpectedly had a daughter. Like most married women at the time she did not go out to work and did not want to, and until I was about twelve she gladly undertook many maternal tasks for my mother. She looked after us in her home when we were ill, and as we got older saw us on and off trains, took us to buy school uniform, sit school entrance exams and took us on holiday. She adored my brother, who was a handsome, easygoing child, with blue eyes and blonde curls, then a requisite of childhood beauty. My hair was irredeemably fine and straight and I was hard to love, being not only a very faddy eater but also much given to tantrums. Nevertheless, she was kind to me when I was ill. I remember her taking me into her bed when I woke up with terrible earache. But for most of the time, as long as I can remember, I hated her, bitterly resenting her taking the place of my mother.

Unsurprisingly we did not remember our early years as happy. When I made this comment to my brother Michael some years ago he replied, 'We had a bloody awful childhood'. Michael's response astonished me. Whilst I was undoubtedly a difficult child, he was gentle, even-tempered and good-humoured and, I had thought, took the vicissitudes of our childhood with equanimity. As a child I was intensely jealous of him and the clear preference for him that I believed everyone felt. I can't remember him ever being punished, whilst I seemed to be constantly scolded and punished for wilful naughtiness. I remember deliberately immersing a wax doll in hot water, which damaged it irretrievably – I never liked dolls and was resentful that they were often given to me as presents. I remember, too, having a tantrum in the local department store, Boardman's, when my mother bought me a yellow silk dress which was not the one I wanted, and later deliberately tipping ink over it. At other times I was punished for knocking down Michael's elaborate brick constructions. Michael was not naughty, but he was very frightened of our father. I don't think he hit him, but he used to tease Michael in ways that terrified him, for example, throwing lighted firecrackers at him on Bonfire Night and I think it was this fear that clouded his early years. My father was also given to arbitrary and implacable edicts. When I was six I was desperate to join the local 'Brownie pack'. He would not allow me to do so since it would involve going to church parades and he was militantly opposed to religion. My mother, who was also an atheist, argued on my behalf but despite tears and angry scenes he would not relent.

Michael and me, at the beach.

A major source of unhappiness in our early childhood was illness. I think we must have been ill more often than other children. Certainly, many of my early memories are centred round illness. We had a kind doctor who kept small squares of chocolate in matchboxes to give his young patients, but before the introduction of antibiotics and sulphonamides medicine had little to offer for childhood infections. Tonsillitis, bronchitis and earaches meant days and especially nights of pain – Calpol was not then available. I do have one cosy memory of lying contentedly in my mother's bed whilst tomato soup was warmed for me on a gas ring in her bedroom. But I also remember screaming at night with the pain of ear infections which left me with scarred eardrums. Childhood illnesses like mumps and chickenpox were more severe and long lasting than today, entailing weeks in bed. Operations were frightening because there was no preoperative sedation. I remember going into hospital for a tonsillectomy at the age of five, immediately having a tantrum because of the humiliation of being put in a cot, and screaming at the sight of the instruments and the terrifying gowned and masked people who put me on an operating table and then lowered an anaesthetic mask over my face. Later, however, there was the consolation of jelly and ice-cream.

Before this, when I was about three, both my brother and I developed whooping cough, then a serious illness, and subsequently scarlet fever, which was at that time a potentially fatal and very infectious disease. We were sent to be nursed, separately, in isolation rooms at the local fever hospital. I remember my distress as my mother in a white gown peered at me through a window and the frightening sight of the nurses wearing masks and white gowns over their uniforms when they came into my room. Scarlet fever at that time often resulted in serious complications. In my case it led to rheumatic heart disease, the effects of which lasted for a number of years. The doctors considered it essential that I have months of convalescence involving almost total rest, preferably in the country or by the sea. For this I was sent to stay with my grandmother's younger sister Francie Pedgrift, who lived in Shoeburyness, a village in Essex, now part of Southend. A convalescent home, of which there were many at the time, would have been the alternative but I doubt if my mother even considered it. She always turned first to her family for support. She and her sister had often been sent as children to stay with their maternal grandmother in the country whenever they were thought run down, and they had fond memories of being spoiled. So, no doubt paying her aunt for my keep, she confidently left me with her for several months and I don't remember her ever visiting me.

Auntie Francie, however, was no lover of children. She was a small, plump, very reserved woman who at that time lived with her teenage children, Vera, a pretty, cheerful girl who worked as a shop assistant and Stan, a garage mechanic, who was crazy about motorbikes. They lived in a 'railway cottage', which was not a cottage in the traditional sense but one of a row of tiny terraced houses belonging to the railway company. Auntie Francie's husband had been a railwayman, killed whilst the children were very young by a train as he walked home from work along the line. She supported the family by taking in washing. In the scullery clothes were constantly bubbling in a coal heated boiler or being wrung through a large mangle or ironed with flat irons heated on the kitchen range.

I have very clear memories of the house, which probably mainly derive from later visits. As well as the scullery there were four tiny rooms, two up and two down. The front parlour was almost never used whilst the back kitchen, the setting for the family's daily life, was very dark and crammed with furniture. Even the mantelpiece was crowded, with vases, shells, framed photos and Toby jugs resting on an elaborately fringed velvety cloth. Steep, narrow stairs between these rooms led to two bedrooms. In the front bedroom where I slept a frightening array of stuffed owls in glass cases stood on the chest of drawers. Auntie Francie and Vera shared a brass knobbed double bed with a white crocheted bedspread, with a cot for me at the end of the bed, whilst Stan slept in the other bedroom. There was no bathroom. Baths were taken once a week in a tin bath in front of the kitchen range and we washed in the scullery sink. The privy at the end of the garden, emptied once a month during the night, was full of enormous spiders.

I was far from spoilt. Auntie Francie had to launder mounds of clothes in difficult conditions, and had no time or inclination to keep me amused. I spent the day on my own in a chair in the tiny kitchen – there were no diversions available such as a radio or gramophone and I couldn't yet read. The highlight of the day was being pushed in a wheelchair as Auntie Francie made her laundry rounds in the afternoon. But as well as being overworked she was, I realised later, an irritable, depressed woman, preoccupied, silent, rarely smiling. Wondering if I had exaggerated this unhappy experience, I recently consulted my cousin Kathleen who had also been sent to stay with Auntie Francie as a child. She wrote that she, too, had hated it, since Auntie Francie was very bad tempered and totally ignored her. Vera and Stan, on the other hand, she agreed were lively, cheerful and friendly, but since they were generally at work and as a small invalid I was put to bed very early, I did not see much of them.

These were dreary, lonely months, relieved only by the experience of the pea harvest. This was the time when as soon as the peas ripened farmers collected women each day from the surrounding villages in trucks to pick them. Auntie Francie always went with them – perhaps the work was better paid than laundering or perhaps she needed a break. The women brought their under school age children, who were left to their own devices at the side of the field, and at midday picnics would be unpacked. As an invalid I was instructed to sit on the grass and not to move while the other children played around. An older girl showed me how to make daisy chains and I sat gazing in delight at the wild flowers, which at that time were plentiful in the fields. This was the start of my lifelong love of the countryside.

In my brother's case scarlet fever led to mastoiditis. This was a very alarming complication since the infection in his mastoid bones could have spread to his brain, so both mastoid bones, the bones behind the ear, were removed. He spent months in bed in hospital and when he was discharged he had to learn to walk again. He, too, had a long period of convalescence, in his case with Auntie Ivy. Since she loved him dearly she was delighted to look after him. Her doctor insisted that Michael must eat raw beef each day to recover his strength. This led to terrible daily scenes, which I once witnessed, when all Ivy's skills at coaxing were needed to get him eventually to swallow a teaspoon or two of raw mince. But having come through all this illness from the age of six or seven we were both exceptionally healthy. At boarding school later I used to long to be ill so as to be admitted to the sanatorium where there was an escape from the school routine and rules, but this never happened.

Back at home the relationship between my parents continued to deteriorate, and as my father's periods of employment grew shorter we began a period of moving house. During our earliest years we lived in Earlham Grove, one of the more upmarket roads in the working-class district of Forest Gate. This was in the borough of West Ham, now Newham, where my mother had always lived, north of the Victoria Docks. It was most people's aim to move out of West Ham to Wanstead or Ilford if they could afford to, and since when they married my father was earning a good salary they could presumably have done so. But both of them were entrenched in local union and Labour Party activities – my father had become a West Ham councillor. Moreover, my mother wanted to stay near her mother to whom she was deeply attached, and with whom she had a mutual support system – my grandmother did all her washing and ironing and my mother gave her the affection she did not get from her husband. In addition, my aunt lived only about two miles north. Not only did she supply vital childcare but she did all my mother's mending. This was a major household task when, before the era of synthetics and cheap clothes, socks and stockings had to be darned, torn or worn clothes patched, the hems of children's clothes let down, worn sheets turned sides to middle.

Our first home in Earlham Grove was a large semi-detached house, with a long garden backing on to the railway line. Two holes were cut in our fence at different heights so that Michael and I could watch the trains together. Years later, in conversation with a much younger psychologist whom I met at a conference, it emerged that he had lived in that very house and the holes were still in the fence. His father had been a Rabbi at the synagogue adjacent to our house. By the time I was three or four my parents could no longer afford the rent of this house, so we moved to a much smaller house in nearby Clova Road. At that time there was a great deal of unfurnished property to rent – seventy per cent of people rented their homes, and neither my parents or grandparents ever bought or wanted to buy a house. We moved three times before my parents' marriage broke up, each time into smaller accommodation in ever-meaner streets. The last rooms we rented, in Gower Road, had a redeeming feature. A kind couple who lived on the ground floor had a vine growing up a glass lean-to. The sight filled me with wonder and delight and sometimes they would cut bunches of black grapes for us. We no longer had a maid, of course, but both of us had started at my mother's school at the age of four. Built in 1874, Odessa Road School was a great brick barracks, standing in a bare concrete playground which was unadorned except by the boys' and girls' toilets. It was an all-age school taking over 1300 children, with the infant department on the ground floor. Further up the school my mother taught the senior girls, whilst from above her the senior boys on the top floor would come hurtling down the flights of stone steps at a terrifying speed.

I remember finding school very puzzling. On the wall of the Infants hall was a large placard with a rhyme which we had to chant each day. It read, 'Good, better best, never let us rest, till our good is better, and our better best'. This was easy to learn, but unintelligible. In the classroom there seemed to me a large number of children. There was much chanting of multiplication tables in unison (it was only years later that I realised 'tables' were made up of successive additions) and much standing on our chairs for mental arithmetic and spelling, sitting down only if our answers were correct. This did not distress me, probably my answers were usually right. I remember nothing about the other children or the teachers, unlike Michael, who fell in love with his teacher and vowed that when he grew up he would buy a rose covered cottage for her to live in with our mother.

I have already mentioned that our father, who was supposed to collect us from school, often did not turn up and we had to come back on our own and wait outside the house for him. On one of these occasions I was desperate for a pee, and desperate with the shame of eventually having to use the gutter with a group of boys on the pavement opposite watching. I was quite aware by this time that we had moved down the social scale into treeless streets, with small terraced houses opening on to the pavements. I don't know whether we were explicitly told that the children around us were 'rough' and that we should not play with them, but we certainly absorbed this message. I think my mother, who had emerged from such streets herself, was determined that we would escape them.

Although most of the memories of my early childhood are unhappy or frightening there are also good memories. I have a clear and happy memory of a birthday party when I was three or four and I can still remember the dress that must have been bought for the occasion, blue silk with net over it and pink rosebuds round the waist. I can also remember both our parents reading to us, as they did very often. They passed on to us a life-long love of reading and we both learned to read very early. My mother read and reread to us many times the Christopher Robin verses and stories and *Peter Pan*, my father read us the *Just So stories*, *Treasure Island* and *Kidnapped*. *Kidnapped* was not, of course, intended for young children. I did not understand it and found it very frightening, especially the illustration in our edition of Davie climbing the staircase at the House of Shaws, which ended in a sheer drop. Both our parents knew a great deal of poetry by heart, and often recited it to us. Michael particularly remembered our father reciting Tennyson's 'Morte d'Arthur' in a fine, resonant voice. In the same fine baritone he would sing Gilbert and Sullivan arias, especially 'Willow, tit willow.'

I can't remember playing at all as a child or any adults playing with us. I do remember being awestruck by a toy that seemed to work by magic. It was a clockwork flourmill, from the top of which sacks of flour apparently miraculously descended and then ascended again at a steady pace. Michael told me some years ago that this was a present for my third birthday, which he and my father bought at a local toy shop. At that time every locality had a small toy shop and a doll's hospital where dolls could be repaired. I always disliked dolls and I don't remember having a Teddy bear or other soft toy. But I'm sure we had as many toys as other children at that time, though far fewer than my children, let alone my grandchildren. I remember waking one Christmas day in the bedroom I shared with my brother to see a 'fairy cycle' (a small two wheeler) at the end of his bed and by mine, to my disgust, a doll's pram. I never did have a bike until just before I went up to Oxford. That summer a young woman teacher whom I met at a camp taught me to ride, a process involving many painful falls, bruises and cuts. I never acquired a good balance and though I rode every day at Oxford where there was then relatively little traffic and subsequently in the country, I was apt to wobble perilously and stop by falling sideways.

My mother over eighty years ago was as health conscious for her children as middle class parents are today. Breastfeeding was recommended by doctors and we were breastfed. However we were not vaccinated against smallpox, the only immunisation then available. The vaccination of infants had been made compulsory in 1853 but this was met by vigorous opposition from working-class and some middle class activists. They objected to the encroachment on their civil rights and to the injection of diseased animal products into their children. They argued that this was a cheap substitute for the more expensive preventative measure of improving public sanitation. So vociferous were these protests that from 1898 exemptions were allowed for parents like mine with 'conscientious objections'. But my mother did try to follow public health advice on diet for children. Parents were urged to give their children milk to drink rather than tea, and fruit, especially apples, rather than cakes and sweets. I remember a very moralistic leaflet picturing a smiling, rosy cheeked girl with a glass of milk and an apple next to a sad, pale, peaky child eating a packet of biscuits. This worried me as I detested milk and would not drink it. We were rarely given sweets and not allowed to drink tea or coffee until in our teens. My mother also knew the value of 'roughage' and insisted that we ate the peel, core and seeds of apples, a tidy habit that I succeeded in passing on to only one of my children.

Many of the children she taught lived on a very different diet. Sir John Boyd Orr estimated in 1936 that nearly a third of the population suffered from serious dietary deficiencies. Surveys showed that the families of unemployed and the lowest paid workers ate large quantities of carbohydrates – white bread, potatoes and sugar – with margarine and tea, but very small amounts of protein, vegetables other than potatoes, and fruit. Any protein available tended to be reserved for the breadwinning males. There were no school dinners or milk to supplement the children's diet. I remember being shocked at the poor fare provided at the Christmas parties at my mother's school – the children were given a mixture of half milk and half water to drink, with jelly, paste sandwiches, biscuits and a bag of sweets.

Exercise was understood to be important for children and too much time 'with your head in a book' was disapproved of. But children then were not usually short of exercise. Very few families had a car and without TV or computer games, and with little traffic in the side roads, most children played out in the street or in a park. There was a strong belief in the beneficial effect of sea and country air, which, considering the level of pollution in coal fuelled cities, was probably justified. But there was very little understanding of children's emotional needs. Children were sent away from home for long periods for the sake of their health, often languishing, as I did, for months with few if any visits from their families.

The constant anger between our parents, my frequent bouts of illness, my periods of isolation and separation in hospital and during convalescence made for an unhappy first five years. Nevertheless I had a loving, if too often absent, mother, I was given a lifelong passion for books and no one was intentionally unkind to me. But the next four years were to be worse!

Chapter 2

Family break-up 1932–33

My parents' marriage ended dramatically in 1932 when I was nearly seven and Michael was eight. Some years ago he gave me an account of what he remembered happening. My mother had gone to Edinburgh for a conference, leaving our father in charge of us. He had been out of work for some time and was very heavily in debt. While my mother was away the bailiffs arrived to take possession of our household goods. The downstairs tenants let them into the house, but my father locked and barricaded the door to our first floor rooms and shouted angrily back as the bailiffs shouted and hammered on the door. Eventually they broke in and removed the furniture and other possessions of any value. Michael said that we had been terrified, but extraordinary as it seems I have no recollection of the event. Michael is certain that I was there, cowering with him in a corner, and it is difficult to think where else I could have been.

We were taken to our mother's parents who lived nearby in Margery Park Road and that was almost the last time we saw our father. There was no divorce. Until 1938 the sole ground for divorce was the adultery of either party, always scandalously reported in the press. The procedure was very costly and used only by the well-to-do. It also carried a very considerable social stigma, which as a teacher and trade union activist my mother would have wished to avoid. Although novels and memoirs of the period suggest that pre-marital and extra-marital sexual relations were not at all infrequent they were neither sanctioned nor acknowledged by establishment figures and much of the public. My grandmother instantly severed relations with her niece on learning that she was having an affair with a married man, and this was not seen as harsh. In 1926 Ford motor works sent inspectors to visit their employees' houses to check that they were living respectable married lives.

I find it extraordinary that a return to making divorce difficult is currently being advocated for the sake of the children – marriages as unhappy as that of my parents can only damage children. However, though divorce was then rarely an option, a legal separation, which my mother obtained, was considered respectable, although unfortunate, and it protected her from liability for my father's debts. She never spoke to us of this period in her life. It must have been very traumatic for her to lose all her possessions, many bought from her own earnings. It must also have been humiliating for her to return to her parents' house when her mother had been so opposed to the marriage, foreseeing how damaging it would be.

Why did my mother marry my father? She had known him for six years and must have been as familiar as her mother with his shortcomings. Perhaps she thought she could influence him. What I know of his life suggests that he was the kind of talented, plausible charmer who attracted people and made them want to help him, though in the end he always let them down. He wasn't particularly good looking and like all his family he was quite short, slightly shorter than my mother, who at five foot six and a half inches was unusually tall for a woman at that time. Perhaps part of his attraction was the social circle he moved in, which she must have found very different and much more glamorous than her own. Initially his family circumstances were very deprived. His father, Harry Parker, a mill hand in Oldham, died when his children were very young. His widow, who was both enterprising and a good cook, scraped a living by making pies and cakes, which she sold at the gates of the mill.

She was rescued from poverty by her brother J.R. Clynes who increasingly assumed responsibility for her children, especially the cleverest child, my father. Their father, Patrick Clynes, had come with his seven children to work in the mills at Oldham after being evicted from his smallholding in Ireland. He could barely afford to feed his family but, illiterate himself, he paid two pennies a week for each of his children to attend school. Education was not free until 1891, and even then it was only compulsory until the age of ten. In 1879, aged ten, Uncle Clynes started work in the mills as a 'little piecer'. His job was to run forward the instant a thread on the spindles broke and with his small fingers join the ends together. He wrote in his Memoirs about this experience, "The noise was what impressed me most. Clatter, rattle, bang, the swish of thrusting levers and the crowding of hundreds of men, women and children at their work... I remember meals at which there never seemed to be enough food, dreary journeys to and from the mill through smoke fouled streets, in mornings when I nodded with tiredness and in evenings when my legs trembled under me with exhaustion". But he had been glad to leave school, writing that, 'My school master taught me nothing except a fear of birching and a hatred of formal education.'

Nevertheless in the evenings, despite his exhaustion, he set about educating himself from books, eventually reading Dickens, Ruskin and Shakespeare in the library of the Oldham Equitable Co-operative Society. At the age of sixteen he wrote, anonymously, a series of articles in the local paper about the harsh treatment of children in the mills, arguing that the Spinners' Union was not doing enough to protect them. He left the mill for the local gas works and at the age of twenty-two was appointed organiser of the newly formed Lancashire Gas Workers' Union. In the following year he became president of the Oldham Trades Council. In 1906, when my father was eleven, Clynes entered Parliament as Labour MP for North East Manchester.

Before the Labour Party was set up in 1900 Clynes belonged to both the Fabian Society and the Independent Labour Party. He strongly supported women's suffrage but he was never on the left-wing of the Labour Party. He was one of a minority of Labour leaders who supported Britain's entry into the First World War and he accepted a post in the war-time coalition government. He was made a privy councillor in 1918. In 1922 he was one of the two contenders for the leadership of the Labour Party – the other, Ramsay Macdonald, beat him by only five votes. In the first Labour government of 1924 he was Lord Privy Seal and Leader of the House of Commons and in the second Labour government of 1929–31 he was Home Secretary. Those on the left regarded him as increasingly reactionary. According to his obituary in the *Daily Worker* 'Clynes moved steadily to the right and lived to condemn strikes and to decry shop stewards as "a great and growing menace."'

Nonetheless, when in the face of economic depression Ramsay Macdonald decided in 1931 to cut the already meagre unemployment benefit and form a coalition with the Conservatives and Liberals, the majority of the Labour cabinet, including Clynes, thought this a step too far and refused to join. The general election that followed was a disaster for the Labour Party. The majority of Labour MPs lost their seats, including Clynes, who had held Manchester for twenty-five years. During all this time he continued his quasi-parental role to my father, who was certainly clever and must at first have seemed to have a promising future, assisting him in every way he could and providing him with a London base. For my mother, her relationship with my father who was then a journalist, familiar with leading politicians, had meant an entrée into a more sophisticated and moneyed circle, with wider horizons, than she had previously known. They were married in The Kings Weigh House Chapel, Hanover Square, a far cry from West Ham.

One of my father's wealthy friends, a publisher called Sidney Walton, paid for their wedding reception at the Savoy hotel and their honeymoon in an expensive hotel in Surrey. The couple made frequent visits to the House of Commons and to the Clynes' house in Downing Street, from where in 1924 my mother was rushed to hospital to give birth to my brother, who was given the middle name of Clynes. My father's mother remained in Oldham and died from cancer when I was quite small. I remember meeting her, though, she was short, slim, white-haired and, I was told, elegantly dressed. All my father's family were short, the women not more than five feet tall. Malnutrition in childhood may have been involved, but my own shortness suggests that genetics was an important factor.

In the general election of 1924 my father stood unsuccessfully as Labour candidate for the safe Conservative seat of Richmond. I have a copy of his election manifesto written in a rather pompous, prolix style, which perhaps was then customary for politicians. Politically he sounds like New Labour, *avant la lettre*. There is no mention of nationalisation or the redistribution of income, 'The Labour Party has a programme, not of greed and envy, but one that will benefit all classes and enrich the nation… I do not stand for Communism…the State should not be a mechanism of interference, but a means of co-ordinating effort, preventing haphazard production, and harnessing good-will, science, and expert management.'

The best evidence I have about my father's career comes from a printed C.V. prepared in 1929, when he was thirty-four. It is professionally laid out with a large photo of himself on the cover and small photos on each page, showing him at work in his various jobs as army officer, at an editing desk and broadcasting. At the back are five references and a list of further referees, headed by Uncle Clynes, with his Home Office address. The C.V. would, I think, deter any prospective employer. It is a remarkably vague document, lacking dates and in the case of the section headed 'Education', plausibility. It states that he was educated at Christ's College Cambridge, Ruskin College Oxford, and the London School of Economics, but with no mention of dates or qualifications acquired. I am sure that in fact there were no qualifications and his attendance at Ruskin College and the L.S.E. was only for short periods before he enlisted in 1915.

He lists seven jobs he had held in the nine years since his abortive period as a student in Cambridge – assistant manager of the London-Rangoon Trading Company in Burma, advertising manager of the *Head Teachers' Review*, publicity manager, first for the B.B.C., and then for the London Co-operative Society, first editor of the *Radio Times*, editor of the *Wireless League Gazette*, and labour correspondent of *Industrial Information*. Of the five references, three appear to be publicity handouts when he was newly appointed, the fourth, from the General Secretary of the YMCA, is a testimonial to the 'integrity and moral character' he demonstrated in 'service in an honorary capacity' for them, and only one, from a publishing firm, where he filled a temporary position in their editorial department, is a straightforward testimonial to his work, recommending his 'considerable ability', 'unfailing courtesy' and 'industry'.

Strangely, he did not list his assignments as overseas correspondent for the *Daily Herald*, the Labour newspaper, which included one in Romania when their king abdicated and another in Tokyo at the time of a major earthquake, and he gave only the night editor of the *Daily Herald* as a referee. Nor, more understandably, did he mention his 'ghost writing' of the autobiography of a Labour trade unionist and politician, Will Thorne. He did, however, state that he was a councillor in West Ham and a member of their finance and other committees.

Since most journalists at that time drank heavily he must have been an exceptionally heavy drinker to stand out; he was undoubtedly an alcoholic. A tendency to be casual with the truth, as suggested by his C.V. may not have helped. My brother was sceptical of all his claims, including the claim to have been the first joint editor of the *Radio Times*, but a good deal of research on my part established that this was true.

We did see our father once more, shortly after the marriage break-up, when on two separate occasions he 'kidnapped' first one and then the other of us, in an ill-judged attempt to get my mother to return to him. My brother never spoke of this experience. In my case I remember my father collecting me from the Infant school playground soon after the separation, when I was six years old, and telling me we were going on holiday to Clacton. We stayed in a grand hotel by the sea. I remember falling asleep in a large bedroom, watching my father playing cards with several men I didn't recognise, perhaps trying to raise the money to pay the bill. Meals were brought to our room and my father told me I could choose whatever I liked at each meal. I remember choosing jelly for breakfast, feeling deliciously transgressive. I was not at all frightened, more exhilarated by the experience. It didn't last long – a friend of my father's contacted my mother, who brought me home. As a result of these events my mother decided to send us away from home immediately. I was sent to live with her sister, Ivy, and Michael was sent to boarding school.

My father's career then went into a sharp decline. His wealthy friends, tired of lending him large sums of money which were never repaid, gave up on him, as did Uncle Clynes. He had the double sorrow that his own son, of about my father's age, was also an alcoholic, despite the efforts of several expensive treatment centres. Clynes did not retire from parliament till 1945, after regaining his parliamentary seat in 1935. After our parents' separation the Clynes' continued for a while to send presents to Michael and me. They invited us with our mother to visit them on several occasions in their large, rather grand house in Putney and a house they had right on the edge of the sea in Brightlingsea. Then, I don't know why, all contact ended.

Shortly after his marriage break-up my father was fined and bound over for a year. He had hired a taxi for the evening and paid the driver with a cheque drawn on my mother's account, which she did not meet. The following year he was working as a clerk in a firm of contractors in Watford. After two months with them one morning he found their safe unlocked. He stole the cash in it, £44, immediately left the office to visit the nearest pub, then returned and gave money to another employee to fetch him a bottle of whisky. The theft was soon discovered, my father was suspected and the police summoned. My father asked to go to the toilet, which was in the yard. The policeman waiting outside noticed that he was treading down the cinders on the toilet floor and found the rest of the money hidden under the cinders. Still protesting his innocence my father was arrested and bailed on the surety of a clergyman. My father failed to appear for trial and the Reverend Moran, yet another victim of his plausibility, lost his bail money. Later my father surrendered to the police. I found an account of the trial in the files of the *West Herts and Watford Observer*, 1934, after coming across a letter to my grandfather from the irate clergyman.

At his trial his lawyer pointed out that it was such a stupidly carried out theft for a man of his intelligence that it must have been done under pressure of 'domestic worries, worries of having sunk down from such a high position, and general demoralisation caused by the effect of the worry and the war wounds.' It was true that my father had been wounded in the war and it may have been the case that his problems stemmed at least in part from his war experiences. His drinking problem was not referred to at his trial, presumably because his lawyer judged this would not help his case. Impressed by the defence arguments and perhaps by my father's conduct in court the judge decided to treat him leniently and bound him over for three years, with a request to the Police Court Missionary to help him find employment and keep in close touch with him.

As I read the newspaper reports I felt sick with sadness that my father had been reduced to such a pathetic state. I know very little of what happened to him thereafter. His fortune improved for a while. My aunt told me that in the late thirties he was press officer for an organisation set up to campaign for a National Theatre and before that, appropriately perhaps, press officer for the Scottish Distillers' Association. My mother never spoke of him and Michael and I understood that his name must not be mentioned. This silence aroused my curiosity, although not Michael's, and I often searched my mother's drawers for information. When I was about ten I found a recent letter from him to my mother, begging her to take him back. Since he gave an address nearby I decided to go and see him, I think

I just wanted to find out what kind of a man he was. However, I lost my nerve outside the house, unable to think what I would say to him – 'Hallo, I'm your daughter' seemed absurd – or what I would say if the landlady opened the door. Instead I kept returning to wait outside the house in a terraced treeless street, hoping that he would come in or out, but he never did. By the next school holidays – I was then at boarding school – I had for some reason lost interest.

Nowadays it is considered important for children to retain contact with both parents but in the 1930s there was little understanding of children's emotional needs. My mother was determined that we should have no contact with, or knowledge of, our father and her friends respected this decision. He never made any attempt to contact me but Michael learned, years later, that on his eighteenth birthday our father had sent him a congratulatory telegram, which my mother destroyed. My father must have looked out for news of our family because, I was told later, he attended my mother's funeral in 1950, though he did not approach us. The following year he went to one of Michael's election meetings in the safe Conservative seat of Kensington and suggested that they meet for tea in the Strand Palace Hotel. Michael told me that he agreed out of politeness (Michael was always very courteous) but there was nothing he wished to say to him, and they just chatted about the forthcoming election.

We did not see our father again, and in the late fifties Michael was notified that he had died. He was at that time working as a clerk in the Reading gas works and lodging in a nearby council house. The landlady, looking through his papers, discovered Michael's address. It seemed that my father had come back from work, found the house empty, put a kettle on to boil in the kitchen-living room without lighting the gas and sat in an easy chair. When his landlady returned he was dead. There was no letter, and no attempt had been made to seal the room, so it was assumed that he had been careless with the gas, and then fallen asleep. The Coroner's verdict was accidental death.

The landlady showed us his bedroom. It was small and virtually bereft of personal possessions, except for four books by Horace and Herodotus, which I took away. The gas works sent two people to represent the office at his funeral and according to his landlady no one else, apart from herself, had attended. I felt deeply unhappy, sick, and irrationally guilty that my father, who had shown such promise as a young man, should have been reduced to what seemed a non-life, without friends or interests, whilst Michael and I were happily married and enjoying our professional careers. Michael regarded this as sentimental nonsense, and took the view that what had happened to our father was his own fault. When years later I took Michael a copy of the newspaper account of the trial he did not want to look at it. I find it difficult to believe that he was, at heart, indifferent to the father who had so frightened him as a child and then disappeared. He had certainly not forgotten his unhappy early experiences but I think that he walled them off, protecting himself from the painful feelings they would have aroused.

To return to the story of our childhood, I spent the first six months after the family break-up with Auntie Ivy, attending the same Infant school as my cousin Kathleen. Care within the family is nowadays considered the best solution for children who cannot live at home and it probably often is. But my own experiences of it with, earlier, Auntie Francie, and subsequently Auntie Ivy, were both unhappy. Not only had Auntie Ivy and I never got on, I had also to contend with the jealousy of my younger cousin. Whilst I was resentful at being sent away from my mother and disturbed by the break-up of my parents' marriage and the events leading up to it, Kathleen was resentful at having to share her parents and her home, and even her bed, with a cousin she did not like.

When we were adults and met amicably Kathleen told me that I used to act as though I were superior to her and that I treated her as an 'underdog'. She complained that I read all day and refused to play with her, telling her that her games were childish. Moreover she maintained that whilst my clothes had been bought at Daniel Neal's (an expensive children's shop) her clothes were always made by our grandmother. If she complained about me to her mother she was told that she must put up with me because my life had been so unhappy. However she said that Michael, who stayed with them for the Easter holidays, was kind and gentle to her and willing to play her games.

I remember Kathleen principally as someone hostile, who used to pinch me surreptitiously when the opportunity arose. I don't remember feeling superior to her but it is true that I never played with her and at the age of seven obsessively read all day. I did, though, hate their little terraced house, which opened on to a narrow, treeless road. We had recently been living in just such a house and street ourselves, but I was aware that this had been a step down in the world and that friends of my parents and the Clynes' lived in much pleasanter surroundings. My major problem, though, was Ivy's assumption of my mother's role. She seemed to me such an inferior version of my mother that I found it hard to believe what Ivy often emphasised to me, that they were sisters. Poor Ivy suffered all her life from the knowledge that my mother was prettier, more intelligent, a public figure and her father's open favourite. Even in extreme old age she still maintained her hatred of her long dead father and still complained bitterly about his favouritism.

By the time I was eight or so I had decided that Ivy was definitely stupid. Of course she was not, but she was badly educated, ignorant and very opinionated. She had left school at fourteen and worked in a clerical job (she never learned to type) until she married and became a full-time housewife. Her reading was confined to popular romances and the *Daily Mail*, yet she had strongly voiced opinions and prejudices on every subject, which could not be shifted by reasoning or appeals to evidence. Hardly had her parents or sister begun to talk than she would contradict them, usually from a position of complete ignorance, provoking endless arguments in which she soon became very excited and angry. Sometimes I felt that she was only happy at these times but I early declined to engage in pointless wrangling with her. Perhaps the arguing developed as a way of competing with her sister and asserting her independence, along with buying the *Daily Mail* and taking a great interest in the Royal Family, whilst her parents and sister were dedicated socialists and anti-monarchists.

She was a hot tempered woman and a tyrant within her own house, constantly scolding, criticising, demeaning and ordering around her husband, Will Rayment, and her daughter. Moving to her house meant exchanging one kind of unhappy family for another. There were no quarrels in this household because Ivy exercised unquestioned power. Uncle Will was very quiet, sweet tempered, patient and unassertive. I never remember him arguing with Ivy or defending himself, or us, against her criticisms or getting cross either with her or with us children. This did mean, though, that we had no defender or advocate. The best he could do for Kathleen when Ivy shouted at her was to take her off to his garden shed to play the violin with him. He worked as a riveter in the London and North Eastern railway yard at Temple Mills, Leyton, starting as a rivet boy at the age of thirteen and ending as foreman. He was very clever with his hands and spent hours making soldiers from molten lead for Michael. There was a serious intentness about everything he undertook. On Fridays he brought his pay packet, unopened, to Ivy and she gave him some pocket money back. He never drank alcohol or went to a pub.

However, he did have a life of his own. After they had moved out to the suburbs with financial help from my grandmother he became a keen gardener. He was a good musician, until the war earning extra money (which he handed over to Ivy) by playing with a dance band in the evenings – he could play both the piano and the violin. He was also a Mason. When he retired, no doubt to escape spending the day with Ivy, he found through his Masonic connections a job as a uniformed messenger for a firm of City jobbers, an occupation that later became obsolete with the development of the internet. I thought it was a demeaning job for an expert craftsman but he enjoyed it and took pride in the responsibility of the post. When he eventually had to give this up through ill health he took up marquetry, producing very skilled work. Despite being completely subservient to and bullied by Ivy in domestic situations, in his work or when involved in his crafts, of which he was proud, he showed self-respect and dignity. Anyone who has read *Great Expectations* will recognise his strong resemblance to Joe Gargery.

As a child I thought only of my own unhappiness in this household and not about how it must have been for Kathleen. A few years ago she wrote to me, 'I was very unhappy as a child, I cried a lot, and was always frightened of displeasing my mother, nothing that I did satisfied her. I longed for you and Michael to become my brother and sister, but my mother was always telling me how much more intelligent you were than me, and that you were better educated and superior'. She now saw her mother as a very unhappy, friendless woman for whom she had felt little affection, whilst she had loved and enormously pitied her father.

Ivy's life was extraordinarily narrow. Her social network was entirely confined to her family, including Norfolk cousins whom she would occasionally visit. As Kathleen said, she had no friends, though she would chat to neighbours in the street and watch them with interest through her window. Most of her considerable energy was spent on housework, about which I think it would be fair to say she was obsessional. For example, she not only constantly washed all the woodwork in the house – doors, skirting boards, etc.– she then polished it. As soon as their income allowed she paid another woman to come in once a week and help her move all the furniture out of one room at a time so that she could clean underneath it. Personal cleanliness was also very important to her. She boasted that her aprons were spotless at the end of the week, and when she had finished cleaning her house in mid afternoon it was an unalterable part of her routine to undress, wash thoroughly (it was usual then to bath only once a week) and change all her clothes.

Kathleen attributed Ivy's unhappiness to her intense jealousy of my mother, about whom she would nonetheless boast to the neighbours, and to her belief that she herself had married beneath her. When Kathleen became a nurse Ivy placed her hopes on Kathleen marrying a doctor. She was furious when Kathleen chose instead a man who was a bank clerk. He was exceptionally kind and patient, very like Will, and later become a bank manager. I think Ivy's husband and daughter by not fulfilling her fantasies experienced the worst of her – it is of course not uncommon for people to do serious harm to those closest to them whilst being a source of good to others. Now, I can appreciate the good she did. She was devoted to her own mother and despite her jealousy she was endlessly helpful to my mother. She adored my brother though she was unable to like or cope with me, and whilst we both visited her in her old age Michael did so more often than I, and was still fond of her.

Her lack of friends was not because she was reserved or depressive. She was, in fact, a very extravert, talkative woman, but all her emotion was invested in her extended family. When she was not angry she was cheerful and could even be high-spirited, joining enthusiastically in such dances as 'The Lambeth Walk' and 'Doing the Hokey Pokey' when the opportunity arose. From 1943, when women from eighteen to fifty were required to do some form of essential war work (before this, the upper age limit had been thirty), she took on the job of canteen cashier and general assistant in my mother's dockland school. She bathed children who needed it and consoled and bandaged others, always with kindness and warmth. But as soon as the war ended she retreated into her home. To the chagrin of Kathleen the years spent looking after Michael and myself seemed to have been the highlight of Ivy's life, which she relived endlessly thereafter in dramatic retelling to anyone who would listen.

I remember nothing about the Infant school I attended with Kathleen. By the age of seven, perhaps earlier, I had stopped playing and in fact I have no recollection at all of ever playing, either alone or with Michael. Instead, I spent most of my time reading. One book, which I still retain, inscribed 'A prize for a good reader', was given me when I was six at my former Infant school. Entitled *Teddy's Ship*, it is about a boy who is shipped off to stay with rather hostile relatives after his father dies, since his mother has to go away to seek work. It all ends happily and it is obvious why I kept rereading it. Two memories stand out from this bleak six-month sojourn with Ivy. One was of the terrible wrath I evoked by stealing from her purse, a pointless crime since I had no opportunity to spend money, and one which even provoked a sad, disappointed look from Uncle Will. The other was the thrill of winning a box of chocolates as first prize for good handwriting (the last time my writing was thought good) in a competition organised by Rowntrees.

In September 1933, aged seven and a half, I started at the boarding school which Michael had just left, and he moved on to another boarding school.

Chapter 3

At boarding school in the 1930s

The worst three years

Nowadays a woman who leaves her husband, especially one with the convenient working hours of a teacher, is likely to move to a smaller home and bring up her children on her own. I am sure that my mother never saw that as an option. Her union and political activities, which often took her away from home, were much too important to her. In any case she had a great desire to give us a better education than she had had, or was then available in West Ham. At that time classes in primary schools were very large, ninety per cent of children had only elementary school experience, and only one per cent of children in state schools went to university. She decided, therefore, to live with her parents and to send us to boarding school.

Although seven now seems very young to send a child to boarding school at that time it was the customary starting age. What is extraordinary is that my mother managed to pay the fees for two children. It is true that, having persuaded the authorities that she could no longer be considered a married woman, she was given a permanent teaching appointment, but the salary of a non-graduate woman teacher – there was no equal pay then – was very low, twenty-twenty-five per cent lower than that of men similarly qualified. Part of the explanation is that she earned extra money and wore herself out by travelling all over the country on behalf of the National Union of Teachers, after school, at weekends and in the school holidays. She was much in demand as a public speaker, but she was also very successful at missions requiring enormous diplomacy, such as dissuading mentally disturbed teachers from pursuing court cases against their local authority. She herself claimed that the difference in price between the first class railway fares which she claimed for, and the third class tickets which she bought (a custom that was then widespread, and I'm sure she didn't consider reprehensible) paid our school fees. Even though the fees of the first schools we went to were comparatively low this explanation is not really plausible. However, I was recently told by a disapproving teacher that my mother was given money by the Teachers' Widows and Orphans Benevolent Fund, having persuaded them that her position was the same as that of a widow.

The first school I attended, which Michael had just left after a term and a half, was a small boarding school for girls called Quarndon House in the Suffolk seaside resort of Felixstowe. There were about twelve boarders and ten to fifteen day girls, all aged between about eleven and sixteen. A great friend of my mother's, Leah Manning, knew the owner, Miss Stevenson, who took us as a special favour. Michael, a small boy entering a girls' school, was taken at very short notice after the 'kidnapping' crisis for a term and a half only, whilst I was accepted the following term on a permanent basis, despite being much younger than the other pupils. There was only one other full-time teacher, Mrs. Madden, who was also the Matron. Both these teachers seemed to me fat, ugly and old, although they were probably in their forties or fifties. Miss Stevenson was short, stout and white haired, forever reclining in an armchair in loose floral printed dresses, which failed to disguise her wobbly fat. Mrs. Madden, usually dressed in tweeds, was also stout but taller, more active and muscular, with a sallow dark appearance, as though she never washed. Visiting teachers taught drawing, the piano, singing, gymnastics in the winter and Greek dancing and tennis in the summer. No public exams were sat. Most of the girls were the daughters of Suffolk farmers who had no academic ambitions for their daughters, but probably thought that attendance at a boarding school would give them a social cachet.

The school was in a large detached red brick house with tennis courts in the garden. I had never been in such large rooms before. Crossing the drawing room to meet Miss Stevenson on my arrival seemed to involve covering a vast distance. She made no attempt to put me at my ease but addressed my mother. When my mother left I felt totally abandoned, especially when I found that for the first time in my life I was to sleep in a room on my own. The room was very small and bare, it had probably originally been a dressing room, furnished only with a bed, wardrobe and chest of drawers. Because I was still considered a semi-invalid with a 'weak heart' my bedtime was to be half past five. Fortunately I did not realise I was at the start of the worst three years of my childhood.

The school was run like an Edwardian upper middle class household, with maids who wore different caps and aprons in the morning and afternoon, and children who were not expected to talk at meal times unless spoken to. The boarders all sat round a very long table for meals with one teacher at each end, and the maids waited on us and swept the crumbs off the table after meals with a special little pan and brush. They were not allowed to talk to us. All this was a far cry from West Ham but I swiftly adjusted to the differences even in small things. For example, jam was served in little glass dishes, not from a jam jar, and you had to spoon it on to the edge of your plate and not, as we did at home, put it directly on to your bread. I quickly learned that this habit and many other things we did at home were considered 'common', a term much used by the middle classes at the time to denigrate the customs, clothes, accents and behaviour of working-class people.

Pupils had to use a side entrance and the servants' narrow back staircase, rather than the main hall and staircase which were reserved for Miss Stevenson and Mrs. Madden. Just inside the side entrance was the cloakroom, where we each had a hook and a pigeonhole for shoes. When we went out we changed into laced outdoor shoes and inside we wore buttoned 'house shoes,' or court shoes for girls of fourteen and over. How I longed to reach that glamorous age! A 'shoe boy' sat in the cloakroom polishing the shoes each morning. We wore two sets of underwear, a vest and over that a 'liberty bodice', which was an over-vest with longitudinal sewn-on tapes on to which suspenders could be fastened for stocking wearers, and two pairs of knickers, white 'linings', and over them longer, baggy brown knickers with elastic in the legs and a front pocket. Over these we wore a brown uniform dress. After lessons ended in the afternoon we changed into non-uniform dresses, which had to be brown but could be of any design, provided they were 'plain'. My mother, not yet sensitive to the nuances of such rules, had one made for me with embroidered orange flowers on the bodice, a very bad start to my school career. The dress had been made, free, by students of dressmaking at the West Ham Municipal College. The principal was a good friend of my mother's and getting help of various kinds from her friends was one of the ways she made ends meet.

On the ground floor were the dining room, kitchen, the boarders' recreation room and the largest room, Miss Stevenson's drawing room. When I first arrived with my mother we were given tea there with thin cucumber sandwiches, which I'd never seen before and was never given again. The only occasions when I entered the room thereafter were when I had been particularly naughty. Behind these rooms was a ground floor annexe with a cloakroom for the daygirls, rooms for piano practice and a small hall for drama, singing and dancing. Upstairs there was a library; a classroom for the girls under fourteen, furnished with desks, presided over by Mrs. Madden; the dormitories and presumably the private rooms of the two teachers. The other class, of girls from fourteen to sixteen, was held downstairs round the dining room table, with Miss Stevenson in charge.

There were no blackboards since, because of the wide age range, there was no group teaching. The day was divided into the usual forty minute periods for different curriculum subjects, and each pupil worked on her own at her own pace through the appropriate text books. At the end of each chapter were questions, to which you had to provide written answers at an acceptable level before being allowed to move on to the next chapter. In theory you could ask for help, in practice this was discouraged. On the first day my English book instructed me to underline certain words. I had no idea what underline meant and sat petrified for a long time, ashamed of my ignorance, and fearful of being scolded or scorned for asking. No talking or moving around was allowed, just silent, solitary study. Under this system if you found schoolwork easy you could make rapid progress – I found myself much in advance of other pupils in most subjects at my next school. If not, you could get desperately discouraged. In my last term, aged ten, I was stymied by a Geography exercise, unable to move on for the rest of the term because I couldn't copy correctly, without tracing, a detailed map of the City of London. I can still see it in broad outline. Week after week I wrestled hopelessly with this assignment, knowing I would never succeed The highlight of the week for me was the literature lesson when Mrs. Madden read to the under-fourteens from an assortment of classics, ranging from Cranford to the Greek myths.

Non-academic subjects were taught to the whole school in a group, which even with the day girls never exceeded about twenty-five pupils. We were taught drawing (but not painting) by a visiting teacher. This experience was as discouraging for me as the map copying since the assignment was to copy rather difficult abstract designs, for example the Greek key design, or sometimes to draw a group of cylinders and cubes, which I found frustratingly difficult as well as boring. We were also taught needlework, which included learning to darn the very large holes we got in our woollen socks and stockings, using a 'mushroom'. Darning is basically fine weaving with a needle, being careful not to pucker the sock, and I was never very good at this or other forms of sewing.

There were no team games such as netball. In the winter a visiting master taught gymnastics once a week but otherwise we had very little exercise apart from a weekend walk 'in crocodile', two by two. In the summer there were sedate Greek dancing lessons, for which we wore sleeveless green tunics girdled at the waist, and tennis lessons from which I was excluded, as I was from gymnastics, because of my 'weak' heart. We were also taken to the sea to swim if the weather was good – the school was only a couple of blocks from the sea front. We were not allowed to sit on the beach and were quickly shepherded back to school.

We were given substantial meals – both teachers were distinctly stout – which, as was usual then, included almost no fruit and no salads. The cooking was institutional and meals were often an ordeal for me. Breakfast consisted of lumpy porridge and a cooked dish such as bacon and sausages or eggs, and bread and butter. Lunch was a meat dish of some kind, overcooked and usually in thick, tasteless gravy, sometimes with heavy dumplings. On Fridays there was boiled fish. The second course was always a sponge or suet pudding. The only meal in the week which I enjoyed, and looked forward to, was the Sunday lunch with roast meat and potatoes. Vegetables, mainly cabbage or carrots, were boiled and overcooked. For tea we were given bread and butter and jam and dripping or cress sandwiches. Supper may have been a cooked meal but I never had it because of my early bedtime. In my last year, though, I was given a tray in the schoolroom, which throughout the summer term was only too often a slimy dish of stewed rhubarb and custard.

My mother hoped that boarding school would cure me of my food fads, which up to a point it did. The rule was that everything you were given must be eaten before you could leave the table. From the start I refused to eat porridge or dripping or drink milk and after many tears and much punishment I managed to persuade my mother to have me exempted from them. There were other foods that I found disgusting, especially boiled onions and suet puddings, from which I was not exempt. I often spent much of the afternoon in the empty dining room, gazing at the bunches of fruit and flowers in the elaborately patterned wallpaper, unable to eat the food on my plate. I tried wrapping the food up in a handkerchief, stuffing this in the pocket of my knickers and later emptying the contents down the lavatory, but the sticky clothes would be discovered when the washing was done and punishment would follow. Supervision in the school was total. Although I left the school eating a much wider range of food than when I entered, to this day I can't drink milk or eat the foods I refused to eat then. Sweets were not allowed at any time but the other girls were given squares of chocolate after their supper. These were kept in the dining room sideboard and on one occasion I stole some, and was of course found out and punished.

The school routine proceeded with deadly monotony. There were morning and evening prayers with hymn singing, which the maids attended. On Saturday we went for an escorted walk through the town in a crocodile, but we were not allowed to go into shops or taken to the sea front. Occasionally we went in a coach to visit churches in nearby villages. As I know now, the Suffolk country churches are very beautiful, but at the time one church seemed to me as boring as another. On Sunday mornings we went to church and in the afternoon wrote letters home. After tea we were sometimes taken to the church hall to hear a talk with lanternslides by a visiting missionary, a welcome diversion from routine. Although Felixstowe has a busy port we were never taken to see it nor did we ever go into the surrounding country, except on the annual picnic. Once a year on Whit Sunday we got up early and were taken into the country to have a picnic breakfast of hardboiled eggs, before going to the church service. This event was looked forward to by everyone with much excitement.

There were no half terms but parents could visit once a term on a Saturday. I longed for this day each term, when I would have my mother to myself for hours on end. When it came it was almost too wonderful to bear. My mother, who despite her small income enjoyed giving us occasional extravagant treats, would take me to lunch in the best hotel in Felixstowe, a grand hotel overlooking the sea. I marvelled at the large dining room, the well-spaced tables, the chandeliers, the thick carpets, the male waiters and the delicious food, including dishes I had never eaten before – my favourite was apple fritters. It was here I first heard and puzzled over the expression 'catching the waiter's eye.' Then we would walk round the beach and the shops and have tea in a café. My mother would buy me sweets, some of which I would smuggle into school, only to have them detected and confiscated later. I would be in floods of tears as she left.

For booklovers there were undoubtedly very good aspects to the school. Mrs. Madden always read to us at the breakfast table, working her way through large numbers of Dr.Dolittle books. I loved them at the time and because of this read them to my older children in the fifties and early sixties. By the seventies I found them too ineradicably racist to read to my younger children. The school had quite a large library from which we could borrow books whenever we liked. It was composed entirely of Victorian and Edwardian minor classic novels and Edwardian children's books. The children's books were virtually all weepies for girls, such as *Anne of Green Gables*, *A Girl of the Limber Lost* and *The Wide Wide World*. They were generally about girls whose mothers died or went away, leaving them with harsh or unsympathetic friends or relatives. All of them had a moral message and a happy ending. The majority of the books, though, were Victorian or Edwardian novels intended for adults. Those that I liked best were historical novels, for example Harrison Ainsworth's *Old Saint Paul's*, Dumas' *The Count of Monte Cristo*, Scott's *Ivanhoe*, Bulwer-Lytton's *Harold*, *The Last of the Saxons*, Kipling's *Puck of Pooks Hill* and most exciting of all, the *Scarlet Pimpernel* series, by Baroness Orczy. From these I got a real, if distorted, sense of history and a lifetime interest in it.

The books would look very unattractive today. They were uniformly covered in faded and fraying navy blue cotton, and their extensive vocabulary and leisurely style would defeat most contemporary children. But I read them voraciously and with great enjoyment. Books were my saviours, a crucial escape into another world. When I was nine or ten I developed a love of poetry. I spent some of my free time copying out and learning by heart my favourite narrative poems, notably 'Morte d'Arthur', 'The Lady of Shalott' and 'The Highwayman', all of which had an elegiac tone. Comics and schoolgirl magazines were strictly forbidden. During the holidays I devoured a weekly magazine called *The Schoolgirl*, which followed the adventures of a group of girls at boarding school, in the manner of a modern 'soap'. I was fascinated by these girls and their same age school classes and dormitories, team games, tuck boxes, passionate friendships, enmities and adventures, all totally unlike Quarndon House. Once I persuaded a daygirl to bring me in her copy of *The Schoolgirl*, but there was the most terrible scene when this was inevitably discovered.

None of the other girls were great readers but they managed to occupy their free time quite happily with rather limited resources. Card or board games were forbidden and there was no radio or music of any kind – the pianos could only be used during practice times. We played paper and pencil games, such as Consequences. Some girls did knitting or embroidery, we all drew with coloured pencils, usually girls in historical costumes, and we kept leather bound albums. Like the other girls I had two albums, one for cigarette card photos of film stars, collected during the holidays, the other a kind of Victorian memento album. On each of the differently coloured pages friends were asked to write a few lines or do a drawing, and girls vied to have the most luxurious looking album and the most interesting contributions. The older girls amused themselves, as was the custom at that time, by telling fortunes from tea leaves or reading palms. In the winter they told ghost stories, inducing an exciting degree of fear, now produced, I suppose, by horror movies.

The best part of school life was the drama. Every year we rehearsed and acted a play. During my last year in the school, when I was ten, *Hamlet* was put on for relatives and friends in the local Winter Garden theatre, with its stage, spotlights and dressing rooms. I was not considered old enough to be given a part but I attended all the rehearsals and fell in love with the theatrical experience. Watching every rehearsal from the wings, weeping, I learnt sections of the play by heart through absorption. I was enthralled by the language, much of which I couldn't have understood. But I did understand the tragedy and the excitement of the play, the beauty of the poetry and the magic of acting, when a perfectly ordinary girl turned as you looked at her into Ophelia or Hamlet. I'm sure that taking part in a properly rehearsed performance is the best way to introduce children and adults to Shakespeare, infinitely superior to reading aloud in a classroom or even going to watch a professional performance.

But most of the time I was desperately unhappy. Every minute of our lives was regulated in a strict routine, and any infringement was punished. I doubt whether modern penitentiaries are as tightly regimented. We had no access to radio, gramophone, newspapers, magazines or comics, no games were provided in the recreation room, we were not allowed into the garden except in the summer to play tennis (which I was excluded from, because of my heart condition) and we were not allowed to mix with the day girls outside of lesson time. We were not allowed into our bedrooms during the day but had to stay together in whatever place was designated at that time. We were not allowed to have any personal possessions other than clothes in the bedrooms. I would smuggle books into my room under my clothes and hide them under a mattress, but sooner or later they would be discovered. We were not, of course, allowed out of the building unless with staff, nor allowed to make or receive telephone calls.

Punishment involved receiving the anger and scorn of Miss Stevenson, who was icy at the best of times, and being deprived of privileges. There were really no privileges I had that I could be deprived of, and I could hardly have been sent to bed any earlier than my usual time of half past five, so in my case the punishment was to forbid me to read outside the classroom, usually for a whole week. I would be plunged into despair and desperately seek for any printed paper, even the leaflet inside a toothpaste box. I could not imagine how anyone could be so cruel.

One reason that I was sent to this school was that my mother assumed that it would be more homelike than a larger school. However, small size does not guarantee homeliness. Throughout my time there I cannot remember either of the teachers ever treating me with kindness, let alone affection. Whilst they were both cultured, well-educated women, I think they must have disliked children and to be fair they did not normally take children under eleven. I suspect that they ran the school as a way of providing themselves with a life style – large house, servants – they could not otherwise have afforded, rather than for any great interest in teaching or children. Certainly, I never saw them show any care, or even interest, in any of their charges. In particular they disliked me, or so I thought, forever singling me out for criticism or punishment and never praising me for what must have been good schoolwork. Fortunately the piano teacher was a very kindly woman and I looked forward with longing to the nice things she would say in my next lesson. Despite my lack of musical talent my time with her was the highlight of my week.

Because I was the youngest girl by at least three years I had no friends to compensate for the lack of maternal care. One might have thought that the older children would have made a pet of me. One of them did tend to protect me, a gentle auburn haired girl called Fay, whose plight was much worse than mine. She was one of the white child victims of the Empire, domiciled in the dreadful school on her own throughout the holidays with only occasional visits from relatives, not seeing her parents, who worked in Malaya, for years. But none of the other girls took any interest in me. I could not have been a very appealing child, always in trouble, always with my head in a book, and always fitted out as cheaply as possible by my hard-up mother, with my clothes not quite right and all my possessions – soap, sponge bag etc.– the cheapest available, a pad of Woolworth's writing paper instead of a leather writing case. My fingers and sometimes my clothes were chronically smudged with ink. Ball point pens did not arrive in England until 1946 and fountain pens were expensive. Children had to learn the skill of dipping pen nibs into inkwells set into their desks, without splashing or smudging ink on their paper and clothes or spoiling the nibs of their pens. I was not a fast learner in this respect.

Moreover as much the youngest I spent most of the time on my own. We all worked on our own during the lesson periods, but whilst the other girls slept in dormitories – which I never saw, since it was against the rules to go into someone else's bedroom – I slept in a room on my own. Because I was sent to bed absurdly early I missed much of the after school recreation period. But I think I felt this isolation most acutely when my bedtime was raised from five thirty to six or six thirty. From then on, before going to bed I was sent alone to the deserted schoolroom at the far end of the empty first floor, where the maid brought me a supper tray and left me to eat and then go to bed on my own. These experiences, which followed the earlier experiences in the isolation hospital and at Auntie Francie's, probably shaped me for life. I learned to be self sufficient, to be on my own, not to depend on company, and to look for comfort in books rather than in people.

When I reminded Michael a while back that I had spent three years at Quarndon House he asked me how I could have stood it, he had barely survived a term and a half there. In his case he had the additional problem of being bullied by Mrs. Madden's son, a boy of his own age who was then living with her. By the time I started he had been sent away to boarding school. For Michael, however, leaving Quarndon House was indeed a case of out of the frying pan into the fire. He was sent to a boys' preparatory school in another seaside town, Seaford, in Sussex, called Charmandean College. It was one of the numerous private schools which undertook to prepare boys for minor public schools for rather low fees.

We were all astonished when in his first school holiday, aged just nine, Michael returned home with 'public school' manners. He leapt to his feet every time a woman came into the room, insisted on walking on the outside of the pavement, a now forgotten mark of a man of the middle or upper classes, and took off his school cap (which he wore with pride) whenever he met a woman. All this seemed bizarre, like the customs of a strange tribe when transplanted to West Ham, but it delighted my grandmother, who had never before received such treatment. However, during the January term he developed the most terrible chilblains. Like many others in pre-central heating days I too developed chilblains every winter, but Michael's were much worse, and bled persistently. It emerged that the boys' quarters were never heated at all. What we did not know, because he didn't tell anyone, was that he was bullied unmercifully by the other boys and probably caned by the masters – boys' schools were much worse places than girls' schools in this respect. His gentle nature, which made him so appealing to adult women, did not serve him well at this school. He became deeply unhappy, culminating early in his second year at the school in what was called a 'breakdown.' He must have been in a bad way for a school with such a tough ethos to summon my mother in the middle of term to take him home. At the time I was only told that he was ill. Years later I learned that he had sat and cried for days on end, but he never spoke of this experience.

Probably my mother took Michael to a doctor, but what saved him was her decision to send him to a very different kind of school, which dramatically improved both his physical and mental health. The Forest School, near Gods Hill, in the New Forest, was in all respects the antithesis of Charmandean College, and it is extraordinary that two such different schools co-existed. It was similar to A.S.Neill's famous school, Somerhill, in its libertarian approach but instead of being based on psychoanalytic theory it was inspired by the ideals of the Order of Woodcraft Chivalry, which meant caring in the deepest sense for nature. The Order was founded by Ernest Westlake, a Quaker, in 1916. The horrors of the First World War led him to believe that in order to avoid the total collapse of civilisation children must be brought up in close contact with nature, rooted and grounded in woodcraft. They should 'learn by doing' and by living in harmonious social fellowship with children and adults of both sexes. The adults' role was to stand back, 'teaching by being', ready to give guidance where necessary, but allowing children to learn from their own experience with the minimum of adult intervention.

Jean Westlake, his daughter-in-law, describes in a memoir of the early thirties how she followed this principle with her own children. When they were living in London her five-year-old son asked one day if he could go on his own to the zoo. She sent him off at ten o'clock with a postcard in his breast pocket with his name, address, and phone number on it, a picnic lunch and tea, a note book and pencil, and enough money for his bus and admission tickets and for an adult to phone her if necessary. He got back at quarter to five, as it was beginning to get dark, his notebook full of drawings. Later, when they were living in the New Forest, she sent her three children aged seven, nine and ten, to camp on their own in the woods some distance from their home. When she returned some days later to pick them up she found a tidy campsite, clothes drying on the bracken, one child gathering wood, one washing in the river, and the third returning from a shop near the forest with biscuits for tea. Today she would probably be prosecuted for neglect, but she succeeded in making them very self-reliant. In 1926 a splinter group who argued that the Order did not do enough for working-class children started 'The Woodcraft Folk', which continues till today to organise activities for children in many localities. They are quite similar to Cubs and Scouts, but without the religious and 'patriotic' input.

In 1930 Westlake's son set up The Forest School, to put his father's educational ideas into practice, although the training in self-reliance was not so extreme as in his own family. He appointed as headmaster Cuthbert Rutter, a devout Quaker and a Cambridge graduate, who had been a housemaster in a borstal. The school was small, all age and coeducational, housed in a group of single storied wooden buildings in a clearing in the New Forest, which extended downhill to the river Avon. Most of the staff were young and unpaid, and therefore changed frequently. They lived with the pupils, and staff and children addressed each other by their first names. Several artists and writers sent their children there, including Robert Graves and Ben Nicholson.

Sandyballs, Forest School.

Each morning there were lessons in school subjects, which children did not have to attend if they so chose. There were no organised games. Instead, the pupils could climb trees, build tree houses, dig for clay and make pots with it, gather wood for fires, dam streams, swim in the nude in the river, do woodwork with one teacher or art with another, rehearse for a play or a performance of a Gilbert and Sullivan opera or simply hang around. The few rules that existed were made by the pupils in a general meeting. Every summer they went on a ten-day trek, carrying rucksacks and taking tents in a handcart. In this setting Michael rapidly regained his health and happiness, though like most of the pupils he tended to attend primarily the lessons he liked, in his case, English and history. He also memorably played Pooh Bah in a performance of *The Mikado*.

The contrast with Charmandean College must have been mind blowing, but Michael told me years later that he felt instantly at home and remembered only being very happy there, quickly making friends for the first time in his life. When my mother saw this, despite having little sympathy with the school's educational theories and methods she decided to leave him there for two years, which was as long as she felt it safe to neglect his formal education.

Unlike Michael, whose experiences must have been much worse than mine, I did keep telling my mother that I hated school. She never took this seriously. She probably thought that though I naturally missed her I was doing very well academically, and flourishing physically, no longer prey to the illnesses of my early years and because of the forced feeding no longer the food faddist I had once been. I often thought of running away from school, of course, but without any money – we were not allowed to keep money – or even knowledge of how to get to the railway station, I did not see how it could be done. Still, if I had been desperate or brave enough, I could have tried.

After three years at Quarndon House my mother decided to move me to another boarding school and the unhappy part of my childhood came to an end. My misery at Quarndon House remained such a strong memory that about ten years ago I decided to try to exorcise it by revisiting the school. I had reckoned without sixty years of urban growth and redevelopment. Felixstowe had become a city, the largest container port in England. I could not match it to my recollections. I couldn't remember the name of the street the school was in, and Felixstowe was much too big to wander around with the hope of coming across the school. As a port Felixstowe had been heavily bombed during the war and it seemed likely that the area where I had thought the school stood had been redeveloped. I appealed to the Planning Officer but he had no records of the period. He said that there had been many small private schools in Felixstowe before the war, which were all evacuated in 1939, and most had never returned.

I thought the building might have become a nursing or old people's home but he could not trace any current institution called Quarndon House. So the episode remains intact in my memory, the two teachers, long dead, unforgiven.

Life improves at a girls' public school

The school to which my mother decided to move me was Bedford High School for Girls, an independent (i.e., private) girls' school founded in 1882 to provide girls with an education similar to that offered in boys' public schools. I wasn't given a reason for the move but I expect she thought that it was time for me to attend a school with a higher academic standing, where the girls took public examinations and were prepared for careers. In some ways my new school was very different from the previous one, in others, quite similar. Instead of twenty-five pupils there were seven hundred, most of them daygirls, a change I found exciting rather than frightening. Dr. Westaway, the headmistress, was very remote from the younger pupils and I doubt if I ever spoke to her. She seemed both impressive and kindly as she presided in an academic gown over the huge school assembly, with hymns sung to an organ accompaniment.

I quickly decided that the new school was in most ways a great improvement on Quarndon House. Instead of working on my own I was in a class of twenty or so girls of my age, with each subject taught by a different teacher. The atmosphere was very competitive, which was entirely new to me. The three or four classes within each year were grouped by ability, e.g. IIIa, b, and c, and a list was posted in the classroom at the end of term showing each pupil's position on each subject within the class. Since I usually came first in most subjects I found this procedure elating. On the other hand there was gym and a great deal of sport, three whole afternoons a week, netball and hockey in the winter terms, cricket and tennis in the summer. Since my heart was now considered to function normally I was not only allowed, but required, to take part in these activities. I took an instant dislike to them, with their balls hurtling alarmingly in all directions. The 'team spirit' seemed to me absurd and I refused to join in the cheering and support for the class/boarding house/ or school teams. In girls' public schools at that time it was *de rigueur* to enthuse about games, whilst academic prowess was of little account. I don't think it ever occurred to me to conceal my contrary stance, which was, of course, a recipe for instant unpopularity.

For boarders there was a big disjunction between life in the main school, where most girls in your form would be daygirls, and the much more intense social life of your own boarding house. There were several of these houses scattered around the neighbourhood of the school, mine was 'Quantocks' in Linden Road. Each took about thirty girls aged eleven to eighteen – as before I was the youngest, but only by a year. They were large, red brick, Edwardian houses, very like Quarndon House, but bigger. Each was presided over by a housemistress, a middle class woman in her forties or fifties, often a widow. She was not a teacher. Her job was to be responsible for our general welfare and discipline, and to liase with the school and the parents. She said prayers in the evening and grace before meals, and inspected our drawers and lockers at frequent intervals to check that they did not contain forbidden objects and were arranged with military precision. This was supposed to inculcate a lifetime habit of tidiness. In my case, it was only in old age that I came to see the beauty as well as the utility of everyday order.

Our housemistress at Quantocks was thin and elegantly dressed. She often wore a hat indoors, as though she were in transit, and she had the manner of a slightly irritated county lady. She seemed remote and detached and had little individual contact with us unless we transgressed. It was the matron and assistant matron who were responsible for our day-to-day care, getting us up, seeing us to bed, looking after us if we were ill, running our baths, escorting us as we walked in a crocodile to and from school, dosing us daily with Radio Malt (a cod liver oil product) and weekly, whether we needed it or not, with syrup of figs, a laxative. Cuts and grazes were treated by the painful application of iodine. Although Matron was in a quasi-maternal role she was quite stern and unmotherly. The assistant matron, who was probably only about eighteen, showed more signs of humanity but was completely subservient to Matron. All our meals, including lunch, and our recreation and homework took place within the house. We did not mix with girls from other houses, and out of school contact with day girls was forbidden, presumably because they were allowed to do all the things we were not – go around on their own and go into shops and cinemas.

In this and a number of other ways Quantocks was run on similar lines to Quarndon House. For example, no possessions other than clothes were allowed in the bedrooms, the uniformed maids were not allowed to speak to us, Sunday was the usual dreary boarding school round of church in the morning and writing home in the afternoon. However, I was delighted to discover that life in Quarndon House did have some resemblances to boarding school life as depicted in my favourite magazine, *The Schoolgirl*. We wore the traditional uniform of navy blue gym tunics (sleeveless square necked dresses, with box pleats falling from a yoke and a girdled waist) worn with white shirt blouses, school ties, navy overcoat or blazer, and navy velour hats with the school ribbon round the brim. We juniors did not object to wearing these unprepossessing clothes, in fact, I remember feeling quite proud of the new uniform. We slept, with girls of about our own age, in six-bedded dormitories divided into cubicles, with curtains which we drew when dressing and undressing. In each cubicle there was a bed, chest of drawers and a washstand with a china bowl and jug of cold water. The maids brought round hot water in the morning.

There was a rota for our weekly baths – there were no showers in the school, or in most homes at that time. The large bathrooms had two baths, each, like the bedroom cubicles, surrounded by curtains. Modesty was certainly a feature of girls' schools at that time, and extended to menstruation. In the bathroom was an untitled register where girls had to tick off each month the days when their periods started and stopped. Since I knew nothing about menstruation when I arrived at the school I was puzzled and curious about the reasons for this register, but nobody would tell me. Later, when my periods started during term time, I was alarmed by the bleeding and not reassured when sent by the Matron to the housemistress, whose embarrassed explanation –'it means you are getting to be a woman'– conveyed nothing to me. When I got home for the holidays I found my mother had put out for me a packet of sanitary towels and a booklet that explained menstruation, but she never spoke about it and nor, so far as I can remember, did any of my friends.

Not only did the boarding house resemble in many ways the boarding schools depicted in schoolgirls' magazines, we also consciously tried to increase the resemblance. On one occasion the girls in our dormitory decided to have a midnight feast modelled on those we had read about. Some of the girls had a hidden reserve of money and we persuaded a daygirl to buy us jam tarts, buns and sweets, which we hid on a shelf in the disused dormitory chimney. Unfortunately the housemistress brought her small dachshund with her on her daily inspection round and he smelled the food and pulled it down. We were in serious trouble but I don't remember what form the punishment took, probably being deprived of our pocket money – it was not a very punitive regime.

Downstairs there were several recreation rooms, called studies, fitted with lockers for private possessions. Here twelve girls of about the same age did homework after school, supervised by a prefect – no help was given – and then amused themselves till bedtime, which was not as ridiculously early as at Quarndon House. The youngest girls in the house acted as 'fags' to the house prefects, who at eighteen seemed like rather glamorous adults. Unlike the fags in boys' public schools from where the practice was copied our duties were fairly light, mostly fetching and carrying, for which we tended to be rewarded, if only with a smile. It was expected that one would have a 'crush' on one's prefect and look forward to waiting on her, and indeed it was the prefects, rather than the staff, who provided some maternal warmth to the youngest of us.

In the dining room we sat at tables with six girls of similar age, waited on by maids and presided over by a house prefect. We could not choose with whom we sat but unlike Quarndon House we could chat freely to each other. The food was much the same as at Quarndon House, and as badly cooked, but this was no longer a problem for me as we were not forced to eat it, a hugely important liberation. Tea, as at Quarndon House, was bread and butter and on some days jam – on jam-less days girls often piled sugar on their bread. At neither of my boarding schools were cake, biscuits or scones ever served. Great stress was placed on good table manners. We were expected to pass food to everyone else at the table but forbidden to ask for it to be passed to oneself. At times this could be frustrating, but I have subsequently been to dinner parties where I wished others had been taught this rule.

And if there was, for example, one slice of pudding that was larger or for some reason more desirable than the others, or only one helping was left, everyone was supposed to, and did, press their neighbours to take it.

Unlike Quarndon House we were given pocket money according to age, which we could spend on sweets from a kind of stall run by the prefects in the corridor after lunch on Saturdays. I started off with two pennies in the old currency with which I always bought either two Milky Ways or the then aristocrat of the sweet world, a Mars bar. Once a term there was a 'study tea', just for the members of the study, when we each told the matron what we would like her to buy for our tea for six pence. With this sum I could order a chocolate éclair (extraordinary luxury) and one or two crumpets. Treats like these assumed great importance in a regime with few indulgences and helped to make the school much more tolerable than Quarndon House. On reflection, I think it was the element of choice that made these events especially important. Whilst the contemporary emphasis on the value of choice is taken to absurd lengths, the lack of choice in boarding school life at that time was so extreme that to choose once a week between different kinds of sweets became an exciting event.

There were other small improvements on Quarndon House which made life less restricted. On Saturday afternoon the older girls could play their own records in the dining room and we were all allowed to sit round and listen. Here I learned the contemporary popular songs I never heard at home, such as 'Alexander's Ragtime Band', 'Tea for Two', and 'The Isle of Capri'. (The term 'pop songs' was a product of the 1950s). In the garden, besides tennis courts there were small plots for anyone who wanted to grow flowers, and there were swings hanging from several of the trees. My attempts to grow flowers were not very successful but I loved swinging, which could be either exhilaratingly active or a solitary, dreamy experience. On Sunday evenings after tea the Matron read to us and we could always freely use the house library. Instead of the Victorian minor classics of Quarndon House this library was composed largely of novels (screened by the house mistress) by twentieth century authors such as G.K. Chesterton, Hugh Walpole, John Buchan, Georgette Heyer and Arnold Bennet, as well as the Sherlock Holmes books. There were no children's books, nor, as was also the case in Quarndon House, any schoolgirl stories such as the Chalet School series, and teenage fiction had not yet developed. It is amazing how many books I read at boarding school where all reading had to be done amidst the gossip, laughter and quarrelling of twelve girls.

However, reading was no longer the central and only enjoyable part of my life, as I had for the first time acquired friends. My two best friends were Margaret and Irene, both a year or two older than me, but in the same dormitory and study. We were very close friends and after I left the school we corresponded for a year or two, gradually losing touch. Looking back, I think we were drawn to each other because we were all three seen as outsiders, who although not necessarily and at all times unpopular did not quite fit in and were not much liked by most of the girls. I was probably the most unpopular because of my outlandish and openly voiced objections to sport and the 'team spirit' and school rules in general, and the unorthodox views on politics and religion I advanced in my second year. Margaret was probably considered an outsider because she was very religious. Whilst conformity to religion, including a mild degree of fasting during Lent, e.g. giving up sugar, was universal, Margaret was thought to pray and fast to an excessive degree. Moreover she was a weekly boarder, i.e. she went home at weekends. At the time the practice was very unusual – she was the only one in our house – and disapproved of by both staff and pupils. Presumably this was because to admit that it is better to go home than to stay at school would undermine the whole mythology of the 'boarding school spirit'.

Her parents had both been missionaries in China, her father was a doctor, her mother a midwife, and on returning to England they opened a maternity home in Hitchin. It was from Margaret that I learned that babies didn't emerge somehow from the navel, as I had believed. She would imitate her father shouting, 'Push, Mrs. Robinson, push, just as though you were going to the lavatory', and we would collapse with mirth. Bedford High School had half term holidays, long weekends once a term in which we could go home from Friday afternoon to Monday evening. I was always invited to stay by one of my new friends on these occasions, most often by Margaret. Her parents lived above their maternity home, a large house with big grounds in which we could roam. When I went to stay with her we were given money to go off for the day, perhaps to keep us away from the patients' screams. Margaret's religion didn't interfere with our schoolgirl pleasures. We would go to the cinema or a local private sports club with an open-air swimming pool, and in the summer we would lie beside it, eating ice-creams and large bars of chocolate, reading and chatting.

Indirectly, Margaret was responsible for my becoming an avowed atheist at the age of eleven. I had always found the frequent prayers and church services at both schools painfully boring and meaningless. I knew that my family were atheists and that neither Michael and I nor my parents had been christened, but I had never thought much about religion till I met Margaret and her family. Here for the first time were people for whom the church practices were not habits but deeply significant and who consciously tried to live their lives in the light of their religious beliefs. I was impressed and decided that I too should be a Christian. I had long discussions with Margaret about God and our future life as medical missionaries. Some time later I was preparing for a difficult piano exam (I never played well) and prayed frequently and passionately to God to help me pass it. When I failed I was totally shocked and immediately decided that God couldn't exist. This was an opinion I have never shifted from, though subsequently I had rather better grounds for holding it. The only person I talked to about this cataclysmic change in my belief was Margaret, who was distressed. I suppose that my family, who had been amused by my aspirations to be a medical missionary, must have noticed that I said no more about it. I did, however, continue to believe that in some way I wanted to spend my life helping others.

My other best friend, Irene, could hardly have been more different from Margaret. Whilst Margaret was tall and plump with a long plait, Irene was small, shorthaired and thin, with a very sallow complexion. I think her outsider status was due to an impression she gave of being unchildlike, almost adult, in a way that was hard to define. She was sceptical, amusingly cynical, and definitely not at all religious. Until recently her parents had managed a coffee plantation in Guatemala where she had spent most of her life. She had been taught at home, free to roam around for much of the time. I stayed with her several times in the school holidays and it seemed to me that her mother treated her almost as an adult. She did not question us about where we had been, tell us what to do, or send us to bed at a particular time. Because Irene was not used to school she found the restraints of boarding school life exceptionally irksome and the 'boarding school spirit' and passion for sport ridiculous. But, unlike me, she kept these views to herself, and was probably seen only as lacking the required amount of enthusiasm.

Under an oath of secrecy she told me of a sexual experience with a Guatemalan boy who worked on the estate and explained to me how babies were conceived. At first I refused to believe her, the process sounded absurd and disgusting. I had to believe her when I read a science book for children with a chapter on human reproduction which my mother gave me a little later. She herself never spoke to me on this subject or referred to the book. She must have wanted me to be informed on sexual matters, but could not bring herself to talk about them. Irene and I were both film fans, in the holidays reading magazines like *Picturegoer* and sending for photos of film stars to paste in our albums. When I stayed with Irene her mother, like Margaret's, would send us off for the day. She gave us enough money to have lunch in a restaurant, wander round the shops and go to the cinema. On one occasion we went straight from seeing a film in one cinema to seeing another film in a second, feeling enjoyably decadent.

I had two other school friends whom I stayed with on occasion, though they were not such close friends as Margaret and Irene. Bunty left the school when I did, in 1938, to join her parents in India. Remembering her, I realised that the parents of three of my four friends at this school worked or had worked in overseas colonies, which must have provided a significant source of employment for the middle classes. The fourth friend, Stella, lived alone with her father, a psychiatrist, in Southampton. When I stayed with them one summer holiday he took us out to restaurants each evening for dinner, an entirely new experience for me, where I was introduced to such exotic dishes as devilled kidneys. He was generous in giving us money to amuse ourselves with during the day, but I felt uneasy in his presence – he was too curious about our lives, even asking about our dreams.

It seems absurd that parents should send their daughters to a school where they were under constant surveillance and not allowed, even at eighteen, to go out except in a crocodile, or to visit at any time shops, cinemas, or cafés, whilst they happily let them loose on their own all day in the holidays. I, also, would go around the neighbourhood quite freely at home, and from the age of seven I went to and from boarding school on my own in the train. Ivy would take me to the railway terminus, and the train guard would come and tell me when I had reached my destination. Luggage was not a problem as it was always sent in advance in a trunk.

Unlike girls of eleven to thirteen today we did not talk about boys, clothes or, of course, make-up or dieting, nor did the other girls of our age in the house. Irene told me about her sexual experience in Guatemala but that seemed an outlandish and one-off event and she seemed to display no further interest in boys. However, the emotional life in Quantocks was quite intense. Most of the younger girls had 'crushes' on older girls or teachers, or were 'stage-struck' on a film star. Friendships were close, but sometimes the 'study' peer group would turn on a girl with great cruelty, mocking and isolating her, and in that situation her friends, unable to withstand the group pressure, often deserted her. But in our case I don't think our outsider status worried us, we saw it almost as a badge of superiority. The boarding house authorities clearly, though not explicitly, disapproved of close friendships, although they were crucial in making the boarding experience tolerable. Matron assigned us to dining room tables away from our friends, and lists were put up each week of pairs of girls who were to walk together to and from school and on weekend walks, rarely putting friends together.

Although the boarding aspect of the school predominated in our lives, life in the classroom was also important to me. This was not, I'm afraid, for the interest of the lessons, which were humdrum, but for the pleasure of coming top of the class. We did not really get to know the day girls or the boarders from other houses as we had to hurry back to our own house at lunch time and at the end of the day. But my lack of prowess at team games and gym, and my vocal objections to them, gave me a certain unpopular notoriety amongst the day girls. Added to this, early in my second year in the school, when I was eleven, I became labelled a 'Red'. The occasion for this was a classroom discussion of socialism which arose because of a local election. The teacher and the pupils were united in their scorn for, and hostility to, the Labour candidate, attitudes that seemed to be taken for granted in the school. Having grown up in a socialist household this incensed me, especially since as a result of many discussions at home I had by this time decided that I was a socialist myself. So I got to my feet and at some length held forth on why Britain should become a socialist society. I was unabashed by the general hostility to my views, and in fact I felt quite brave, and proud of myself, enjoying the role of agitator.

It is, perhaps, surprising that my mother sent us to schools where the espoused political and religious values were so different from her own. I suppose she felt confident that in the long run her influence would prevail, as indeed it did. I remember clearly my hurt feelings when at the age of about eight I bought a needle case with a photograph of the Queen on the cover, as a present for my grandmother. She set it aside after the first glance with a contemptuous expression, not even pretending to like it. I chose the present in innocence, because of the magnificent robes of the Queen, not knowing then that our family was anti-royalist, or even that there were different attitudes to royalty.

Although at eight unaware of political attitudes I was certainly aware of class differences. Class awareness and hostility was a marked feature of social life before the war. People immediately appraised the social class of anyone they met, and judged them accordingly. To a much greater extent than today class could be identified by clothing. Working-class men tended to wear flat cloth caps and, especially at home, collarless shirts without ties, their wives, crossover floral overalls. Accents, manners, your post code, the school you had attended, your meal times, what you ate and drank, your leisure pursuits, were all sure markers of social class. Middle class people regarded themselves as ladies or gentlemen, and despised working-class people as 'common', 'vulgar' and 'rough', and tried to keep their children from contact with them. They never, as often happens today, sent their children to the local primary schools. Working-class people, for their part, considered the middle class 'snobby', 'stuck up' and unable 'to let their hair down'.

I had some awareness of these differences at least by the age of six, as we moved into 'rougher' streets. When I arrived at Quarndon House at the age of seven I was quickly aware that the tables had been turned. As I took in the large house and garden, the maids waiting at table, and the different way in which almost every aspect of daily life was conducted I felt uncomfortably aware that staff and pupils alike would despise my home and many of the ways of life that I had taken for granted. I don't remember anything ever being said by the other girls, it was more that I knew that everyone could see that my possessions were inferior to theirs – the Lux soap instead of Pears, the Woolworth's writing pad instead of a leather writing case. On returning home, however thankful I was not to be at school, I now saw it through the eyes of my fellow boarders. Whilst scorning their political views I quickly absorbed their class prejudices.

Home, as I will explain later, was living with my grandparents, working-class people who had left school at 11 or 12. I knew that my friends' fathers did not, like my grandfather, sharpen their cut throat razors on a leather strop each day before shaving in the kitchen and that their last meal of the day was not tea at five o'clock. I felt that these working-class ways were inferior and that I could not possibly invite my friends to our home, but at the same time I felt guilty at having such thoughts. I remember Irene's mother's comment, which made me feel ashamed but also angry with her, when in answer to the question, 'Where do you live?' I answered 'Forest Gate'. 'Where's that?' 'E7'. 'Good Lord'. Years later – as children we never discussed such matters – I found that Michael's feelings had been very similar. He told me that he came home from the Forest School with letters of invitation to stay with school friends during the holidays, which he destroyed on the way, because he felt he would not be able to ask them back. I'm afraid I gladly accepted such invitations, knowing I would not reciprocate.

I am sure that neither of us ever felt ashamed of our mother, who was more or less perfection in our eyes. It was our grandparents and their home and way of life that we could not help seeing through the eyes of those who would look down on them. It is of course possible that my mother did realise that we would have such problems, but did not let them impede her major aim, which was to provide us with the opportunity of moving into the professional classes. At no time did she disclose this aim to us, or urge us to work hard in order to achieve it. I think she felt confident that if she put us on the right ladders we would climb up them and escape from West Ham.

Life at Quantocks was very much better than it had been at Quarndon House. At ten, I was much better able to cope without my family than at seven, and whilst the staff were emotionally distant I never felt as I had at Quarndon House that they were hostile. I was no longer isolated for much of the time because of my age and 'weak heart', and, most important, I had friends of about my age to whom I could look for affection and support. The regime was less punitive, I was less often in trouble, and not deprived of books as punishment or forced to eat food I disliked. Surveillance was slightly less total than at Quarndon House and a few 'treats' were provided. Nonetheless we were extremely constrained by rules, almost every aspect of our lives was regulated, including who we sat with at table or walked with to school and the routine was rigid and unvarying. I think it's fair to say, though, that the majority of girls accepted this regime without complaint. Irene and I, as incorrigible rebels, were in a very small minority.

Looking back, I'm struck also by the cultural impoverishment of our lives, which was worse than at Quarndon House. We never took part in drama or were taken to theatrical performances, or were shown slides of works of art or taken to places of historical interest, or indeed taken anywhere except to walk in a crocodile in the town. We had no access to newspapers, magazines or the radio, apart from one occasion when the senior girls were invited into the housemistress' drawing room to hear King Edward v111's abdication speech. We were all taught the piano and there were occasional concerts of classical music in the evening at school, which the older girls could attend. But we were given no opportunity to paint, or walk in the country, ride bikes or horses, or ice skate, watch birds or cook or dance or do any crafts other than knitting and embroidery, nor could we learn by listening to, and taking part in, the conversation of intelligent adults.

The regime seemed designed to turn out conventional, obedient, well-mannered, reasonably well-educated girls, but not girls who thought for themselves or were given to questioning or were creative or independent or aware of the wider social environment. However, since we spent a third of the year at home and came from a variety of backgrounds the socialising process could not be, and was not, a hundred per cent effective. But I fear that five years of such schools left a permanent and damaging imprint on me.

Recently I sent for a prospectus of Bedford High School to see what changes had occurred. The pupils today lead extraordinarily more varied lives than we did seventy years ago. No doubt aiming at an international market, the prospectus states that students from all cultures, religions, and countries are welcome, and girls are encouraged to take the International Baccalaureate diploma instead of A levels. The boarding houses are equipped with extensive ICT facilities and girls are asked to bring their own laptops. Weekly boarding is encouraged, and those who remain at school are taken at the weekends to the theatre and cinema and to towns like Cambridge and Brighton. Quantocks is now a boarding house for sixth form girls only. The school provides fifty-five different clubs and activities for both day and boarding pupils, including, as well as the usual drama, music, singing and sports clubs of all kinds, jazz, tap dancing, and ballet, trampolining, football, rowing, self-defence, and a rock band. It is depressingly symptomatic of what is wrong with our society that these activities are provided for girls who are already privileged, rather than the inner city children who are in much greater need of them. But these privileges do not come cheaply. The fee for day girls is now over £9,000 a year, and for boarders over £17,000, plus extra amounts for music, dance and drama.

Chapter 4

A socialist family in the 1930s

During the five years I was at boarding school, when I was between the ages of seven and twelve, Michael and I spent our school holidays with my mother's parents, Tom and Edith Kirk, in West Ham. My mother was also living there but we saw rather little of her. All three adults were loyal Labour Party supporters. At that time political loyalties were polarised, strongly class-linked, and fiercely held. Unlike new Labour today they were declared socialists. They had a clear moral aim, never far from their minds – the creation of a society based not on profit and inequality but on social and economic equality, freedom and justice. All three were activists. For them, politics was not just a matter of voting for the Labour Party in elections and reading the Labour newspaper, the *Daily Herald*. It was rather the medium in which they lived. Their work and much of their leisure time was bound up with union, municipal or co-operative activities. Trade union activity was then an important form of left-wing politics. Membership was much higher than in many countries, trade unions were a major training ground for labour politicians, and they served as a social glue which bound workers together. In my family the rights and wrongs of individual strikes were never discussed, we were automatically on the side of the strikers. Politics, whether national, union, or municipal was the major topic of conversation, especially when my mother was present. As a young child, I found the conversation boring and hardly listened to it.

But by the time I was eleven I was aware that the international news, far from being boring, was alarming. The Spanish Civil War of 1936–39, when Franco led the landowning, Catholic, monarchists in an armed insurrection against the elected Republican government, became a burning issue for the British left. The Tory government policy was one of non-intervention, largely because they were unwilling to ally themselves with the Soviet Union and the Communist parties throughout Europe, who had immediately offered the Republicans support. Initially, the policy of non-intervention was backed by the right-wing leaders of the Labour Party. It soon became clear that this meant, in effect, abandoning the Republic to the onslaught of Franco's fascist allies, Hitler and Mussolini, who had not hesitated to intervene on the side of Franco. But even after the German air force bombed Madrid, and almost totally destroyed Guernica in 1937, the Tories refused to supply the Republicans with arms. The left were outraged and many young men saw the defeat of fascism in Spain as a cause for which they were prepared to risk their lives. The Government attempted to prevent them from going to Spain to join the communist-led International Brigade, but two thousand young British men did so, many dying, before the Republicans were finally defeated in 1939. Hundreds of thousands of Spaniards on both sides had been killed in the war and thousands more Republican supporters were executed after the war ended.

Despite their anti-communism my family were in favour of intervention, although my mother, who had strong pacifist tendencies, felt torn by the issue. She did become involved in the evacuation and subsequent care of 4,000 Basque children from Bilbao in 1937, organised by one of her closest friends. This was Leah Manning, who had been a Labour MP and was an advocate of British military intervention. The authorities in Republican Bilbao, threatened with starvation by a blockade and fearing the onset of bombing, tried to find homes abroad for 20,000 children. The British government, unwilling to compromise its 'non intervention' position, was reluctant to admit any of them but Leah mobilised powerful all-party support. One crowded shipload of children was finally admitted, with the proviso that the Government would give no financial aid to the scheme. Two years later, with war imminent in Britain, most of the children returned home or emigrated to Central America. But Leah Manning's help was not forgotten, and in 2002, twenty-five years after her death, a square in Bilbao was renamed 'Plaza Mrs. Leah Manning.' The Spanish Civil War not only demonstrated the military prowess of the fascist governments, it was also a chilling illustration of a new military strategy, that of targeting aerial bombardment at a civilian population.

Equally chilling was the simultaneous news from Germany of Hitler's expansionist aims, and his anti-semitic and anti-left repressive measures, including the setting up of concentration camps. These were not yet extermination camps – they were initially set up to imprison and intimidate left-wing opponents. But we children were not as frightened as we should have been by these developments. Probably this was mainly because until the Munich crisis we did not understand their implication for Britain. Another factor may have been the lack of dramatic immediacy in news presentation at that time. Television has brought world events as they happen into the living room in a quite astonishing way, and the hyped up, personalised style of news reporting in all the media gives it a greater emotional impact than the matter of fact, impersonal style of radio and broadsheets in the past.

It was evident to me from the age of about ten that our family's political attitudes were very different from those of our teachers and our friends' parents. For example, in our family it was taken for granted that the police were to be feared and distrusted. I think this had a lasting impact on my brother. As a junior barrister in the early fifties, at a time when the integrity of police evidence was generally taken for granted, he tended to regard it as suspect. Whilst most families paid at least lip service to religion and the church, my parents were militant atheists. Royalty was generally revered at that time and at least until the sixties. The expectation that families would gather together, especially on Christmas Day, to listen to the king broadcasting was unquestioned, but derided in my family. Everyone except my family stood to attention during the national anthem, which was played at the end of all performances at the theatre, cinema, or concert halls – we busied ourselves instead putting on our coats. Against the prevailing code of behaviour, my mother encouraged us to drop our litter in the streets and our tram tickets on the floor of trams, in order to help keep the cleaners in employment. Unemployment was high throughout the thirties and keeping people in work was more important to her than civic tidiness. But we were aware that our family did not simply reject mainstream attitudes. They had strongly held alternative values and aims, which they believed would ultimately succeed, and which gave purpose to their lives.

My family's attitudes were born from their personal experience of the violence with which the state had confronted trade union and socialist, and indeed feminist, activities, during my mother's lifetime. Marches and demonstrations were at times met with charges from mounted police, armed with batons. During the General Strike armoured cars drove round London, and troops set up camp in Hyde Park. In 1932 an unemployment protest march, meeting police opposition, turned into a riot in the Romford Road, at the end of my grandparents' street. For most of my grandfather's adult life he had been a militant trade unionist, ready to take on the police. I realise now with regret that I know very little about this side of his life. He was not one to talk to children and Michael and I disliked him too much to talk to him any more than was necessary, or to question him about his past. So far as we were concerned, he was notable for his outbursts of temper and his bouts of drunkenness. Generally, he took very little notice of us, although when I was eight or nine he made a determined and unsuccessful attempt to improve my handwriting. He had learnt a very fine copperplate script at school and was shocked by my inelegant joined-up print.

His own father had been politically active. When I was about ten I drew up his family tree, which I still have, with information supplied by my grandmother. He grew up in a Norfolk village, Acle, near Upton. His own grandfather, a shepherd, had moved to Norfolk from Scotland in about 1830, and the shepherd's son, my great-grandfather, was at various times a shepherd and a peddler. But by the time my grandfather, Tom, was born he had become, and remained, a farm labourer. He was also a committed trade unionist, which took courage in a period when farmers, fiercely opposed to the unionisation of their workers, could sack them and dispossess them from their tied cottages at will. As secretary of the Norfolk branch of the National Agricultural Labourers Union, founded in 1872, he secured a rise of two shillings a week for the Norfolk farm labourers. He married Elizabeth Griffiths, whose father was Welsh and mother Irish.

Elizabeth, my grandfather's mother, had been 'saved' by Sankey and Moody, American evangelists who visited England frequently between 1872 and 1892. Sankey was a Gospel singer and hymn composer, Moody a preacher, and together they were probably even more successful than Billy Graham, addressing crowds outdoors of up to 20,000. Sankey would start the meetings by singing in a voice said to be of great volume and richness, Moody would then preach and Sankey would sing again as sinners came up to be saved. They interpreted the Bible literally and preached the 'Three Rs' – Ruined by Sin, Redeemed by Christ, Regenerated by Salvation. They inspired Elizabeth to save sinners herself and she became an itinerant Sunday preacher, much in demand in the Norfolk nonconformist chapels for her fiery sermons. She believed that her own children, like all others, needed to have the sin they were born with beaten out of them. A generation later when Auntie Ivy, as a girl, stayed with her, she always had a cane on the table during meals. This she used to beat her grandson Granville who lived with her, severely disabled by polio, and any other children who did not eat what they were given or who spoke at meals out of turn.

As her husband got older his fighting spirit deserted him and he took permanently to his bed, long before he died in 1910 at the age of seventy. Auntie Ivy believed that there was nothing wrong with him, and he had simply found a way to escape from his wife. However, Ronald Blythe, of Akenfield fame, told me recently that farm labourers before the First World War were often literally worn out before their time by long hours of heavy labour in all weathers, on an inadequate diet. Towards the end of the nineteenth century many of their sons joined the army or sought work on the rapidly developing railway network to escape this fate. At the age of thirteen my grandfather, who had left school at eleven, escaped both rural servitude and his oppressive mother by running away to sea. He never returned to the village, and became a lifelong socialist and atheist.

He was born in 1871 and was thus about the same age as my father's Uncle Clynes. Materially, he was probably less deprived. He did not have to start work in the mills at ten or grow up in the terrible pollution of a mill town, and he didn't go hungry as a child. But whilst Uncle Clynes came from a close knit, supportive family and could identify the mill owners as an outside force oppressing him, in my grandfather's case it was his own parents who denied him affection and his mother who physically abused him. Perhaps it is not surprising that as an adult he had serious personality problems. He did not survive many years as a ship's boy – the discipline on board was as brutal as it had been at home. On returning to land he found work in Essex on the railways, then a rapidly expanding industry, and eventually became a signalman. As an inveterate rebel he quickly became involved in trade union and political activity, which at that time was met by the violent opposition of the state.

The 1880s had experienced a revival of socialist ideas in Britain for the first time since the days of the Chartists. The middle of the decade saw the formation of the Fabian Society and of two socialist parties, the Marxist Social Democratic Federation (SDF), led by Hyndman, a socialist intellectual, and the more pragmatic, non-Marxist Independent Labour Party (ILP) led by Keir Hardie, a miner. A savage depression had dragged down wages and raised unemployment. The militant Marxist SDF became the dominant force on the left and many socialist leaders and commentators, including Engels, thought at the time that revolution was an immediate possibility.

The SDF leaders mobilised and drilled the unemployed. On November 13 1887, later known as Bloody Sunday, the police attacked a large demonstration of unemployed workers, killing two and injuring others. A week later the SDF leaders, headed by William Morris, led another march of unemployed workers in an attempt to storm Trafalgar Square against the police. Alfred Linnell, a young clerk, died from injuries inflicted by the police in the struggle. It was deaths like his, as well as others in Ireland, that led a young Irishman, Jim Connell, to write in 1889 what later became the Labour Party official song, *The People's Flag* ('it shrouded oft our martyred dead'). Contemporary Labour politicians look ill at ease singing this song, a relic and reminder of the revolutionary roots of the Labour movement, a time when William Morris wrote:

"Not one, not one, nor thousands, must they slay,
But one and all, if they would dusk the day".

However, thousands did not rally in support of revolution. Instead, the next two decades saw the development of militant trade unionism, in which my grandfather played a part. Before this time trade unions had been mainly respectable associations of skilled workers, e.g. the United Signalmen and Pointsmen, and tended to function as little more than friendly societies. Now unskilled and semi skilled workers, subjected to appalling working conditions, flocked into new unions led by socialists, who had no hesitation in calling strikes and organising marches. Between 1888–89 strikes by the match girls, the new gas workers' union and the newly unionised dock workers were all successful. A great struggle with the old craft unions followed to create large, powerful new unions, which would include all the workers in an industry. My grandfather's union, The National Union of Railwaymen (N.U.R.) was finally formed from the amalgamation of several small unions in 1912, and union membership doubled in the next eighteen months.

In 1900 the trade unions, with the Fabian Society, the SDF and the ILP set up the Labour Party. Its stated aims were not socialism, let alone revolution, but to get MPs elected who would fight for legislation to protect the unions. In the 1906 election twenty-nine Labour MPs (including my uncle Clynes) were elected. There was already one socialist MP, Keir Hardie, the ex-miner, leader of the ILP, who had been elected for West Ham in 1892. He famously took his seat in Parliament wearing his working clothes and cloth cap, escorted by a large procession of his constituents, with a brass band playing. To the fury of the Establishment one of his first actions was to oppose the vote of congratulations to Queen Victoria on the birth of a grand-daughter, because the House had sent no condolences to those bereaved in a recent Welsh mining disaster.

In 1894 at the age of twenty-three my grandfather, Tom Kirk, married, and headed for West Ham, then a major centre of left-wing activity. He at once became involved with Keir Hardie in the local ILP, as well as in the struggle to set up the N.U.R. West Ham was the first local authority to elect a Socialist council in 1898, and my grandfather served on it from 1910 onwards, first as a councillor, then as an alderman. He remained a West Ham, rather than a national, trade union leader, probably held back by his hotheadedness, short temper and tendency to bluster. Although a militant trade unionist, always ready to lead a local strike, and a republican, he knew nothing about Marxism and was bitterly opposed to the Communist Party from its inception. Tall, extravert and good looking, with a hail-fellow-well-met manner, he was a great street corner orator. His style would today be thought ranting, and was perhaps absorbed from his hell-and-damnation preaching mother.

When the First World War broke out it was supported by most Labour leaders, including Keir Hardie, and by most national trade union leaders, who voluntarily gave up the right to strike. But it was opposed by many of the local leaders, including my grandfather. Unofficial strikes took place and became more frequent from 1917, and in 1918 a national rail strike successfully improved wages. As unemployment grew after the war mounted police rode down demonstrators in Trafalgar Square. The advent of a minority Labour government in 1924 failed to stop the frequency of railway and other strikes, and it was defeated in Parliament after barely a year in office.

The failure of the General Strike of 1926 put an end to my grandfather's militant union activity. Along with thousands of militants all over the country he was dismissed from his job. Michael thought his employers must have welcomed this opportunity because of his drunkenness, but it does seem unlikely that he could have survived for many years as a signalman with a serious drink problem. On the other hand my grandmother told me wistfully on one occasion that he could have been a stationmaster 'if it hadn't been for the drink'. At the time when we moved in with him, seven years after he was sacked, he went every day to the local pub, which he used as a kind of club, a place to meet friends and pass a large part of the day. Quite often he had a bout of drunkenness, when he would stagger home or be brought home by fellow drinkers. Sometimes they left him at night collapsed on the front door step. If he was still on his feet he would come in the house shouting in a blind rage, hurling anything he could lay his hands on across the room. Even now, I find the smell of beer on a man's breath nauseating. I don't believe my grandfather ever physically attacked anyone but he was a terrifying spectacle to us children, huddling away from him in another room. The next morning he would groan loudly that he could not get up without a drink. Even if we had not been anxious about class differences his unpredictable drunken bouts would have made it impossible for Michael and me to bring friends home, and nobody in the family ever suggested it.

He never got another job but he continued to be secretary of the local branch of the N.U.R., and on reaching the age of sixty-five became active in the Association of Old Age Pensioners. He managed to earn some money from his work as a West Ham alderman and commissions from the N.U.R. as well as by writing articles for its journal, the *Railway Review*, which I read recently in the British Library newspaper section.

They included an anti-communist series on 'British Workers and Soviet Russia', which was 'aimed principally at those foolish persons who picture an industrial inferno as an earthly paradise,' a series on 'Buying Britain's food', and another series on 'West Ham: The first socialist municipality in Britain'. His very basic education at a village school had stopped at eleven, but like Uncle Clynes he was a member of the last working-class generation to educate themselves after leaving school by extensive reading in the evenings. In his case, apart from Dickens, who was then still immensely popular, he mainly read books advocating socialism, such as Robert Blatchford's *Merrie England*, and contemporary socialist novels by Jack London and Upton Sinclair. But he also acquired some knowledge of economics and a considerable knowledge of current world affairs. By the time I knew him he read only Labour and trade union newspapers and periodicals – I never saw him with a book, and he owned very few. However, he continued to write easily and with gusto.

His somewhat high-flown style must have owed much to his early religious indoctrination. For example, writing about the likely future course of the Soviet Union he alluded to Bunyan's *The Pilgrim's Progress* – 'But like the by-way to Hell that Christian and Hopeful found even at the gate of the Celestial City itself, the road may yet lead in the other direction. For there is in Russia that which George Brandes described as the "darkly mysterious."' The George Brandes he referred to was a radical Danish writer then famous for his sayings, which are still relevant, such as, 'It is useless to send armies against ideas.' Today, there must be very few railwaymen able or likely to scatter their writing with such allusions. The self-educated workers of the past were simply better educated than workers today. But my grandfather, like most people at the time, was deeply anti-semitic, writing that 'the Soviet can no more suppress the international Jewish organisations for moving and conserving wealth than could the kings of the middle ages.' Both of my grandparents and my aunt used the terms 'Yid' and 'Darky' frequently and disparagingly, though they had met very few Jewish people and hardly any black people. At that time West Ham, which my grandparents rarely left, was a solidly white working-class district, except in the docklands. But I never heard my mother make any anti-semitic or racist remarks.

Both Michael and I intensely disliked our grandfather. In my case, certainly, the feeling amounted to hatred. Although he could be genial, he had a bullying manner, was quick to anger, and his drunken rages frightened us. Christmas afternoon was an especial ordeal. At that time pubs opened as usual on Christmas morning, and my grandfather would return in the afternoon when they closed, having missed, thankfully, Christmas dinner. He would be in an exceptionally aggressive mood. He would shout obscenities, rage against Christianity, abuse everyone, and start throwing things around. My mother, who was the only one who could handle him and had any sympathy for him, would eventually persuade him to go to bed and help him up. My grandmother, although her whole demeanour expressed her hostility, never complained about him in front of us children. The only even implicit criticism I heard her make was in relation to his meanness, when she advised me, 'Whatever you do, don't marry a mean man.' Notoriously, he was said to have only once in his life given a present to anyone, when he gave my mother sixpence for getting a free grammar school place.

I had an extra reason for hating him. He sexually abused me one day when we were alone in the house, when I was about ten, picking me up and laying me on a bed. This was all the more frightening in that the episode began by his usual bullying mode changing to flattery and a smiling joviality, like the wolf's transformation into Red Riding Hood's grandmother. Like most children I never told anyone of this experience at the time. I told my cousin about it recently, and she told me that he had 'tried it on' with her, and that when she was an adult her mother, my Auntie Ivy, had told her that as a child he had abused her. I was astonished – how could my aunt not have warned my mother and grandmother that I was at risk? I suppose I should not have been astonished – there was a complete taboo in our family, as in many families at the time, on any reference to sex. It seems to me very likely that sexual abuse of this kind was, and perhaps always has been, not uncommon.

After our grandmother died at the age of seventy-five Michael and I never saw our grandfather again. He lived on his own for a while, though there were some rumours of a 'lady friend' moving in. As he became infirm the council persuaded Auntie Ivy to take him to live with her. This arrangement was inevitably very short lived – both had fiery tempers – and he spent the rest of his life until he died, aged eighty-nine, in a council old people's home. Neither Michael nor I ever visited him or went to his funeral.

I knew my grandmother, born Edith Mary Collins, very much better than my grandfather, or indeed, than my mother, because I spent so much time with her, and most of her life was contained within her house. In personality and physique she was the opposite of her husband. Whilst he was tall, broad, blonde, blue eyed, and outgoing, she was short, dark, slight, and shy. He had a loud, blustering manner, whilst she was reticent and soft spoken, offended by coarse language and behaviour, and decidedly prim. She had grown up in what was then the village of Prittlewell, now a suburb of Southend, in Essex. Her mother, who had been widowed young, supported her children by working as a midwife in cooperation with the local doctor. She delivered babies on her own, without any nursing or midwifery training or qualifications, which were not then required by law. She continued this work into old age and is said to have delivered a baby, returned home and died. Auntie Ivy, who was a sickly child, (though she lived to her late eighties) was often sent to stay with her to benefit from the country air. She remembered her in sharp contrast to her paternal grandmother as warm and indulgent, spoiling her outrageously. If Ivy didn't like the dinner she would be given a penny to buy a bun at the village bakery.

Edith, my grandmother, left school at twelve and was apprenticed, she told me, to 'the best milliner in Southend', walking the three miles to work and then home again, before and after working from 8a.m. – 7p.m. Two of her brothers worked on the railway and it was through them that she met my grandfather, Tom Kirk. At the age of twenty, in 1894, she made what was surely the greatest mistake of her life and married him. Soon afterwards they moved to West Ham. As a country girl she was shocked to find stale eggs and rancid butter in the shops. In 1906 *The Jungle*, by Upton Sinclair, was published. It vividly described workers falling into machinery and being ground up along with animal parts for use in meat pies and sausages. Other accounts described 'raspberry' jam being made from swedes, with wooden pips and colouring added.

Horrified, from that time she bought no prepared food but made all her own jam, cakes, biscuits, mince pies and Christmas puddings. She cooked with the dripping she made, and would not allow margarine (which she thought of dubious origin) in the house or minced meat or sausages. She decided to keep her own hens, which she did all her life, and she got her country relatives to send her fruit in the summer. The only tinned foods she bought were those she could see the composition of – peas, fruit, and salmon – and there were no shop-bought sauces or packets of Bisto in her kitchen. It was a matter of principle with her to buy not only food but virtually everything except clothes, which she made herself, at the Co-operative Society. It had been set up to sell pure unadulterated food, was controlled by its members, and treated its staff fairly. She was, in fact, an organic consumer before her time.

She was also a committed socialist and like my grandfather strongly opposed to the monarchy and religion. In her early-married years a whole way of life was available to socialist families in the Clarion movement. In 1891 Robert Blatchford, author of 'Merrie England', started *The Clarion*, a penny Socialist weekly with not only political and anti-religious articles, but also regular features on music, theatre, books, sport, a Children's Corner and a Woman's Letter. It soon achieved a circulation of 90,000. *The Clarion* promoted a William Morris style of socialism, stressing the immorality and ugliness of capitalism, and advocating a society which would be not only equal and just, but one where people would live more satisfying lives, closer to nature, making and using beautiful objects. Meanwhile, *The Clarion* encouraged socialists to spread the gospel and gain mutual support by joining one of the Clarion clubs, which sprang up all over the country. There were cycling clubs for young people, who on Sundays cycled together into the country, their saddlebags full of Clarions to sell or give away, and also Clarion rambling clubs and Clarion holiday camps, and choral singing clubs, which organised concerts of socialist songs – Gustav Holst became the first conductor of the Hammersmith Socialist Choir.

At about the same time a network of Socialist Sunday Schools spread all over Britain, where children were taught socialist ethics instead of religion. The first school opened in London in 1892 and by

1912 there were 200 schools throughout Britain. They were set up by socialists as an alternative to the long established church and chapel Sunday schools which most working-class children attended. Those who worry that without religion there can be no morality should study the ten secular commandments that were taught:

Love your schoolfellows, and make happy those in sorrow.

Be grateful to your parents and teachers, and love learning.

Do some kindly deed each day.

Honour good men, be courteous to all, bow down to none.

Stand up for what is right, but do not be revengeful.

Try not to be cowardly, and always help the weak.

All good things are produced by the toil of hand and brain. Whoever enjoys them without working steals the bread of workers.

Speak the truth at all times, and do not believe what is contrary to reason.

Love your own country, but do not hate or despise other countries, and strive to abolish war.

Look forward to the day when all the men and women in the world will be free and live in peace.

The children were also taught the importance of collective and militant struggle. I have my mother's copy of the *Socialist Sunday School Song Book*, which includes many rousing militaristic songs such as:

'Onward friends of Freedom

Onward for the strife

Each for all we struggle

One in death and life'

as well as the famous revolutionary songs – 'The Red Flag', 'The Marseillaise', 'England arise, the long long night is over', 'Arise! Ye starvelings from your slumbers'. However, there are just as many songs advocating pacifist, internationalist principles, for example:

'Nation with nation, land with land,
Unarm'd shall live as comrades free;
In ev'ry heart and brain shall throb
The pulse of one fraternity.'

It has to be said that these lack the rousing tunes of the more revolutionary songs. Throughout all the songs there is a celebration of fraternity, equality, and liberty, as in:

'Hail! Dawn of liberty, Day of equality
When all mankind shall be bound in fraternity.'

The songs specifically written for children do stick in the modern gullet, for example:

'We're a band of little Comrades
Walking in the path of truth;
We are marching onward onward,
Through the flowery land of youth.
Marching onward up to Manhood
When we mean to join the fight
Of the weak against oppression
In the battle for the right.'

There are two more verses, and a refrain:

'And we practice as we go
On the little things we meet;
Carrying Granny's parcel for her,
Guiding blind men o'er the street
Lifting up the fallen baby,
Helping mother all we may
Thus as little duties meet us
We perform them day by day.'

After she acquired a car my mother would beguile long journeys by singing these songs to us. Both she and my aunt were, of course, sent regularly throughout their childhood to the nearest Socialist Sunday School. The experience made no impact on my aunt, who became a dedicated *Daily Mail* reader and royalist as soon as she left home, but it left my mother a convinced, idealistic socialist. As a teenager she graduated from the Socialist Sunday School to become an enthusiastic 'Clarionette', cycling every Sunday into Essex with her local Clarion cycling club. The heyday of these groups was before the First World War. When war broke out *The Clarion* strongly supported it, and in consequence lost the majority of its readers. The circulation dropped rapidly from 90,000 to 10,000. Blatchford moved increasingly to the right, and eventually became a Tory and a supporter of the Empire.

After the First World War my grandmother represented the Labour Party for many years on the local Board of Guardians, an elected group of ratepayers who administered the local workhouse (the experience left her with an abiding fear of entering one) the boarding out (fostering) of children, and poor relief. These boards were abolished in 1929 to be replaced by Public Assistance committees, but the poor law system was not finally abolished until 1948. Despite her shyness my grandmother was very determined and had a powerful sense of duty. It was this presumably, which led to her standing, successfully, for election as councillor in 1924. She must have won by virtue of being on the Labour Party ticket, it is difficult to imagine her making public speeches. She also held office in the local Co-operative Society for many years.

Always a supporter of women's rights, though she had not been an active suffragette, she wanted my mother to have a career that would give her the economic independence that she herself never achieved, and she helped her to do so in many practical ways. By 1933 when we went to live with her my grandmother was still involved with the West Ham Co-operative Movement, but no longer active in the Labour Party. However she retained an interest in politics and every Saturday until her death at the age of seventy-five she bought a copy of the Communist *Daily Worker* from a young man who called at her house. This greatly annoyed her husband, always a fierce opponent of the Communist Party. We used to tease her that she bought it because of the charm of the young men and I think this was partially true – her life had been sadly lacking in charming young men.

She used to speak nostalgically of the laughter and high spirits in the house before her daughters married, when she also had two lodgers, sometimes young men, sometimes young women, who shared the largest bedroom and lived as members of the family. By the time we moved in with her she was, I think now, chronically mildly depressed. And some time after my mother, Michael and I finally moved out of her house she became seriously depressed, staying in bed for many weeks, refusing to speak. Although her daughters always faithfully visited her once a week she had no other relatives within reach and she seemed never to have made friends to compensate for her loveless marriage. I can't remember anyone outside the immediate family and an occasional woman friend of my mother's ever entering the house, apart from Florence, another dressmaker, who succeeded the lodgers, renting the largest bedroom as a work room. My grandmother did no more than nod to the neighbours. I don't know whether this was because of her reserved personality or because she didn't consider them respectable. At the time I knew her she never went out other than for her work or essential shopping. Her only diversion was reading. Most evenings when she had finished work she would settle down with a book, sometimes Dickens, more often a very sentimental novel by the prolific interwar novelist Warwick Deeping.

She did, however, get happiness from caring for her beloved animals. As a child she had a pet lamb, which she said did indeed follow her to school, and as a girl she used to go the local Big House to help groom the hounds. In London she always had a cat, sometimes a dog, and she was fond, individually, of each of her eight hens. If one was ill she would bring it in the house and keep it in a cardboard box by the fire, wrapped in an old cardigan, dosing it with teaspoons of brandy. Like many working-class women of her generation who had seen the terrible effect drunkenness had on family life, she was a teetotaller, that is, she thought any consumption of alcohol was wrong and she had taken The Pledge never to drink it herself. Still, she had a great belief in the efficacy of brandy for sick animals and kept a small amount hidden away in a medicine bottle. She made a little money selling eggs to the neighbours, but of course she never ate her hens.

Her married life had always involved working very hard. Because so much of her husband's money was spent on drink she had early decided that she would have to earn money by taking in lodgers and doing dressmaking at home, to ensure that the rent was paid. Like the general run of dressmakers at the time – now they are almost an extinct species – although competent, her clothes were decidedly unstylish. As soon as we were old enough to realise this my cousin and I begged our mothers for shop bought clothes but were very rarely given them. Instead, until the outbreak of war, my mother got most of both her own and my clothes, apart from school uniform, made free of charge by students at the then West Ham Technical College.

My grandmother's mornings were mainly spent in heavy physical labour. Coal had to be carried into the house from the coal shed. The kitchen range, used for cooking, and heating the room, had to be lit every morning, black leaded and frequently stoked with coal. There was no running hot water so kettles had to be constantly refilled and kept simmering on the range. The weekly wash was a formidable task. A fire had to be lit under the clothes boiler in the scullery to heat the water, stains first removed by rubbing on a rubbing board before plunging them in the boiler. Then the laundry, heavy with water, had to be wrung through the mangle on the back porch and hung to dry in the garden or kitchen. Without a vacuum cleaner mats were cleaned by hanging them on a line in the garden and beating them with a kind of racquet. Food had to be cooked for the hens, and the hen run had to be cleaned out. Every day my grandmother cooked a two-course midday meal for her husband and daughter, and in the school holidays, for Michael and me.

Except on washing and ironing days my grandmother managed to fit some of her dressmaking into the morning. She would peddle furiously on her treadle machine or sew by hand with a row of already threaded needles stuck in her blouse, her lips terrifyingly clenched over an array of pins. She was quick and bustling in everything she did, never sitting down till the evening. As soon as the midday meal was finished she would quash any tendency to linger by getting to her feet, saying, 'This won't buy the baby a new bonnet.' In the afternoon she worked for the Co-op, walking briskly round the neighbourhood, calling on members to collect their contributions to the Christmas and funeral clubs. She also made cakes in the afternoon and in the summer large amounts of jam, and if she had time, she did more dressmaking.

My grandmother never cut corners on cooking, which was particularly time consuming in the summer, when peas had to be shelled, runner beans sliced, gooseberries topped and tailed, blackcurrants destringed, and jam made. She did, however, give housework a very low priority, as had her mother, the village midwife, and as my mother was to do in her turn. The usual extent of her housework was to quickly sweep the kitchen floor and perhaps run over the mats in the hall with a carpet cleaner, occasionally beating them in the garden. She sometimes dusted, but she certainly never undertook spring-cleaning, or polished or 'turned rooms out'. I don't think the house was actually dirty, but my grandmother disliked housework and did as little as she could get away with. However, she was concerned that the outside of the house should always look clean. The front door was kept dusted, the front step frequently whitened, and – my mother's only contribution to the housework – the windows kept clean. It used to terrify me to watch my mother cleaning the outsides of the windows, sitting on the first floor window sills, facing inwards, her legs held in place by the lower window sash. My grandfather's only contribution was to polish all the shoes.

My mother had bought my grandmother an electric oven, kettle, fire and iron, to free her from the labour and dirt of the kitchen range, but she hardly ever used them. She was unwilling to give up the all day warmth of the range, the comfort of its open grate, the permanently simmering kettles and the tremendous heat of the oven, which produced her excellent roasts and Yorkshire puddings. Sometimes she used the electric hotplates to make pancakes, but for the most part she had learnt how to manage without modern aids and felt no need for them. She did not want an electric iron, because she had perfected the skill of keeping several flat irons at different heats on the hob. She kept food cool in the summer in a larder with outside ventilation and had butter dishes that cooled by water evaporation. There was no 'weekly shop' – without cars or refrigeration food was bought daily. Working-class women would run over to the nearest shop, or send out a child, middle class women would phone the local shop with an order and deliveries would be made swiftly by a boy on a bike. My grandmother visited the local shops in the course of her afternoon work round, and it helped that the Co-op milkman called twice a day, the Co-op baker daily, and the greengrocer several times a week.

I thought of my grandmother as old, and I suspect she did too, but she was only fifty-seven when we first moved in. Like many women of her age and class she retreated early into a kind of old age uniform. She wore longish black skirts and subdued blouses with a brooch at the neck, usually covered when in the house by a patterned crossover apron, or in the evenings by a shawl. Outside she always wore a black coat of rather shiny broadcloth and a black hat, which she discreetly trimmed – neither she nor her daughters ever went out without a hat. Even her umbrella was black, though its handle was in the form of a bright green parrot's head, which both horrified and fascinated me. She wore her hair, which had been very dark and was now grey, in a bun. She made all her own clothes including her coats, and unlike my grandfather who was quite vain, she seemed not interested in her appearance as long as she looked clean and respectable.

To be respectable was then a key concept, distinguishing not only individuals, but classes, or sub classes – the unrespectable section of the working-class was scorned not only by the middle class, but by the respectable working-class. These were generally skilled workers, the labour aristocracy – it was difficult to maintain respectability on a very low income. It involved a cluster of virtues, including thrift, self-discipline, hard work, sobriety, living within one's means without charitable assistance, and sexual propriety. Within the house respectability required tidiness, cleanliness and a certain standard of housewifery, such as the use of a tablecloth for meals. My grandfather, apart from always being clean and smartly dressed, was decidedly unrespectable, whilst my grandmother was, of course, the acme of respectability. She often warned us against going out in less than spotless underclothes or in stockings that needed mending, in case someone should see them if we were knocked down by a bus or car. Amongst her other oft repeated and surprisingly pragmatic tips for dealing with life's hazards were, 'Never go out without at least sixpence in your pocket', and, 'Be good, but if you can't be good, be careful'.

Unlike my grandfather she was certainly not mean. Out of her hard earned savings she bought me an amethyst necklace for my twenty-first birthday and she saved to give Ivy money towards a deposit on a house. But she was extremely parsimonious and the ultimate anti-consumer, reluctant to see any expenditure she considered unnecessary.

If we were out she would refuse my mother's invitation to have tea in a café, arguing that it would be a waste of money, and in any case the milk would not be fresh and the cakes would not be made with butter. If absolutely dragooned into having a meal out she would sit at the table calculating how much more cheaply she could have made each dish at home, and she could not be laughed out of these attitudes. A preoccupation with saving money was, admittedly, a perfectly rational response to the desperate hazards of working-class life before the advent of the welfare state. But in my grandmother's case this preoccupation had become an obsession, perhaps because of her deeply ingrained Puritanism. When she died at home at the age of seventy-five, still working as hard as ever, she left savings of about £500 in bank notes hidden in the house. Auntie Ivy knew where the money was and quickly retrieved it before my grandfather could find it.

I don't know when relations between my grandparents deteriorated but there was no love or affection between them when I knew them. My grandmother's constant disapproval of her husband was palpable, but rarely expressed, and she did not respond when he angrily shouted at her. They talked to each other when necessary, they shared the same views on religion, politics and society, but they certainly never chatted or went anywhere together. It was clear that she was disgusted by his drunkenness but she made no comment in my presence, and maintained an attitude of quiet dignity during his tirades. It infuriated him that she would not give him any of the money she earned. Sometimes, desperate to buy a drink, he would search the house whilst she was out on her rounds for money that she might have hidden, and if he found any he would take it and go out.

But I doubt whether, despite his hot temper, drunkenness, and meanness my grandmother ever seriously contemplated leaving her husband. Even though he didn't give her enough money to run the household, without the contribution he did make, at a time when there was no child or housing benefit or income support, she could not have managed to bring up her children 'respectably'. Equally or more important was her belief that no respectable woman would break up her marriage. Socialist and atheist she may have been, but in other ways she was deeply conventional and very prim. When her niece formed a relationship with a married man she would no longer speak to her.

Sex was a taboo subject in the household and I think that her sexual relationship with her husband must have been unsatisfactory, and ended early. Certainly, as soon as her daughters left home she moved into a separate bedroom, a very unusual arrangement in a working-class family, and she undoubtedly passed on to her daughters a distaste for sex.

Although in my late teens I began to respect and sympathise with my grandmother, as a child I did not like her. I thought her cold and distant and I resented her substituting for my mother. My cousin's judgement recently, which had not changed over the years, was that she was 'stern and Victorian, not like a grandmother, not affectionate.' However, there must have been another side to her – the same woman was remembered by Michael, whom she dearly loved, as 'warm and affectionate', and her daughters were very attached to her. She was very proud of my mother, but, unlike her husband, she was careful never to give any sign of preferring her over her sister.

Despite my grandfather's shortcomings as a husband and father, my mother as a girl admired his political and trade union activities. She used to distribute leaflets for him at election times, accompany him to public meetings, and when he took his soap box to a park or street corner she would go with him to 'start a crowd' and lead the applause. She took easily to public speaking and soon became much more effective than her father. All her life she retained a degree of sympathy for him, shared by no one else in the family. It must have been because he was in some ways a role model to her that as soon as she started to teach she became active in the National Union of Teachers and the local Labour Party. Physically, too, she resembled him. She was a good-looking woman, of above average height for the time, slim all her life, with an erect carriage. She had blue eyes like her father and thick fair hair that, until it was bobbed after she left college, was long enough for her to sit on. She was the clever younger daughter, who went to a grammar school and a two-year Teachers Training College, then the best career option for bright working-class girls. There was never a possibility that she could go to a university, but she did not repine about this, although she was determined her children would go. She passionately wanted to improve the education of working-class children, and later I describe some of her ideas about education.

My mother was undoubtedly a feminist of her era. The suffrage movement finally achieved its aim in 1928, when women under thirty were given the vote. By that time my mother was thirty-one, with two children. But women still experienced discrimination in many areas. Many fewer women than men entered higher education, the professions and skilled jobs, they were paid less for doing the same work as men, and married women were often regarded as dependents of their husbands, for example, they were not able to apply for a mortgage. My mother actively campaigned for equal pay, which was not finally achieved by teachers until 1961, after her death, but nine years before the Equal Pay Act was passed in 1970. However she did not join the National Union of Women Teachers because they were almost entirely concerned with gender equality amongst teachers, whilst my mother's priority was to end class discrimination in education.

She was, however, very aware that working-class women were even more oppressed than working-class men. She despaired at the low expectations of the girls in her school and the narrow opportunities open to them. Almost all on leaving school at fourteen did meaningless repetitive work on the production line of the local Tate and Lyle factory, until, seeking freedom from their parents and a higher status, they married and brought up their children, now dependent on their husband's handouts. My mother certainly did not believe that men should occupy the leading positions in society, she herself was a head teacher, an excellent public speaker and in 1938 president of the National Union of Teachers.

She very rarely spoke to us about the past. We learned about our father and the family history from my grandmother and aunt. My mother's mind seemed to be always on the present and the future. She was determined that both Michael and I should have the best education she could give us, which would lead us to successful and useful careers. She did not in any way discriminate between us, or have lower or different expectations of her daughter, and she did not want either of us to marry until we were well established in a profession. She had returned to full time work herself whilst I was still a baby, and rather despised women whose interests were mainly confined to their homes and families. She could not imagine that her daughter would be content with such a life.

But it was only after her death that the 'second wave' of feminism in the sixties and seventies argued that personal relationships between the sexes reflect gender inequalities in society. Although she certainly didn't believe that women can only find fulfilment in child rearing and domesticity, she accepted without question the traditional division of responsibilities within the family. When at forty-three she set up house with a male partner she did not in any way abdicate her role in decision making. But she did unquestioningly add to her work load the roles of cook, shopper, cleaner and general housekeeper, even though she was working much longer hours and with a wider range of work responsibilities than her partner. Unlike some later feminists she was very interested in clothes and her appearance, and, far from having any general hostility to men, most of her friends were men, who tended to find her very attractive. She also had a few good women friends, but they were all single women, who, like her, were involved in politics and in their own work. Typically, at social gatherings my mother would be deep in discussion with the men about political, union, or municipal policy and strategy, whilst their wives would be at the other end of the room discussing their children and homes.

My mother resembled my grandmother in little except a propensity to hard work. Far from being prim and puritanical she smoked and drank, though very moderately – her cigarette case only held five cigarettes. Between the wars for a woman to smoke cigarettes suggested that she was modern and liberated – although no respectable woman would smoke in the street – and I think it was for that reason, rather than any addiction to nicotine, that she sometimes smoked. My mother was not, unlike her mother, introverted and depressive. On the contrary, she was socially confident, vivacious, and smiled a lot. It was often said of her that 'she could charm the birds off the trees', and she emanated such a feeling of vitality that even when very ill with cancer she seemed, receiving visitors, to be the most alive person in the room. Despite her very limited income she loved to treat us to occasional extravagances – a taxi ride or a meal in a restaurant. She was also very ambitious both for herself and even more so for us children, for whom she made great sacrifices. The money she earned working long hours after the end of the school day was spent on our school fees, not on herself. She liked clothes, and I'm sure that she would have preferred to buy them in Oxford Street, but to save money she had them made by students at the West Ham Technical College, and although she always looked attractive her clothes lacked a fashionable edge. Another economy was to have her hair washed and set, not very professionally, by a neighbour, and she had no jewellery until, a few years before her death, she bought a ring.

Fortunately, although she resembled her father physically and in some ways he was a role model for her, she did not inherit his explosive temper and bullying manner. Before their marriage broke up our parents always seemed to us children to be shouting at each other, but thereafter I don't remember my mother ever behaving in this way. In fact she was very skilled at defusing situations and finding a way to achieve her ends, whether by means of her extraordinary charm, or by diplomacy, or manipulation, or where necessary making a decisive intervention, even if this made people angry. When my cousin Kathleen decided she wanted to train as a nurse, her mother, Auntie Ivy, refused to allow this, on the grounds that she needed her at home, despite the fact that the two of them constantly quarrelled. My mother, who Kathleen told me 'she adored all her life', knowing the futility of arguing with her sister, simply contacted the London Hospital herself and helped Kathleen to get a place.

An example of my mother's ingenuity in achieving her ends was told me by a member of her staff. It has something of the flavour of an Ealing comedy. It arose from her frustration at being unable to persuade the West Ham Education Office to allocate her funds to buy books. This was 1948, when war-time conditions still prevailed, and even the supply of blackboard chalk was rationed. My mother decided to force the hand of the local authority by giving an interview to the *News Chronicle*, describing the difficulty of teaching without the most basic materials. The report appeared under headlines the next day, to the fury of the Education Officer, who ordered an immediate investigation of the school's resources. My mother was alarmed because every classroom in fact contained a cupboard full of books, but so old, tattered and out of date that they were useless. She hurried into school to get the cooperation of the head of the parallel boys' school, which occupied the top half of the building, and the two of them, with members of her staff, swiftly moved these tattered books into the back of his cupboards. When the officials arrived she received them cordially, though without retracting her complaint, and invited them to look for themselves. Finding an almost total absence of books, despite searching every cupboard in the school, they grudgingly allocated her the funds she needed, to the delight of her staff. It is understandable that a woman so skilled and determined at getting what she wanted would make enemies from time to time, but she won more friends than foes.

The same teacher told me that my mother was generally loved by the staff, who referred to her affectionately behind her back as 'Elsie Vera', her first and middle names – at that time no teacher would have addressed the head by her first name. One or two of her staff were said by my informant to loathe her, because, it was suggested, as women of similar age, education and background, they were jealous of her success. She was said to be always accessible and fair, though 'she wasn't a person that you could take liberties with.' She knew how to delegate responsibility and she looked after her staff, helping them to get promotion and go on courses. She arranged little celebrations for them and persuaded the dinner ladies to give the youngest teachers, who were always hungry in that post-war period, larger helpings. I was told by one of her staff that having a head with her unusual qualities, who was famous throughout West Ham and the N.U.T., helped to compensate for working in a bleak Victorian building in a deprived, bomb damaged area, and made them feel 'a little special'.

My mother was an intelligent woman with an especially high social intelligence. She was not an intellectual, she was not interested in theories or in discussing or reading about ideas, but rather in trying to put into effect what she believed to be right. She had not been well educated. Her two-year teacher training course was probably equivalent to, or below, today's A level courses, and she was not interested in, or knowledgeable about the arts, history or science. I never knew her go to an art gallery, theatre or museum or listen to music. My grandmother, anxious that her talented daughter should study and go to college, had sheltered her from household tasks so that she was completely impractical, without any domestic skills. As an adult she had no leisure time in which to develop new skills and interests, but her mind was stocked with the poems she had learned as party pieces, and the Socialist Sunday School songs she had learned as a child. In what little leisure she had, mainly on trains, she read contemporary fiction and always liked to have a novel to hand.

I occasionally saw her in two of her public roles, the eloquent public speaker and the strict teacher whose pupils kept their heads down and worked very hard. But at home we only saw the loving mother who moved in and out of our lives like a fairy godmother, dissolving sulks and tears with her charm and warmth, though not often with hugs and caresses – physical affection was rarely displayed in our family. Probably it was her very unavailability that contributed to her magic – apart from the summer of 1940 I did not live with her day in and day out until I was sixteen, and Michael never did. Hers was not a love that brought me security, though. This was not only because she was so often unavailable but also because I was convinced that like everyone else she must prefer Michael, so cheerful and even tempered, whilst I was universally considered difficult. When I was an adult she once told me 'I didn't really want to have Michael, but I was so happy when you were born, I longed to have a daughter'. I was not only pleased but astonished that I had been wanted.

When I was about eight I developed a theory that my mother, who to me was so very unlike her parents, had in fact been adopted by them from some highborn and glamorous couple. This fantasy became a strongly held belief but I never spoke of it to anyone and it had faded away by the time I was about ten. I can understand its plausibility. Compared with her parents and sister, my mother was so good looking, so well dressed, so loving and charming, mixing with such grand people in exotic places, that she did indeed seem to come from another sphere. It is only recently that I was able to see that my grandparents were in their different ways remarkable people who had struggled to make the most of the limited opportunities available to them. They, and my mother, handed on to Michael and me a commitment to the political ideals they believed in so deeply. I think we were fortunate in being brought up with a sense of purpose, a sense that we should be involved in helping to improve the lot of others as well as ourselves, and, what is, alas, rare today, a belief that, with struggle, a more equal, just, free and humane society would emerge.

Chapter 5

High days and holidays 1933–39

A lonely time: 1933–36

Grateful as I was to get away from my first boarding school, home life seemed decidedly drab. Probably the main reason for this was that we did not in fact see much of our beloved mother. I shared her bedroom, and the best part of the day for me was getting into bed with her first thing in the morning, whilst she drank the cup of tea brought her by her mother. I would lie there contentedly, marvelling at the gurgling noises that always came from inside her. Since the holidays in state schools were shorter than ours, during part of our holiday she would be teaching. She almost always came home for the midday meal, walking briskly the half mile or so from school. She did this partly because she went as little as possible into the school staff room – she found the other teachers very narrow minded and conservative. When I consulted Michael about how much our mother was at home during our holidays apart from this he said, after reflection, 'sometimes on Sundays.' At the end of her school day, and at weekends and virtually all of the time during her own school holidays she was presumably at meetings or conferences. Perhaps, I have thought recently, she might have been with friends or with one of her many admirers – could she really have had so many meetings to attend?

My grandmother was thus, in effect, a foster mother to us for five years, and Michael once remarked to me that she had brought us up. I was taken aback by the comment – we lived in her house, and she fed us, but I resented her substituting for our mother too much to have thought of her in that role. On further thought I realised that she may have had a greater long term influence on me than my mother, of whom we saw so little. But my grandmother was always preoccupied and in a hurry, and I can't remember her ever chatting to us, let alone playing, reading or telling us stories. Occasionally I could persuade her to talk to me about her childhood. Like the rest of the family she was not physically affectionate and never cuddled children. Like her sister Francie she was quiet, reserved and somewhat depressive, as well as extraordinarily busy, so that looking after us must have been an unwelcome burden, undertaken to help the daughter of whom she was so proud. I don't think it ever crossed her mind that we should be taken out, stimulated, or occupied. She was never unkind, did not punish us except by scolding, and she only scolded us if we were wasteful or did something that created extra work for her, like spilling milk on the tablecloth. She simply left us to our own devices, as was usual in working-class families. This would not have been a problem if we had had friends nearby, but although there were plenty of children living in the street, indeed, next door, we were not allowed to speak to them. Probably this was because my mother feared we would acquire their accent – we were never given reasons for adults' edicts. In any case we did not feel any inclination to know them, they looked decidedly 'rough'.

Unfortunately Michael and I were not at all close at that time. I think he was happier than I because he was very fond of our grandmother. But like me he must surely have been preoccupied at some deep level with wanting to see more of our mother, loathing our grandfather and hating boarding school, though we did not confide in, or indeed, talk much to each other until we were older. Yet our interests and activities were quite similar. We both read a great deal, I would often read a book a day. Reading was immensely important to me as a child, especially under the age of about twelve. It was a way of escaping from a lonely or unhappy situation into other lives. I would read, with tears streaming, sad stories about abandoned or orphaned children whom I could identify with, or I would read enviously stories about the fun children had in large happy families or I would be absorbed in the exciting adventures of adults in historical novels. I read with passion and excitement, and though I am still a compulsive reader, unable to leave the house without taking something to read, the pleasure is never as intense, my abandonment to a book never as total, as when I was a child. Michael was a less compulsive reader and had wider interests. He read history and books about sport, rather than novels. He was very keen on sport, especially cricket (as an adult he spent as much time as he could at Lords) but I was totally uninterested in it, and only reluctantly agreed to bowl at him in the little back yard. He collected cigarette cards of cricketers and read about their lives. He followed football, supported West Ham United, and as he got older went to their home matches, and he listened endlessly to the football results on the radio. Even today, hearing them by chance makes me shiver with remembered boredom.

Temperamentally, too, we were very different. Michael was always calm and good natured, whilst I frequently got cross. Once, exasperated by his refusal to be ruffled by my anger, I threw a glass of water at him, which he dodged, laughing infuriatingly. During this period I was subject to some extreme fears. I was terrified of daddy longlegs, insects that seemed to come into the house quite frequently and I would run out of the room if I saw one. If I were alone in the house I would rush into the garden and stay there, if necessary for hours, till someone returned. The family could hardly avoid knowing about this fear but I concealed my fear of going to bed. No one came to tuck us up or put our lights out, we were told to go, and went. Michael slept in the room next to the kitchen, but the first floor where I slept was dark and my bedroom seemed frighteningly far from the light and warmth of the kitchen, myself unprotected against a menacing intruder. I always made sure that I had a potential weapon, a cricket bat after I acquired one at school, by the side of my bed. I realise now that I was only subject to these fears at home, not at school, and that they stopped after we moved away from my grandparents. They may have been related to a fear of my grandfather.

It wasn't until I was about fourteen that Michael and I drew together. Before that we led parallel lives, not quarrelling much, but not conversing much. We frequently walked to the public library together, sometimes each day, and went together once or twice a week to the public swimming baths. Every week my mother gave us sixpence each to go together to a matinee at the local cinema, and we both read film magazines and became very knowledgeable about Hollywood film stars. Michael was a particular fan of Deanna Durbin, then a teenage singing star. The cinema was an important part of most people's lives at that time – thirty million people went at least once a week before the war. The experience offered much more than a film. With your ticket you bought several hours of entertainment in a palatial interior – cinemas were in fact often called 'Picture Palaces'– with thick carpets, marble walls and staircases, glittering chandeliers and soft seats. They were a warm retreat on a cold day, a cool haven when it was hot outside. There was always, as well as the main film, a 'B' movie, made on a small budget without star performers, a newsreel, and often a cartoon. About mid-time there would be an 'intermission,' when a cinema organist wearing a frock coat or tails magically rose up with his organ, playing the while, from a sunken pit. Sometimes during the intermission there was live singing or dancing on the stage. At matinees tickets were very cheap, even for adults. Unemployed men could afford to go, and working-class women brought their babies and pre-school children, whatever the film, not only, I think, to escape into the fantasy life of the stars, but to spend a brief time in the palatial, spacious interior and the physical comfort of the cinema.

If Michael and I wanted to see a film with an 'A' certificate, which children were not allowed into except with an adult, we just approached a woman in the queue with our sixpences and asked her to take us in. On one occasion when I was twelve we were desperate to see 'Gone with the Wind' and somehow acquired the money to see it in the West End. I don't think my grandparents ever went to the cinema, and my mother went very rarely, so it was no use asking them to take us. Uncertain whether our usual tactic of asking an adult to take us in would work in such a grand locale, I borrowed one of my grandmother's hats and stood on tiptoe at the box office. I must have looked absurd, but at any rate we were admitted.

Trams, succeeded in 1937 by trolleybuses, ran past the end of our road, but when we were younger it never occurred to us to break the tedium of our lives (as I experienced it) by exploring other parts of London. Between the age of seven and ten was the only period in my life when I have suffered long periods of boredom. I'm not sure whether the feeling should be described as boredom, it was so intense. Often I would lie in bed, seeing no reason to get up, listening to the monotonous street calls of the rag and bone man with his handcart, and feeling despair. I think now that this despair was really due to the lack of a close friend or affectionate adult – I was perfectly happy when staying with school friends later, although we spent the days much as I did at home, reading, swimming, and going to the cinema. I would have liked to help my grandmother, but she was far too busy and impatient to show me how to sew or do household chores and refused to let me help her. It is true that when she did occasionally send me to the shops I always failed. Sent for potatoes, I asked for all the small ones, thinking they would be like new potatoes; sent for butter, I bought expensive English butter, thinking my grandmother would want the best, and, exasperated, she had to go out and change the goods, scolding me severely. She did ask me to help her fold the sheets, and sometimes to feed the hens, which I did reluctantly, hating the smell of the hen run, and apprehensive of their beaks. Their run took up most of the back garden. There were no flower beds or grass in the garden –it was not a garden people sat in, more a yard for the hen-run with drying space for the washing. My grandmother had no time for gardening, and the only flowers were a pink rambler rose which grew over an arch outside the back door, with lilies of the valley, my mother's favourite flower, underneath. A magnificent cultivated blackberry bush covered the side fence.

Whilst my grandmother was out on her rounds for the Co-op in the afternoons I often wandered around the house, vaguely searching for hidden information. I had a strong and justified feeling that there were many secrets in the family, especially about my father, though I don't think Michael ever felt this. Once I found a letter from my father pleading for the marriage to be reinstated, once a love letter to my mother from someone unknown to me. The likeliest hiding places were in the bedroom I shared with her, but I would also scan the 'front room', which contained a piano, used only for my reluctant practice – I learnt the piano for five years at boarding school and have never played it, or any other musical instrument, since.

Apart from this the room was used only at Christmas or on the rare occasions when my mother invited a friend round in the evening. It had a carpet square bought by my mother, the only carpet in the house, a three piece suite and a large, glass fronted bookcase containing my mother's books, of which I can only remember several volumes of Aldous Huxley's novels. The room had a silent, unlived in feeling, and I used to think wistfully about how it must have been in the past when my mother and aunt, young and unmarried, gathered round the piano with their friends for singsongs and solo singing. My mother was not a great singer and her contribution to these occasions had been to recite from memory long dramatic poems, some by Longfellow and Tennyson, most by poets no longer known. Many of them came from a book called *Hasluck's Recitations for Ladies* which I still have, although, alas, it does not include her favourite 'The green eye of the little yellow god.'

Behind the front room was my grandmother's dressmaking room with her treadle machine and the curvaceous Edwardian-looking dressmaker's form; Michael slept there during the holidays. Beyond that was the kitchen and then the scullery which housed the sink, coal-fired clothes boiler and a large larder, and opened on to a back porch where the mangle and the hens' foodstuff were kept. The kitchen was where the life of the house went on, mainly because no other rooms were heated, except the front room at Christmas. The bedrooms were always cold, as was the bathroom, and the tap water, except at the time of the weekly baths. Then an Ascot gas water heater was lit in the bathroom, and a paraffin stove, which cast a complex and beautiful pattern of shadows on the ceiling, was brought in. I can't remember us washing at other times – probably we were sent to wash our hands on the way to bed, but washing occurred much less frequently than today. My grandmother would remark if we got dirty, 'You have to eat a peck of dirt before you die.' The kitchen was more like a living room than a modern functional kitchen. It was heated by a coal-fired range, which had a fire visible, glowing through the bars of a small grate, and also fuelled the built in oven and the kettles and pans permanently simmering on the hob. In the summer disgusting strips of sticky paper hung from the ceiling to catch flies, still plentiful because of the dung from the horses which still drove carts up and down the street.

The kitchen was quite small. Much of it was taken up by a large table covered with a heavy floor-length tasselled golden chenille tablecloth, a good hiding place when we were very young. It was made by one of my grandmother's brothers, a skilled carpenter. I still have a small mahogany table he made. The kitchen table was not just a dining table. My grandmother used it for preparing meals, and when covered by a thick layer of blanket, for ironing, and my grandfather wrote letters at it. These were never dashed off but carefully organised, with pen, ink, paper and blotting paper lined up, and slow and serious consideration was given to what was written. My grandparents' collection of about twelve books were housed in a small hanging bookcase. There were books by Dickens and socialist writers like Jack London, Upton Sinclair, and Edward Carpenter, and a memoir, 'My life's struggles' by Will Thorne, ghost written by my father. Will Thorne, a gas workers' union leader, was taught to read and write by Eleanor Marx and was for many years a Labour MP in West Ham. The room also housed a long dresser, a desk, too small to work at, where stationery and correspondence were kept, a large walk-in cupboard for bread, cake, and dry goods, a small fireside chair by the kitchen range where my grandmother sat in the evenings and a larger, leatherette covered armchair for my grandfather. This left very little space to move around. Anyone else had to sit at the table, or as was more often the case, stand around, arguing.

It was in the kitchen when I was eight that it was discovered I was very short-sighted. My mother called from the scullery to ask me the time on the large wall clock, which, despite sitting a few feet away, I could not see. Many bitter tears followed when I was told I must wear glasses. Wearing glasses was a great stigma then, especially for girls. There were absolutely no role models of women looking attractive in them and children who wore them were always teased. Whenever possible I took them off. At Oxford this led to my apparently cutting people in the street whom I knew quite well. My grandmother's kitchen was also where my grandfather would polish everyone's shoes, and prepare to go out, brushing his bowler hat and his coat with great concentration. Before that he would sharpen his cut-throat razor on a leather strap and shave with caution, peering into a small mirror on the wall. It was in the kitchen that my mother would curl her hair with curling tongs heated on the range and my grandmother would iron with flat irons, spitting on them first to test the temperature they had reached, and hang the washing across the room to dry when it rained. Family rows and arguments took place in the kitchen, and local and national politics and union business were discussed and explained to Michael and me if we asked.

I remember the house as dark and dingy. I think my grandparents can have taken no interest in its appearance. All the woodwork was dark brown and the distempered walls were never redecorated. The floors were covered with a nondescript lino and small mats, except for a carpet square in the front room. There was one picture in the house, a black and white print of 'Hope' by the nineteenth-century English aesthetic painter Watts. It depicted a blindfolded woman wearing a Grecian tunic, draped despondently over the top of the globe, holding a broken lyre. It is in fact rather a beautiful, romantic image, especially in its original subdued blue-grey and yellow tones, but I did not understand its symbolism and it seemed to me simply puzzling and depressing. Though evidently not to Nelson Mandela, who is said to have had a copy of it in his prison cell. Poor lighting levels must have added to the gloom of the house. When we first moved in the house was lit by gas. This was soon replaced by electric light, a single central ceiling light in each room, fitted with a fairly low powered bulb.

On Sunday afternoons my mother when at home would often take us with her to visit her friends, all of whom were involved in education or local politics. We were usually given a splendid tea and there might be some diversion for us from the boring adult conversation – one couple had a table tennis room. But no one minded if we sat and read our books. My favourite couple, the Coles, were a delight to visit. Their house was full of interesting objects, including a full sized suit of armour in the hall, and their unconventional life style was totally new to us. After a meal they put all the dishes in the basement and washed up together only when they had run through their large collection of crockery. The Coles were wonderfully warm, plump and jolly. Though they must have been married for over twenty years they often held hands – it was the first truly affectionate, supportive marriage relationship I had seen.

In 1936 my mother bought an Austin seven car. It was very small, designed to compete with the motorcycle and side-car, but it had a roof that opened. My mother's mileage would have been subsidised by the N.U.T., but I don't know how she paid for the car, still an impossible aspiration for most people. At that time only twelve per cent of households had cars, compared with seventy six per cent today. Perhaps the N.U.T. lent her the money. We found the car a liberation. It meant that we could travel much more widely at weekends and could visit many more of my mother's friends. Two of them, Lillian de Lissa, principal of Gypsy Hill Teachers' Training College, and Leah Manning, an N.U.T. official, formerly a Labour MP, had beautiful Tudor cottages in the country. Sometimes we would just drive to the nearby Epping Forest to look at the autumn leaves or wild flowers, and after we acquired a puppy we would take him to run around in the forest. My mother, although she walked briskly, took no great pleasure in walking, and after acquiring the car I think that she took very little exercise.

During my three years at Quarndon House Michael, Kathleen and I were taken by Ivy to spend two weeks of our summer holiday in Shoeburyness with Auntie Francie. My grandparents never in their lives had a holiday away from home, but by the 1930s it was common for skilled workers to spend a week or two at the seaside, staying in a boarding house. Uncle Will got free travel on the railways for his family once a year, so after our stay at Shoeburyness they would go to Cornwall, Devon or on one occasion Belgium, to make the most of the opportunity. My mother must have paid Auntie Francie to put us all up, but it was probably still the cheapest holiday she could organise. It never occurred to me to wonder why my mother did not take us herself; now I suspect it was because she would have found it very tedious. The arrangement with Auntie Francie was for bed and breakfast only. My mother hired a beach hut for the fortnight, one in a long row of small chalets on the beach. Inside were a small bed, a table and chairs, and a Calor gas cooking ring and outside there was a veranda, where you could sit on deckchairs, and hang up wet costumes to dry. We would set off for the beach hut after breakfast whatever the weather, have lunch and tea in the hut, and wash there before going back to the house at night, when we were put straight to bed.

The days were an unvarying routine of playing on the beach, swimming, and in my case reading. The beach was a strip of sand and shingle, with none of the cliffs, rock pools, or dunes that featured in children's books. I found these holidays quite boring, I think because, unlike Michael and Kathleen, I was not interested in playing on the beach with the other chalet children. But the hut had the fascination of an oversized Wendy House, so that living there seemed in itself a kind of game. Sometimes on the way back in the evening Ivy would buy us bags of chips, under a vow of secrecy. My mother didn't allow us to patronise fish and chip shops, which at that time were not at all trendy, but emblematic of the working-class life she was trying to rescue us from.

Michael and me,
aged about 11 and 9.

Holidays 1936–39

After I started at Bedford High School in 1936, at the age of ten, holidays greatly improved. No one from the school lived near me, but quite often I was invited to stay with one or other of my new friends. And I acquired someone to love at home, a beautiful Irish setter puppy, Timothy Shawn, whom I persuaded my mother to buy. We did not realise that he would grow into a very large dog, totally unsuited to life in West Ham. He was very good-natured, and the women in the family loved him very much, but he was never properly trained. He would greet unsuspecting callers at the front door by putting his front paws on their shoulders, lick the ice- creams of babies in prams, and sniff out and eat any chocolate that entered the house. So possessive was I of my mother that I would feel intensely jealous when she caressed him. It mostly fell to Michael, who had never wanted him in the first place, to exercise him, which is perhaps why, whilst I was left with a lifelong affection for dogs, Michael most definitely was not. When we left my grandmother's house to live in a flat we clearly couldn't take him. He was too strong for my grandmother, and my aunt, another dog lover, took over his care.

In the summer of 1936, when I was ten, my mother drove Michael and myself and a friend of hers, Billy Spikes, to Barmouth in North Wales. We stayed in a guest house, which in facilities and cost was somewhere between a boarding house and an hotel. Car journeys were much more hazardous then. Driving tests and a 30 mph speed limit in towns had only been introduced in 1934, and in 1936 there were 2.4 road fatalities a year per thousand vehicles, compared with 0.1 today. Spikes did not drive, and my mother had not yet passed the driving test, but she was never a great one for sticking to the letter of the law. Still, she drove carefully, and by today's standards, very slowly indeed. Spikes was head of a West Ham grammar school, a physicist, educated in Cambridge and Germany. (Because I later came to dislike him very much, I prefer to refer to him by his surname). For the first time I found myself in close contact with a well-educated person with wide interests, and I was impressed. His idea of a holiday was not to sit on a beach. He took us to see castles and we went on long mountain walks, and climbed in our ordinary school shoes to the top of Snowdon, which, alas, was shrouded in mist. I reminded Michael of this some time ago, but he had forgotten the excitement of this achievement. For him, seeing the film of the H.G. Wells book, *The Shape of Things to Come*, was the highlight of the holiday. Spikes taught me some Welsh, and also some German, and because he flattered me and talked to me as though I were an adult, I didn't feel jealous at having to share my mother with him. Michael, however, was noticeably cool towards him, though polite.

The following year we drove without Spikes to Cornwall, again staying in a guest house near Newquay, where most of our fellow guests seemed to be teachers. We were very excited at learning to surf, inexpertly, on surfboards. Although there was relatively little traffic then, the two-lane roads, the absence of bypass roads and my mother's preferred speed at that time of 20 mph, made for a very long journey. However, she kept us entertained with her long verse recitations, and her repertoire of old music hall songs, such as 'Daisy, Daisy, give me your answer do' and 'I do like to be beside the seaside', as well as songs from her Socialist Sunday School. The next summer, 1938, we did not go away with our mother, since, as President of the National Union of Teachers, she went on an official visit to the USA, travelling by sea. The first transatlantic passenger air service was not inaugurated until the following year and was not widely used until the 1950s. The highlight of her tour was being driven through New York with the flamboyant, radical Mayor La Guardia in his official car, sirens blazing to clear the traffic ahead. To my indignation Michael and I were sent with Auntie Ivy and Kathleen to stay in a private hotel on the Isle of Wight, which I resented and found intolerably boring.

As well as going away with our mother, we now camped for two weeks every summer. Michael's new school, the Forest School, at the start of the summer holidays held a camp in their grounds in the New Forest for pupils, ex-pupils, and their brothers and sisters. We slept in sleeping bags on ground sheets, in our own small tents, and ate in the open, mainly, as I remember, grated cheese, grated carrots, raisins and bread and jam, the huge tins of jam swarming with wasps. When it rained we retired to our tents and read, or visited another tent. The camps were run on the principles of the Order of Woodcraft Chivalry (see Chapter 3). These emphasised the importance of living close to nature and acquiring the skills needed to live in woods. Instead of religion we were to learn to live and work together, children and adults, peacefully and in harmony, and this, it was hoped, would spread to the rest of humanity. How innocent and idealistic the reformers of the interwar period seem today.

As in the Forest School we were organised in approximate age groups – Elves, Woodlings (my group), Trackers, Pathfinders. In order to move up to the next group you had to pass woodcraft tests, e.g. identifying, and judging the height of trees, laying and following forest trails, and tests that were easier for townies, such as carrying complicated verbal messages accurately from one end of the woods to another. Much of the day was spent practising for these tests, but we also built dams in the river, swam, and when it was the turn of the work group to which we were assigned we helped cook, wash up and clean around. Just outside the school territory was a primitive shop in a converted stable, exactly like one in an old cowboy movie, where we could buy sweets. It smelled of candles and paraffin. I was introduced for the first time to the delights of sweetened condensed milk, which you could suck up after 'Grandpa', who ran the store, had made two holes in the tin with a nail. At night there was always a campfire, with cocoa and singing. The songs were a rather strange assortment, my favourites were 'Miss Otis Regrets', a haunting Cole Porter song, and two nineteenth-century comic songs which can still be found in U.S. folk song books.

One, the Darkies' Sunday School – 'Young folks, old folks, everybody come/ Join the darkies Sunday school and have a bit of fun/ Bring your sticks of chewing gum and sit upon the floor/ and we'll tell you Bible stories like you never heard before'– consists of a long list of send-ups of Bible stories, for example: 'Adam was a gardener, and Eve she was his spouse/They got the sack for stealing fruit and went to keeping house/ They lived a very quiet life and peaceful in the main/ Until they had a baby and started raising Cain'. The other favourite, 'Abdul Abulbul Amir', about a fight between a Moslem and a Russian hero, also had a large number of verses. 'The sons of the Prophet are brave men and bold/and quite unaccustomed to fear/ but the bravest by far in the ranks of the Shah/ was Abdul Abulbul Amir'. He challenges a Russian hero, Ivan Skavinsky Skavar, to a duel, in which eventually both are killed. The tone seemed to be comic more than tragic, I suspect because of the implicit chauvinist assumption that foreigners with such outrageous names can't be taken seriously.

Once every year we played the 'Night Game', which everyone who attended the school or the camps remembers with either exhilaration or, as in my case, terror. We were woken at 10p.m. and divided into two teams, each with their headquarters, some distance apart in the woods and mounted with a flag. The game was to crawl silently in total darkness through the undergrowth (often prickly) to capture the flag or flags of the other team.

These camps were the highlight of the year for me from 1936 until 1939. I loved the beauty of the woods, which wound downhill to the river and I loved living in the open air all day, even sleeping on the ground. Back at home, for the first few days I insisted on sleeping on my bedroom floor. I loved the variety of activities, the campfires and the pleasure of meeting the same children each year. Almost for the first time I met boys other than Michael and promptly fell in love with a silent, handsome dark haired boy, two years older than me, who completely ignored me. I don't think I minded that, it was enough to enjoy falling in love, an experience I didn't talk about to anyone. I also made new friends.

One was a very beautiful girl of my own age from Sri Lanka – she and her brother, children of an Embassy official, were the first non-European people I'd seen. Another was Mina, a pupil at the Forest School who was then about sixteen. Michael adored her, and she took me, too, under her wing. She was a pretty, blonde, enthusiastic girl, generous and decided in both her opinions and her affections. After she left the Forest School at seventeen, without, like the other pupils, taking any public examinations, she immediately got married and several times invited me to stay with her. She and her husband, Zed Dienes, who was writing a doctoral dissertation in maths, were living on the £2 a week Zed's father gave him. They rented a tiny farm labourer's cottage, the middle one in a row of three, in a small village called Moreton, near Thame. Zed later became a Professor of Mathematics and invented the Dienes blocks, a devise to help children understand maths.

Zed grew all their vegetables and fruit in their garden, there were apple trees, and, partly to save money, they were vegetarians. Either from ignorance or lack of interest they lived on a very unappetising and monotonous diet of boiled vegetables, apples, bread, margarine and Cheddar cheese. This put me off vegetarianism for many years. On Tuesdays they would go to the market in Thame and on Saturdays to the market in Aylesbury, having planned in advance how every penny would be spent. All journeys were done by walking or hitchhiking, and I learnt for the first time both the pleasure of walking in the country and that you could travel anywhere, if you had no money, simply by raising your arm and asking for a lift.

Some aspects of the Forest School and its camp shocked me – the kinds of behaviour that were acceptable seemed extraordinary. Swearing (which I'd only ever heard before from my grandfather) was frequent and tolerated by the staff without comment, bathroom doors were not locked, pupils wandered round, and swam, in the nude, no one bothered about dirty clothes or faces, the 'manners' that I had been taught were not observed and the children didn't talk respectfully to adults. Everyone seemed very happy under this regime but it was a difficult adjustment to make for two weeks in the year. Although by the age of ten I thought of myself as a rebel, I was in many ways very conventional and watched the behaviour of the Forest School pupils with a mixture of horror and fascination. It would probably have been extremely valuable for me to have attended the school and lost my inhibitions and conventional outlook. As it was, despite my enthusiasm for the camps, I did feel an outsider.

In 1938 the school moved to Whitwell Hall, a large house in Reepham, Norfolk, losing the magic of the forest and river. The next year the house was requisitioned by the army and the school and the camps stopped for the duration of the war. The school didn't reopen after the war, but some of the staff and ex-pupils got together to organise an annual summer camp. This expanded into a large enterprise, which still continues, with many different camps each year, some for trekking and canoeing, at Easter and Whit, as well as in the summer. I don't know how much of the original ethos of 'Woodcraft Chivalry' they now retain.

But the Forest School camps had been such an important experience for me that I sent my three older children to them regularly, from the age of about eight or nine until they were about sixteen, and so did Michael. If you want your children to enjoy camping 'sauvage', and living in the open, you need to start them young. Adults, and even teenagers, especially women, coming to it for the first time can be appalled rather than thrilled. As well as sending our children to the camps, my husband, Jack, and I took them camping in France and Italy almost every summer until the year before he died. In that year he and I also spent a long weekend on our own, camping in Burgundy. At first, in the late fifties, there were still undeveloped stretches of the Mediterranean coast where you could camp, but with the mass tourism that began in the sixties we retreated to less popular areas.

At the Easter annual conference of the National Union of Teachers (N.U.T.) in 1938 my mother became its president, the fifth woman to be elected to this position. We went to Margate with her a day or two before the start of the conference so that she could try out her presidential address in the huge conference hall. My mother was a very good and experienced public speaker, often called on at conferences to quell an unruly audience on behalf of the executive committee, and teachers' conferences at that time were very unruly. But on this occasion she was nervous and wanted to rehearse, while we sat in the empty hall and listened to her. Her presidential address was reproduced verbatim in the organ of the N.U.T., then called *The Schoolmaster*, and I recently read it with interest.

Most N.U.T. presidential addresses at the time were concerned with teachers' salaries and conditions, which of course were a concern of my mother also. But she chose to discuss the issues nearest her heart, the education of working-class children and the role of education in the defence of freedom. She began by saying that 'we are witnessing in the world today cruelty and carnage which the more sensitive spirits of our fathers would have found it hard to bear' and went on to say that 'the principle of freedom is itself at stake, and we cannot be blind to the issues that are involved. We see elsewhere the use of education to kill the human spirit and enslave the mind. It must be our aim to liberate the human spirit, by giving children complete freedom to develop the gifts with which Nature has endowed them.' This, she argued, requires freeing children from the effects of poverty, under-nourishment, lack of sleep and overcrowding. It also requires a reform of the educational system. Children cannot be free to develop whilst our schools mirror the class structure of society with the 'fateful examination' at eleven, which labels ninety per cent as failures, and thereafter consigns them to classes of forty or fifty in outdated, ill-equipped schools. She said this situation was deteriorating, rather than improving – the Board of Education's own statistics showed that working-class children had less chance then than six years earlier of a secondary (i.e. grammar school) education.

My mother went on to attack the nature of the education offered in schools, particularly its structuring around examinations. This, she believed, led to too much emphasis on academic studies. Moreover, examinations 'promote self-seeking, selfishness, and competitiveness,' and 'discourage true co-operation and mutual help'. The curriculum should also be reformed, since it was overcrowded, and 'devised by pedantic minds, instead of being fitted to the child.' All this must change if schools are to produce 'free citizens of a free and democratic state, trained in those attributes of moral courage and intellectual honesty which distinguish men from helots.... As soon as we cease to practise independent thought and judgement and to encourage these in our children both we and they will fall victims to the evils of dictatorship'.

In today's context much of this speech would sound amazing. True, criticism of large classes and selection at eleven continues, seventy years later, but Presidents of the N.U.T. and education ministers and officials do not describe the aim of schools as to liberate the human spirit and promote independent thought, moral courage and true cooperation. The emphasis, especially in secondary schools, is now very much on the acquisition of skills and knowledge. Even when SATS testing is attacked, this is because it distorts the curriculum and is a strain on children, not, as my mother believed, because it promotes self-seeking and competitiveness.

At the N.U.T. conference, 1938, aged 14 and 12, with our mother.

Of course, my mother wanted her pupils to achieve. But what drove her almost to despair was the fatalistic way in which the girls she taught accepted (as did their parents) their future as hands in the nearby Tate and Lyle's factory and then as housewives, and she thought that their greatest need was to develop independent judgement and to become 'free spirits.' In her own class she gave a great deal of practical help and support, often after school hours, to any girl with an outstanding talent, most often athletic, in the hope that this would give them a chance to break out of the mould.

She was an early advocate of multilateral schools, that is, secondary schools which all children would attend, although in different streams. She saw them as offering the only way to achieve equality in class size and school facilities, but in 1938 this was still a distant dream. After she became a head teacher herself in a 'senior elementary' school she arranged for the most able pupils to be moved to a grammar school at thirteen. She held no examinations in the school and she tried to broaden the pupils' horizons by introducing French teaching (then virtually unknown outside of grammar schools), organising training for those teachers who were already reasonably proficient in French. She encouraged school outings that both staff and children would be interested in, including visits to the Regents Park Open Air Theatre. She also insisted that school dinners, which served very overcooked vegetables, should include grated raw carrots each day. It must be said, though, that she sent Michael and me to schools where high achievement and exam success were the main, though not the only, priorities, and raw carrots were unknown.

My mother's stress on the preservation of freedom was prompted by fear of Nazi Germany, which the month before had annexed Austria, and was as she spoke threatening Czechoslovakia. It also reflected her humanist socialist views acquired in her *Clarion* days. She was the first N.U.T. president to attend and speak at the annual meeting of the National Association of Labour Teachers, which took place during the conference. I don't know to what extent she carried her audience with her in her presidential address – the responses to her speech printed in *The Schoolmaster* tended to be rather sexist references to her charm, or fine phrases were picked out for approval, e.g. 'the need to make the climate of the child's soul grow sunnier.' This kind of high-flown language seems to have been expected of pre-war public speakers.

We stayed for the first few days of the conference and were the focus of much attention, basking in photo calls, feeling very proud of our mother. I was presented with a gold wristwatch, Michael with gold cufflinks. Our mother was staying in the grandest hotel in Margate and we ate with her, attending some sessions of the conference, whilst sleeping in a guesthouse with our grandmother, who came up to look after us once the conference started. This was my first experience of the luxurious and surely corrupting life style enjoyed by leading trade unionists and Labour politicians. We were amazed to be told by my mother that we could order anything we liked from the hotel's menu, instead of her usual instruction to choose from among the cheapest dishes. During the conference I had my twelfth birthday, and a party was organised for me at the hotel, attended by Michael and by children I had never seen before, the offspring of local N.U.T. members. There was a magnificent birthday cake, presents and party games, and beforehand I was excited because I had not had a birthday party or a birthday cake since I was three or four – I didn't have another till I was seventy-five. But when a horde of strange children filed in I felt embarrassed and horrified, and Michael remembered me looking unhappy and eventually dissolving in tears.

I must have been a strange and objectionable mixture of social immaturity and intellectual precocity. Michael also remembers me arguing at the conference with W.G. Cove, a Labour MP who was paid a retainer by the N.U.T. to represent its interests in Parliament, and a great friend and admirer of my mother's. According to Michael, in the course of the argument, which was about the government's policy of appeasing Hitler, I said, 'Then you are either foolish or dishonest'. Michael, whilst agreeing with my political point, was shocked by my rudeness, and I have to admit that as a child I was often very rude, possibly without full intent. However, I think he may have polished up the anecdote, he liked to present a picture of me as a precocious child revolutionary.

Michael and I attended one more N.U.T. conference the following Easter, 1939, when my mother handed on the presidency to her successor at Llandudno. This time, now aged just thirteen and fourteen and a half, Michael and I were allowed to stay on our own in a guest house and attend the conference whenever we wished. The rest of the time we were given money to go to the cinema, funfairs, etc. The only conference event I remember is hearing Lloyd George, a former Prime Minister and renowned Welsh orator, address the conference –he was then MP for Llandudno. I was sitting immediately behind him on the platform and what I remember most is his shoulder length silver, silky hair, and saying to myself, 'You must remember this. You are listening to one of the greatest British orators.' His voice was indeed musical and his style dramatic, but I can't remember a word he said. Michael, whose memory was phenomenal, years later assured me that the theme was not education, but the need to increase food production because of the threat of war.

I entitled this chapter, nostalgically, *High Days and Holidays*, the title of a children's book by Eleanor Graham published in 1932. I read it many times from the age of about eight, and I still own it. For each month of the year it included traditional rhymes (e.g. 'April showers/make May flowers') and accounts of the ways in which High Days were once celebrated. High Days were pre-industrial holidays, celebrated before Bank holidays were introduced in 1871. Many of them, such as Candlemas day on February 2nd are now forgotten. There were also extracts from children's books such as

What Katy Did, describing how High Days were celebrated in the fairly recent past, e.g. by Valentine and Halloween parties. These were interspersed with accounts of the day-to-day holiday activities of a fictional, and I later realised, highly idealised, Edwardian family, the Roses. There were six children in the family, a father who barely appeared and a mother who was always present, encouraging and supporting the children to devise their own amusements. Despite having a maid and a daily cleaner they were depicted as too short of money for the children to be taken on outings or to the seaside, but the children's creativity and imagination ensured that their holidays were busy and enjoyable. I fell in love with this ever-contented, secure and inventive family, envying them, but unable to think how Michael and I could even begin to emulate them. It's possible that at some less than conscious level the idealised Rose family later influenced my decision to have a large family.

The only High Day our family celebrated was Christmas Day, though at Easter we were each given a chocolate egg. Christmas for me was a mixture of excitement, boredom and alarm. It was a much lower key event than today because the standard of living was so much lower, and the consumer society had not arrived – the term itself was invented in the 1950s, and not in general use until the 1960s. In our family, preparations for Christmas began in the autumn when my grandmother made the mincemeat and Christmas puddings, adding, despite her Pledge, a little brandy as a preservative – one or more of the puddings would be saved to eat later in the year. I was allowed to help clean the dried fruit with flour – it was then a different, less shiny product than now, the fruit still attached to tendrils. About this time she would also make the Christmas cake, which was richer than her usual fruit cake.

Apart from these advance preparations, Christmas was not signalled in the shops or in people's activity until about a week before the event. It was only in the few days before Christmas day that Christmas trees were usually bought. We always had a small, table top one, sadly unlike the Roses', but eagerly awaited, because my mother bedecked it with beautiful jewel coloured glass baubles, carefully saved in tissue paper year after year. It was only then that we made our Christmas decorations. These were very amateurish home made paper chains, interlocking strips of gummed coloured paper, hung round the kitchen. Presents and Christmas cards were also not bought until the Christmas week, often not till Christmas Eve. Cards posted on Christmas Eve were delivered on Christmas Day, when there was only one, instead of the usual three, postal deliveries. Our Christmas chicken – turkeys were too expensive for our family – was bought in Angel Lane market on Christmas Eve.

In our family few cards were sent, although in her union role my mother received a great many. During the week before Christmas we would, with great excitement, go with our mother to a small, superior grocer in Stratford Broadway – not the Co-op! – to help her choose silver balls and 'hundreds and thousands' for the trifle she always made for Christmas tea, and little figures to put on the Christmas cake. This was the only time in the year that we bought biscuits, and we were allowed to choose an assortment from large, oblong, open tins arranged in ranks, one above another, sloping so that you could see the contents. Biscuits, like sweets, were not pre-packaged then. You could choose from any tins you liked, and the biscuits were weighed out and given you in a paper bag.

As in most families, our Christmas Day was highly ritualised. We did not have Christmas stockings and we exchanged presents within the family after breakfast. My grandfather was not, of course, involved in this, he was still in bed, but in any case he neither gave nor was given presents. The pubs opened as usual on the morning of Christmas Day and he would go there till they closed in the afternoon. Michael and I would each tend to be given one or two books, a box of sweets, perhaps an album for sticking in cigarette cards or film stars photos, and some rather utilitarian clothing, like bedroom slippers or a dressing gown. The main excitement of the day was the Christmas dinner, with its once a year menu of roast chicken and Christmas pudding, preceded by Christmas crackers, and attended by Auntie Ivy, Uncle Will, and Kathleen, who would arrive in time for Ivy and my mother to help prepare the vegetables. A fire was lit for the day in the front room – a very rare event – and after dinner we would sit there, until – the frightening part of Christmas – my grandfather would return, drunk, shouting, and abusive, from the pub.

I would silently vow that when I grew up I would never invite relations to visit on Christmas Day – they were boring people, and why would one not prefer to see one's friends? Our family did not, of course, join the millions in listening to the king's broadcast to the nation. The second highlight of the day was playing a card game called Pit, which involves a great deal of shouting and excitement, and was only played in our family on Christmas Day, after a tea of trifle, mince pies, and Christmas cake. Christmas day was the only time in our childhood that I remember adults playing with us, although in the war, as teenagers, we would sometimes play rummy and whist with our mother during evening air raids. Boxing Day was inevitably rather flat, but it was a second day on which our mother would definitely be at home. Later in the week she would take us on our annual visit to the theatre, to see *Peter Pan*, which I thought exciting and quite magical, or to a pantomime.

Food and meals in working-class families in the 1930s

One of my aims in writing this memoir was to contribute towards the social history of the thirties and forties. I often wonder, reading biographies and memoirs, what the people in the books used to eat, and therefore I decided to describe in detail the meals we had while spending our school holidays with my grandparents from 1933–39.

I have already described how during the 1930s the poorest section of the population lived largely on carbohydrates, especially bread and margarine, with cups of tea. Middle class families had what now seems an excessively rich diet with a cooked breakfast, a cooked lunch and a cooked dinner in the evening, and often coffee and cake in the middle of the morning, as well as afternoon tea at about 4 p.m. with little sandwiches, scones and cakes. Better off working-class families, like my grandparents, had a much healthier diet. They had only one cooked meal a day, called dinner, usually served in the middle of the day, and no 'afternoon tea', but instead a fairly substantial uncooked final meal, called tea, when the breadwinner got home from work. Later in the evening they would have tea or Ovaltine and biscuits. This difference in meal patterns was a major marker of social class.

In my grandmother's house the main meal of the day, and the only cooked meal, was a two- course dinner at midday. At that time shops, offices, schools and factories generally closed for an hour, and since the staff tended to live nearby they would hurry home to eat. My mother usually came back from her school to her mother's house. My grandmother was an unusually good cook and did not stint on the quality of the food she bought, so that the meals she provided may not have been typical of those in better off working-class homes.

We knew what the main course would be by the day of the week. I can recommend this system, which I followed with my children, as it simplifies shopping and saves time otherwise spent on wondering what to cook, and arguing about this with one's children. Provided they like the dishes chosen I think that the routine gives them a feeling of security. In my grandmother's case Sunday was the day of roast meat, usually beef, with roast potatoes. Before the meat course the best Yorkshire pudding I have ever known, as light and high as a soufflé, but crisp round the edges, was served as a separate first course with gravy from the meat. The intention of this north country tradition was to fill you up so you wouldn't eat too much of the more expensive meat that followed, but I thought it the best part of the meal. On Monday, which was washing day, there was cold meat, boiled potatoes, and tinned peas. On Tuesday, when the huge pile of ironing had to be tackled, my grandmother made a rich vegetable soup, first boiling bones on the range to make the stock. This smelled truly horrible, but it gave a rich flavour to the soup. On Wednesday she made a pie with stewing steak, on Thursday she boiled bacon with pease pudding. On Friday she cooked fried fish with chips, always using skate, which was then an inexpensive fish. I hated skate, with its soft slimy bones, and refused to eat it, so my grandmother cooked me what she said was plaice (then an expensive fish) but years later she told me was in fact filleted skate. There was always a second vegetable, as well as potatoes.

My grandmother never forced us children to eat anything, nor did she cook us special food. If there was something we didn't like she found a way to disguise it. Before air freight and freezers the range of vegetables available in winter was limited to root vegetables, cauliflower, brussel sprouts, tinned and dried peas and also – though my grandmother never bought these – leeks and 'greens' of various kinds. In the summer there were fresh peas, runner beans, tomatoes and salad. Chicken, which was then expensive (we never ate our hens) we had only once a year at Christmas, rather than turkey, which was still more expensive. I remember the terrible disappointment one Christmas when we were given pork because my grandmother could not afford a chicken that year.

For the second course at dinner there was always a delicious traditional English pudding – a fruit pie, a jam tart, rice pudding, apple charlotte, bread and butter pudding, pancakes with lemon and sugar, and my favourite, 'queen of puddings' – a meringue top over layers of jam, custard and soaked bread crumbs. My grandmother took cooking seriously, and did not cut corners to save time. For example, she improved the flavour of her apricot and plum jam by breaking the stones with a hammer and adding the kernels to the jam. However, she had an amazingly limited range. She only made one kind of soup, and one cake, an excellent fruit cake, and she did not cook stews, pulses, baked vegetable or cheese dishes, pasta or rice, other than rice pudding, or eggs in any way other than boiled for tea. Vegetables were always boiled, apart from potatoes, which once a week were roasted and once a week chipped. We never had sliced bacon, perhaps because my grandmother only cooked at dinner time, and for her this meant a meal of meat or fish and two vegetables. Much standard British fare, such as chops or steak, was beyond her budget, and like most working-class women she did not cook offal, and she never cooked food such as sausages which she had not seen being made. She owned one cookery book, a small edition of Mrs. Beeton, and only referred to this once a year when checking the ingredients for Christmas puddings and mincemeat.

The other two meals were not cooked. For breakfast we had Post Toasties or Force, both similar to corn flakes, and bread and butter. There was, of course, no electric toaster or grill, so toast could only be made at tea time when the stove had got hot and people had more time. The last meal of the day, tea, at around 5.30, was bread and butter and jam, sometimes with fruit cake. There was often also a boiled egg, laid that day, or less often tinned fruit or occasionally tinned salmon – fresh salmon was then extremely expensive, and we never had it. In the summer there was usually salad, lettuce or watercress, tomatoes and cucumber. In winter we made toast with a toasting fork at the coal range fire, the best hot buttered toast I've ever had. For a treat we children occasionally had jelly. Sticks of celery were put on the tea table at weekends in a tall narrow glass celery vase. Sometimes on Saturdays we would go with our mother to the fish stall in Angel Lane street market in Stratford and buy kippers for tea, or smoked haddock, or shrimps, or for my grandmother, cockles and winkles.

One thing my grandmother never made was bread. When she was a child the women in her village baked bread only once a week, so that most of the time it was very stale, and she vowed that when she got married she would never eat home baked bread again. The Co-op baker called daily, and my grandmother always bought a white 'cottage' loaf, made up of a small round very crusty 'bun' sitting on top of a larger, round, less crusty base, so that all tastes could be satisfied. She would butter the bread herself before she cut it, holding the loaf against her body, as you could spread the butter more thinly that way. People were certainly not allowed to butter the bread themselves

Tea was drunk by working-class families at meals, but in our family rarely between meals, since both my mother and grandmother were busy, active women who had no leisure time till the evening. Like most working-class people my grandparents did not drink coffee before the war. We children were not allowed tea. We were given milk or water. Squash or fruit juice were unknown, at least to us, although on high days and holidays we were bought 'Tizer' and 'Ice-cream soda', a drink which had no apparent relation to ice-cream. In the summer we had ice-cream once a week when a man on a bicycle with an icebox attached in front came down the street, selling Walls ice cream. If you put a card with a large 'W' in your front window he would stop and sell you ice-cream cornets. We were not given pocket money till I was twelve, but sometimes we were given a penny to buy sweets at the little local sweet shop. We would stare in the window at the display of what you could buy for a farthing (a tiny coin, worth a quarter of a penny) trying to choose between liquorice bootlaces, gobstoppers, or my favourite, lemon sherbet dips, tiny lollipop which you dipped in a packet of sherbet powder.

In many ways we had a much healthier diet than children today, quite low in sugar and fats, with no additives since we ate very little food that was not prepared at home. Readymade bought dishes were unknown then, apart from fish and chips, though my grandmother cooked these herself. We had quite a lot of vegetables but not much fresh fruit, especially in winter, when instead we usually had tinned fruit once a week. Fruit was very seasonal, mandarins, for example, arriving at Christmas, whilst apples were finished by early spring. During the summer relatives in the country sent up boxes of blackcurrants, and these, together with the blackberries from the garden, and plums, which could be bought quite cheaply, my grandmother made into jam. Other summer fruits such as cherries, raspberries and strawberries were too expensive to buy except for a special occasion, like my mother's birthday on June 19th. My grandmother had no feeling that fruit should be eaten every day, and it was much too expensive to leave around in bowls.

No alcohol was kept in my grandparents' house, other than a little brandy hidden away in a medicine bottle for treating sick animals and adding to Christmas puddings. My grandfather's drinking was done in pubs. Michael remembers that on the rare occasions when my mother had a friend visiting in the evening she would buy a bottle of sherry. Later, in her own home, she kept gin and tonic for occasional drinking. I don't think I ever saw anyone drink wine until I went to Oxford.

A return to West Ham after 55 years

I did not visit West Ham after my grandmother died in 1949 until 2004. Whilst thinking about this memoir I felt intensely curious, and almost impelled to see it again. Intellectually I realised that much would have changed in fifty-five years, but at some less than conscious level I think I believed that I would be able to step back into the past. The first surprise was to find that instead of the massive journey I had vaguely anticipated, matching perhaps, the psychological journey involved, a London overground train would take me from Gospel Oak station, nearby on Hampstead Heath, to Stratford, in twenty-six minutes. Stratford, about a mile from my grandmother's house, had been our nearest shopping centre, with two department stores and a busy street market in Angel Lane. I stepped out of the train to find myself in the middle of a huge travel centre serving, as well as overground trains, the Docklands light railway, the Central underground line and a large bus centre. All this was linked to a conference centre, a sports centre and a shopping mall. The department stores had, of course, long disappeared, and Angel Lane had been enlarged into a main thoroughfare.

Escaping from all this I walked the mile down the Romford Road to Forest Gate. Although there were a few new large buildings I was by then surprised to find that most of the old landmarks remained, including the public library, the baths and West Ham Technical College, now part of the University of East London. The streets where we had lived as children were much as I remembered, but the houses now looked much smarter, freshly painted, with glass porches added, tiled door steps replacing the old stone ones that had to be scrubbed and whitened, the front yards planted with flowers or turned into car spaces, the roads lined with cars. Gradually I realised that whilst the buildings had not substantially changed the population had – the white working-class had been almost entirely replaced by Pakistani and Indian families, most in traditional dress. In the park, which looked much more attractive than I remembered, there were only two white youths in the football match that was taking place. The local bakers, butchers, and greengrocers had been replaced by shops selling *halal* meat, Asian fruit and vegetables and *chapattis*, and there were Asian hairdressers and clothing shops. The cinema had been turned into a mosque, the church at the end of my grandmother's road into a Moslem college.

I went to the first house I remember, in Earlham Grove, intending to ask whether I could look in the garden to see if there were still two holes cut in the fence for children to watch the trains. The house had been converted into flats, and the Pakistani ground floor tenant or owner said he had only been in England for six months, and though he was perfectly friendly his English was not good enough for him to understand my rather strange request. The synagogue next door had been turned into the offices of a building society, still with its star of David cut into the stone work. I looked around for a café where I could have coffee and a sandwich, but the few cafés I found sold only kebabs or burgers. I had never seen, outside of India, such an entirely Asian scene. Forest Gate today seemed much livelier and more colourful than the dreary neighbourhood I remembered from my childhood. When I subsequently looked on the Internet I found that only sixty-nine per cent of the population were said to be Asian, not, as it seemed, ninety per cent. I realised, intellectually, that these changes must have come about gradually, but to me it seemed as though a magic wand had transformed the area whilst I wasn't looking, so that the past had indeed disappeared.

Chapter 6

Day school, the Munich crisis, evacuation and the 'phoney war' 1938–1940

In September, 1938, aged twelve, I started as a day pupil at St. Paul's Girls' School in Hammersmith. At that time children were not consulted about or even given the reason for adults' decisions about their lives, so I can only speculate on my mother's motives for bringing me home. I imagine that she wanted to end the expense of boarding school and thought that I was now old enough to largely look after myself, without imposing too much extra responsibility on her mother. She must have chosen St. Paul's because it had the reputation of being the girls' school with the highest academic standards in London, if not the country, and for sending large numbers of girls to Oxford and Cambridge. It's clear to me now that she was extremely ambitious for the two of us, but I did not realise this at the time and never felt that I was being 'pushed.' Michael, completely recovered from his dreadful experience at prep school, had left the Forest School a year earlier to attend a boys' public day school, the City of London School on the Embankment. This was then more liberal than most public schools and had several very left-wing masters. It had been the first public school to teach science and English literature rather than concentrating on the classics, and it had a strong reputation for public speaking and debate. Michael weathered the transition to a conventional school very well.

How my mother could have found the money for these schools remains a mystery. Both were expensive. The current fees for St. Paul's are about £15,000 a year, for the City of London, about £12,000. School fees, expensive school dinners, uniforms, fares and school books for two children, as well as fencing lessons for Michael, would have consumed all of her salary. Perhaps the Teachers' Widows and Orphans Benevolent Fund helped her. Michael, having missed two years of formal schooling, could not be expected to win a scholarship. I think her strategy must have been that she would find the money for me to go to St. Paul's for a year. I would then be in a good position, because of knowing what was required, to win a Junior scholarship in the summer term and subsequently a Senior scholarship at fifteen, and so it happened. Since I can still remember some of the questions in the scholarship papers, but not in any other exams I've taken, I must have realised their importance. I remember at fifteen having to write an essay on 'Discuss the meaning of civilisation' and feeling thankful that I had recently read (not in school) a Penguin book by Clive Bell entitled *What is Civilisation?* and also having to discuss and analyse a poem by D.H. Lawrence, 'Piano', which I hadn't previously read, and fell in love with.

According to plan, in the summer of 1938 I took the school's entrance examination and was admitted for the autumn term, on condition that during the summer holidays I made up the year of Latin that I had missed. A sixth form boy from the local grammar school was engaged to tutor me and as I then had an excellent memory the task was not a problem. When term started it felt wonderful to have done with the restrictions of boarding school. In the morning I got a trolleybus from the end of our road to Bow Road, which was then the nearest underground station to Forest Gate. From there it was twenty-one stops on the District line to Hammersmith and then seven minutes walk to school. The journey took about an hour and a quarter and would probably be considered excessive by today's parents. But I enjoyed the freedom of travelling round London on my own, and I could do all my learning and reading homework en route.

My elation with the new life that was beginning for me was soon destroyed. The Germans, having annexed Austria in the spring, prepared to invade Czechoslovakia, which was now surrounded by Germany on three sides. The Czechs appealed for help to the French and British, who were disinclined to give it. The majority of the British Cabinet, apart from Churchill and Duff Cooper, argued that we had no treaty obligation with Czechoslovakia. Moreover, our armed forces were in no position to go to war for what Chamberlain, the Prime Minister, notoriously described as 'a quarrel in a faraway country between people of whom we know nothing.' Contemporary historians are inclined to agree that because of the long-standing reluctance of Chamberlain and most of his cabinet to contemplate war with Germany we were not adequately prepared to wage a successful war in 1938. But many on both right and left saw Chamberlain's reluctance as shameful. As Hitler assembled his troops on the Czech frontiers Chamberlain made several visits to Germany, flying for the first time in his life, in an attempt to secure a compromise solution. His extreme reluctance to countenance the possibility of Britain going to war also meant that no civil defence measures had been put in place. On September 30th Chamberlain returned from Munich with a compromise agreement secured at the expense of the Czechs – more than a third of Czechoslovakia was to be transferred to Germany. He assured Britain that Hitler had renounced all war-like intentions against our country and, 'it is peace for our time'. In fact, Hitler merely postponed his invasion of the rest of Czechoslovakia until the following March, meanwhile turning his attention to the expulsion of foreign born Jews and the destruction of Jewish homes, shops and synagogues in the 'Kristallnacht'.

Despite a widespread foreboding of war in the previous few years, when the Munich crisis came in September most people, like the government, had not expected or prepared for it. We would certainly not have gone on holiday to the Isle of Wight in August nor would our mother have visited the U.S.A. then if war had been expected imminently. Most schools, including St. Paul's, had made no preparations for evacuation. On September 25th gas masks were issued, trenches dug in parks and barrage balloons appeared in the sky over London. These were shining silvery balloons, sixty feet long, floating 2,000 feet above the ground to which they were tethered by steel cables. They were intended to discourage dive bombing and low-level air attacks. On September 29th the government announced plans for the evacuation of two million people from London.

My grandmother bought 'iron rations' for Michael and myself to take when we were evacuated, following a list issued by the government. A bar of plain chocolate, which at that time I disliked, was specified and I raged against my grandmother for not buying milk chocolate, finally flinging myself on my bed in tears. On my mother's return, with her usual diplomacy, instead of scolding me for my bad temper she sat on my bed and began to tell me about her day. She described the decision of the local bureaucrats to marshal the pregnant women who were to be evacuated with the blind (at that time a pregnant woman was considered an embarrassing sight) so I was soon laughing instead of crying. The next day, war was averted.

It seems childish at twelve to respond to the threat of war with hysteria about a bar of chocolate, but I think my mother understood that I was really desperately worried about what war would bring. I had a fair understanding of the international situation, but emotionally it was the effect on my own life that concerned me. It was not so much fear of the saturation bombing and gas attacks that were generally expected to follow as soon as war was declared. It was more a feeling of despair that just when I had at last escaped from boarding school and started at what seemed to be my best school yet, I was going to lose all this and once more be separated from my family and my new school. And I felt despair at having so little control over my life, not understanding that in wartime everyone suffers a massive loss of control.

Like that of many other British families, our family's response to the Munich agreement was mixed. Contemporary Tories often accuse the left of a cowardly opposition to the war. But by 1938 the majority of the left, including influential intellectuals and journalists and at this stage the Communist Party, were convinced that war was both right and inevitable and that fascism had to be defeated. The strongest opponents of the war were in fact a section of the right, who saw much to admire in Germany. They believed that it formed a useful bulwark between the Soviet Union and Britain, or thought that the best solution would be a German-Soviet war, which would weaken both. Because of the influence of these powerful conservatives the government, despite Churchill's urging, had made neither military nor civil defence preparations for war.

But opponents of the war were not confined to the right. My mother remembered the horrors of the First World War and the suffering it had caused. In her opinion the war had created, and not solved, international conflict. She was certainly not alone in this. There was a strong pacifist movement in the thirties, which included a sizable minority of the Labour Party, as well as Quakers and other non-political people. The Labour Party had only abandoned its opposition to rearmament in 1937 in response to the Spanish civil war and as late as November 1939 seventy Labour constituency parties supported a call for a truce. So whilst some felt shame at our betrayal of Czechoslovakia, many felt enormous relief that war had been avoided, if only for a while.

For me, avoidance of war meant that I could return to my new school, St.Paul's, which had about 450 pupils aged eleven to eighteen. It tended to attract pupils from well-to-do intellectual families – the daughters of G.D.H. Cole, the left-wing economist, were there with me, Shirley Williams, daughter of Vera Brittain, came later. It had a reputation for welcoming Jewish girls and there was a sizeable Jewish minority, including the daughters of the left-wing publisher Victor Gollancz. During the religious assembly with which like almost all schools then we started each day, a Jewish prefect held a separate assembly for the Jewish girls in a special room, where they also went during scripture lessons. Kosher dinners were provided for them and I don't remember ever hearing an anti-semitic remark in the school. I thought at the time that there was only one discriminatory practice – a Jewish girl was never appointed as head girl because one of her duties was to accompany the high mistress to morning assembly, carrying her prayer book. However, years later I learned that there was an unofficial 'quota' of Jewish girls admitted, and that there was definitely some covert anti-semitism amongst the pupils.

Our school was the sister of the boys' St. Paul's school. It had been built in 1903, apparently without regard to expense, in the style of Norman Shaw. It had the pink bricks with stone facings and the large windows, made up of many small panes, which Shaw favoured. The main rooms and corridors were lined with oak, with decorative Art Nouveau wall tiles, and the floors in the entrance hall were black and white marble. The Great Hall extended to the roof and was overlooked on the first floor by a gallery four rows deep. On the oak platform at the far end of the hall was a large and magnificent organ, a grand piano and a wide pulpit-like, elaborately carved structure where the high mistress stood. Twenty classrooms opened out of the two storeys of the Great Hall, with large many paned windows on both sides, so that they were very light.

The boys' school had been founded by John Colet in 1509 and we copied some of its ancient customs. Originally the boys' school consisted of a large hall, where the boys sat in eight rows according to their achievements, the seventh and eighth rows being the top of the school. Because the master in charge had sat, elevated on a platform, at the far end, he was given the title of 'high master'. Accordingly, we had a 'high' instead of a 'head' mistress and the top two years in our school were called the seventh and eighth forms, but for the purpose of this account I refer to them as the sixth form. We scholars wore brass badges engraved with the head of John Colet and far from being looked down on as 'scholarship girls', we were called together as a group once a term and told we were the intellectual elite of the school from whom much was expected. In order to further diminish the possibility that we would be looked down upon all parents were encouraged to enter their daughters for the examinations if they thought they stood a chance of winning. Those whose daughters did win were asked privately whether they needed to have the fees remitted.

In the entrance hall boards were hung, with the names of the girls who won university scholarships, principally to Oxford and Cambridge, engraved in gilt. The school has always had a reputation for being extremely academic but it was after all its declared aim to prepare girls for professional careers. This was stated in its prospectus from 1920. There was never a suggestion from anyone that there were professions girls should not enter or that they were likely to do less well than boys. Practical subjects, sewing, cooking, pottery, which we were taught at Bedford High School, were not on the curriculum. At the time I assumed that almost of us went on to a university, but I later discovered that only about three quarters did so then, and the others may have felt in some sense failures or misfits. I am often puzzled and slightly irritated by the frequency with which generalisations, like the following by Hilary Spurling, are made, 'Girls of my generation were very restricted. We were educated for marriage, and not for careers.' This was not true of either of the secondary schools I attended, and I am fourteen years older than Spurling.

Although avowedly academic the school's practices were not at that time as competitive as those of my previous school. The parallel classes in each year were not grouped by ability, though within the classes there were ability 'sets' for maths and languages. We were given grades, A+, A, A- etc, rather than marks for homework and exams and not placed in form order, though there was a form prize each year for the girl whose work had been the best all-round. Musical prowess was very highly regarded. There was a separate music wing with a singing hall (concerts were usually held in the Great Hall) a soundproof room for the Director of Music, who played the organ for school assembly, and many soundproof practice rooms. Gustav Holst was Director of Music until he died in office in 1934, to be succeeded by Vaughan Williams and then Herbert Howells. Girls could always get out of games and even lessons if they pleaded an important music rehearsal and they could practice in the dinner hour instead of being turned out into the playground.

Avoiding the playground in the morning break and the dinner hour was one of my preoccupations as a junior. Unlike most of the girls I disliked running around and practicing netball goal shots. I no longer learnt the piano, so I could not escape in that way, but going to the art department on the top floor was sometimes possible. Art was not nearly as highly rated in the school as music, and perhaps sensitive to this, the senior art teacher, a sister of the artist Victor Pasmore, would often admonish the girls for the philistine values of their families. She would point out that if their parents spent less on possessions like cars they could well afford to buy contemporary art. It was also sometimes possible to retreat to the special history library, although the main, large, beautiful and oak lined library was out of bounds in the dinner hour. If all else failed I would sit on the outside steps with a likeminded friend, firmly refusing the prefects' injunctions to exercise.

Far too much time was spent on gymnastics and games for my taste. Both then and now most school children would have envied what I hated – games in our own grounds *every afternoon*, hockey, lacrosse and netball in the winter, tennis and cricket in the summer. As well as this, we had gym twice a week, and swimming in the school baths once a week until the war started, when the baths were closed to conserve fuel. However, unlike in my previous school, academic and musical success had higher status than athletic prowess and I was no longer unpopular for my dislike of games, merely considered eccentric.

The large gymnasium, dining room, kitchen and cloakrooms were in the basement. We each had a tall narrow locker where we kept our gym and games clothes, with a key, which we had to keep on a ribbon round our necks. The school dinners were very civilised compared to those in my earlier schools. Each class had its own long oak table, set with linen runners and linen napkins, and you could sit next to whomever you wished. Before and after the meal Miss Strudwick said a Latin grace. The form teacher sat at the head of the table and we were waited on by maids. There was no question of having to eat the food but, amazingly, it was usually very good. If you felt unwell, or pretended that you did, you could ask for soup instead of the first course and fruit instead of the pudding. Kosher meals were available.

A good deal of stress was placed not only on academic prowess but also on behaving as 'young ladies'. We addressed the staff as Ma'am and had to stand up when any adult entered the room. One member of the class had to meet the teacher outside the staff room before each lesson began and accompany her, carrying her books, to the classroom. At dinner we had to take it in turn to sit next to the teacher and entertain her with supposedly interesting conversation. Once a week we had to sit at a 'French table' presided over by one of the French teachers, where all conversation had to be in French. Unfortunately this practice stopped during the war when the native French teachers left. Food had to be eaten in 'polite' ways – for example, if oranges were served for dessert, we had to cut them round their equator and then eat them with a teaspoon, a difficult accomplishment. We were not allowed to eat in the street or to go into any of the local shops.

We always had to wear gloves outside the school – even during the war we had to wear white cotton gloves in the streets during the summer. We were not allowed to run in any part of the building or to talk in the Hall, corridors, cloakrooms or on the stairs and prefects were posted to enforce this. At the time I regarded these rules as ridiculous, but looking back I realise that they did result in a calm, peaceful atmosphere, which I remember nostalgically. During my six years in the school I used to wander round the building, admiring its large, beautiful and silent spaces.

I recently returned to the school to consult Dr. Bailes, the senior history master who is in charge of its archives. The building seemed as beautiful as before but there had been many additions – a small theatre in the grounds, with a green room, professional lighting etc., rooms full of computers and many more classrooms since there are now 700 pupils. The calm and quiet in the school had disappeared – girls in jeans (there is no longer a school uniform) were running up and down the stairs shouting to each other. They looked much more attractive and sophisticated than the rather 'puddingy', uniformed schoolgirls of my time. The school still has high academic expectations of its pupils, perhaps more so than in my time, and they are expected to work very hard, but they don't just keep their heads down. A great deal of out-of-lesson activity seemed to be going on, concerts and plays were being rehearsed, clubs were meeting, art was being produced, joint arrangements were being made with other schools. There were many non European faces and I was told that three days a week there is a Christian Assembly, one day a Jewish one, and one day a Moslem one, and that the girls could, and did, go to any or all of these as they wished. The dining room is now a self-service cafeteria with a wide range of dishes to accommodate all religious diets. The quaint customs I remembered, such as addressing the teachers as Ma'am and carrying their books, had long ago disappeared. There were a number of male teachers, though no male pupils. There was no longer the massive disjunction between the informality of home life and the formal, and even then very old fashioned, behaviour expected at school in my day, and whilst the peace I remember nostalgically had gone, their school life today seemed much more interesting.

Throughout my own stay at St. Paul's I did not find the school lessons interesting, with one exception. During my first year we had an excellent English teacher, Miss Gibson, a youngish woman with an Eton crop, a crisp, incisive manner and very high expectations of twelve year olds. We read the *Canterbury tales* in Early English and I, at least, enjoyed the strange, poetic language. Sadly, in 1940 she left for America where she married and produced Shakespearean plays in Connecticut. We would still have lost her if she had married in England. It was another twenty years, in the mid fifties, before the school would employ married women teachers. In my first year at St. Paul's I was introduced to science, which was taught in a splendid, separate block with seven large laboratories, built only five years earlier to the specifications of several professors from Imperial College. But the science lessons did not match the splendid buildings – I found them extraordinarily boring. I could work up no interest in determining specific gravity by putting small balls into bottles and even heating substances in test tubes to watch them change colour seemed pointless. Throughout my time in St. Paul's the science teaching was very uninspired. For a period during the war the science block was closed and no science was taught.

I quickly discovered that there were a number of clubs one could join, which put on plays and arranged dramatic readings and lectures from outside speakers and sometimes went on outings on Saturday mornings. Juniors like myself were discouraged from joining by the hurdle of having to first produce an acceptable piece of writing to merit admission, but I succeeded in joining the history club. These clubs played an important part in providing the wide cultural education which some boys' public schools offered. Unfortunately the outbreak of the war was soon to put an end to them.

An unexpected and welcome feature of the school was the 'fog holidays' we were given. Because many girls lived some distance from the school, when fogs were expected to our delight we were sent home after lunch before the fog got too thick. These were not the gentle mists that Whistler and Monet painted but the choking 'pea soupers' of Dickens, thick, dirty and acrid, caused by burning coal, which set everyone coughing. To be out in dense fog when you literally could not see beyond a few inches ahead and had to feel your way home along fences or walls was exciting but alarming and exhausting. When you finally got home you would find that fog had penetrated to every room in the house. 'Fog holidays' continued throughout and after the war. The last great fog was in 1952, the year my second child was born. It lasted four days and killed about 4000 Londoners. The Clean Air Act of 1956 began to control this form of air pollution.

In my experience happiness at school depends most of all on your friends. I quickly made a friend, Teresa Symons, the closest girl friend I had ever had or was to have in the future. We were attracted to each other on almost the first day by our mutual dislike of games and gymnastics – sometimes we managed to evade them by walking up and down the road outside the school during the games period. But we soon discovered that we had a lot else in common. Unlike any girl of my age I'd met before Teresa was very interested in politics, a Labour supporter and an atheist. She, like me, was a great reader and a lover of poetry. My leather-bound, gilt-edged volume of Shelley was a present from her mother for my thirteenth birthday, I gave Teresa a volume of T.S. Eliot when she was 14 and she responded with a volume of Sassoon. We both disliked the petty rules at school, but whilst I would always fight them Teresa was simply privately scornful of them.

Her mother Madeleine, like mine, was a public figure and a socialist, although a Fabian rather than a trade unionist. She did not have a job but like my mother she had many public duties, as a J.P. and a member of committees and government tribunals. She was also a lone mother, like mine, but had never been married – she was addressed as Miss Simons, an extraordinary defiance of convention at that time in a middle class circle. Teresa had an adopted brother who was at boarding school. Like me, she was intensely curious about her father, who was also never mentioned at home, and who at that time she suspected was dead.

There the similarity between our circumstances ended. Madeleine was a very wealthy woman who lived in a large house, 17 Pelham Crescent, in South Kensington. It was staffed by three maids, a cook and a companion for Teresa, always referred to by the two of us as 'the Lady', perhaps to mark her social position in the household. She was a kind of successor to a nanny, but a middle class woman, who saw that Teresa got up and went to bed at the right times, took her to buy clothes, to the dentist, doctor etc., was always there when her mother was out and for the first term at St. Paul's took her to and from school. (I privately considered this ludicrous). Despite, or because of this nannying, Teresa was an independent, strong willed girl accustomed to getting her way. On hot summer days if she announced she could not sleep her mother would take her in a taxi to an evening performance at the Open Air theatre in Regent's Park. On the school's Founders Day we were all required to appear in a velvet dress. Teresa persuaded her mother to buy her a sophisticated black one, though it was then unheard of for a child to wear black, except in mourning, and certainly not black velvet. I'm sure that she was as able as I but her attitude to school work was much more laid back. I think that at some level I already realised that escape from West Ham depended on my doing well at school, but she had no such motivation.

Every day we used to go home together as far as South Kensington on the underground, at first with 'the Lady', who tactfully sat down several seats away from us, later Teresa was allowed to go home on her own. At that time there were first class carriages on the underground, which were often empty during the afternoon, and sometimes we went in them illegally and from sheer high spirits swung from the leather straps. I would often go home with her and visit her in the holidays.

We both developed a 'crush' on Emlyn Williams, then at the height of his fame as an actor and film star. He lived two houses away from Teresa and we would hang about outside his house, waiting to get a glimpse of him. The transition from Teresa's home to Margery Park Road was painful. I relayed home the strange fact that if something was spilt on the tablecloth at Teresa's nobody was scolded, nothing was said, and my grandmother rather tartly pointed out that Teresa's mother would not be washing the cloth. I even felt uneasy about a possible meeting between my beloved mother and Madeleine, who had a social poise, graciousness and queenly manner I'd never seen before, no doubt derived from generations of wealth and power.

A third girl was often with us, Isabel Waley, whose father was Technical Director of the British Film Institute. He was a member of a wealthy intellectual Jewish family, his brother, Arthur, is famous for his translations of Chinese and Japanese poetry. For her thirteenth birthday party Isabel's father hired a room above a restaurant in Soho and after tea showed 'The Gold Rush', the first time I'd seen a Chaplin film. The Waleys lived in the next street to Teresa, the two families were friendly and the girls had been friends at preparatory school, and almost since birth. Teresa swiftly abandoned Isabel for me, but Isabel was a good-natured girl who did not easily take offence and would tag around after us.

A fourth girl, Lilian Horesh, was in our circle of friends. But whilst Teresa and I were proudly defiant outsiders at school because of our opinions and tastes I think that Lilian was a reluctant outsider, who felt excluded by her culture and ethnicity. Her parents were Jewish business people from the Middle East, and she looked decidedly Middle Eastern, with very dark hair and eyes and a dark olive skin. I don't believe anyone addressed racist remarks to her at school but she was aware, as I was not at the time, of covert anti-semitism. She was extremely diffident and lacking in confidence in all areas of school life. Even her posture displayed her unease – she habitually slouched, and held her head down, as though to avoid being seen. When I met her after leaving Oxford I was amazed at her transformation. She had married a solicitor from a similar background, had a flat on the Chelsea embankment, was elegantly dressed, exotically beautiful and socially confident.

Isabel was not considered an outsider by anyone, but she chose us for her friends. We regarded both Lilian and Isabel as 'childish', ourselves as sophisticates and I'm afraid we unkindly made it clear that they could not be admitted to the inner circle of our friendship. Later events were to change all this.

What was most important that year to me was my friendship with Teresa. We were so delighted with each other's company that we parted every day with great reluctance. I can't remember us ever talking about the imminent threat of war, we were absorbed in a kind of love affair. There was no physical component, at that time girls did not embrace each other. It was more that we felt like Platonic twins, separated at birth, who had found each other. Through Teresa and Isabel I witnessed a life style I had never seen before, or indeed, since. I was astonished to find that Isabel's mother had breakfast in bed, brought by a maid, and didn't get up until after the cook had come to take orders. One Sunday I was invited to a family lunch party at Isabel's grandfather's house near Hyde Park. It was a very imposing house, but the detail that remained in my memory was that the toilet paper was coloured, which I'd never seen before. In my previous schools the other girls had been middle class, but they didn't have parlour maids or go for holidays abroad. St. Paul's had a sizeable proportion of girls from wealthy upper middle class families.

As a socialist, I might have been expected to disapprove of these displays of wealth, but I'm afraid I wholly admired them. The houses and furnishings were more beautiful and spacious than any I had known, the children had extraordinarily varied and interesting lives -frequent visits to the theatre, days spent ice skating in a private club in Queensway, horse riding, holidays abroad, country weekends. Now, these experiences are commonplace in many middle class homes but at that time they were confined to wealthy families. Wealth removed many of the sharp edges of daily life. My friends were not, like me, always in trouble for losing their possessions, spilling ink on their clothes or food on the tablecloth. I suppose I envied them, but I principally remember constantly being amazed. Once Teresa and I went into a patisserie near South Kensington station to buy some cakes for her mother. Two elegant and fashionably dressed young women were sitting inside and seeing our unmistakeable school uniform told us that they were 'old

Paulinas'. I gazed with wonder, and thought, ' Will we grow up to be like them?'

But it was not just wonder and admiration that I felt in South Kensington. I also felt definitely uneasy in these unfamiliar environments, afraid of doing 'the wrong thing', aware that these families regarded themselves and their life styles as vastly superior to mine and that the adults were liable to patronise me. It was not comfortable to realise that my family and I were regarded as inferior. I felt defensive about my family, unsure about myself, but also more than ever dissatisfied with the dreariness of Forest Gate and our home, our narrow life, expandable only through immersing oneself in the fantasy of books or films, the continuous tension between my grandparents and the ugliness of my grandfather's hot temper and drunkenness. I was not so foolish as to suppose that the family relations of the wealthy were always harmonious. Although voices never seemed to be raised or cross words spoken in Teresa's home, there was obvious friction between Isabel's parents. But it seemed to me that the possibilities of retreat in a large house, compared to Margery Park Road where all life was lived out in the kitchen, and the consolations that wealth could bring – breakfast in bed, trips to the theatre, etc.– must cushion whatever problems arose. Over the next few years when I saw the Waley family at closer quarters I came to realise that this was not in fact the case- there was a coldness between the parents that money did not ease.

That year, 1938–9, was not only the year of my great friendship but the last 'normal' year of my schooling. When St. Paul's eventually re-opened it was a very changed school.

The breakout of war, evacuation and the 'phoney war' 1939–40

After the Munich crisis the government at last began to prepare for war. Hitler invaded the rest of Czechoslovakia in March and Britain promised to support Poland in the event of a German attack. The forces were rearmed, military conscription was introduced, detailed plans for civilian evacuation were drawn up. During the summer of 1939 we had no family holiday. Probably our mother was involved in plans for evacuating West Ham schools and the N.U.T. headquarters. I went to the Forest School camp as usual but Michael went to an Officer's Training

Corps camp, organised by his school. Then I went to stay for a week or so with Isabel Waley and her family near Kirkcudbright in south west Scotland, travelling on my own by train. The Waleys, anticipating war, instead of their usual holiday abroad had rented a big house in the country near the sea for the summer, taking their servants with them. (Later, as women were conscripted into the forces or essential work, maids virtually disappeared.) The holiday was a decided culture shock, coming as it did directly after the unconventionality of the Forest School camp. I was puzzled by the weird upper middle class conventions, for example a maid 'turned down' the beds at night, an apparently pointless exercise. I did not particularly enjoy the holiday. Later I became fond of Isabel, but we did not have much in common and that summer I was still emotionally tied to Teresa. Isabel had an older brother, Daniel, who became a distinguished medieval historian. He seemed to me both extremely clever and very cruel, delighting in exposing any shallow intellectual pretensions of my own. Her father was ironically distant, with a very dry wit, characteristics I had never met before and found disconcerting, though later I grew to appreciate them. Her mother took very little notice of Isabel and myself. I got badly sunburnt and felt the absence of a sympathetic adult. Isabel, always cheerful and good-natured and decidedly without intellectual interests, seemed a strange anomaly in her family.

I was home by the time the Germans invaded Poland on September 1st, and on Sunday September 3rd at 11 a.m. a querulous Chamberlain, pushed by his cabinet, broadcast to the nation that his peace efforts had failed and war had been declared. I did not feel the despair that had overwhelmed me the year before. Thinking about this difference recently I assumed that it was due to my greater maturity at thirteen, until I read Eric Hobsbawm's autobiography. He was twenty-one at the time of the Munich crisis but he too describes being briefly overcome by a feeling of panic. When the war actually started he too felt quite calm because, he thought, the intervening year had allowed everyone to get used to the prospect of war. We were braced for an immediate onset of bombing and gas attacks. Military planners had privately forecast that there would be 150,000 casualties in the first air attack, but it was another year before the bombing of cities started. No one then envisaged the scale of suffering that was to come – that the war would last for six years and become a world wide, not a local war, and lead to the death of at least fifty million and the displacement of many more and the destruction of whole economies. And we were not to know that, despite our initial fears, and despite the death and destruction that did follow in Britain, our suffering was in the end much less than that in many other countries.

Somehow, though, absorbed in my new school and friends I managed not to think about the war that was coming, except when a U.S. friend of my mother's suggested that Michael and I should be sent to live with her if war came. For once we were given a choice and we both absolutely refused to go. Unlike the Munich crisis, this time plans had been made to put Britain on a war footing. Two days before war was declared, as German troops moved into Poland, two million people began to be evacuated from London – school children, pregnant women, mothers with under-fives, disabled adults, as well as the staff of major organisations, such as the civil service, banks and building societies. Street lighting and station lights were turned off and 'the blackout' began – householders had to see that no light was visible from their houses at night. Any chink of light meant a call from a policeman or air raid warden. My mother, who was by then head teacher of Manor Road Senior Elementary Girls School in the Victoria Docks area, was assigned to take her school by train to Bruton, a small town in Somerset and I went with her. She found chaos. Local people were unwilling to take or having taken, to keep, the children billeted on them, most of whom had never left home before and were desperate to get back. Teaching turned out to be impossible because no building, books, or blackboards were available.

As always, middle class families fared better. Avoiding the mass evacuation on September 1st, Michael had already left with his school on August 30th for Marlborough, in Wiltshire, where it had been arranged that they would lodge with private families in the town and share facilities with a large public school, Marlborough College. Later, my mother drove me to High Wycombe, where we Paulinas were to attend Wycombe Abbey School. In fact, only 182 of the 450 Paulinas came to High Wycombe, the rest had left for other boarding schools. Often their parents had recently bought or rented, if they had not long possessed, houses in the country, where the mothers took their children, finding boarding schools for them later. Alas, this is what happened to Teresa – her mother bought a beautiful Tudor house in the Cotswolds, from whence she was soon sent to boarding school.

About half of the Paulinas who came to High Wycombe were billeted in the town, the other half became boarders in the school. Wycombe Abbey was a very grand boarding school – there were no day girls – set in 160 acres of land, with woods, gardens and a large lake. The central school block had been built in the Romantic Gothic style at the end of the eighteenth century, and was castellated, with turrets at each end. The chapel, built at the same time in the style of a medieval abbey, had statues in niches round its external walls. There were nine boarding houses scattered around the grounds and the girls wore long hooded cloaks, like monks, to move around. The current fee for boarders is £28,000 a year. The ethos of the school was very different from that of St. Paul's. The forms were streamed and the academic standard in the top stream was very high, but there was more stress on religion than at St. Paul's, some of the girls were titled and all were being groomed to enter 'society'. There were weekly ballroom dancing lessons where half the class in turn had to pretend to be men, and we were taught what to say when accepting or declining an invitation to dance and how to make the right kind of conversation.

From the start the arrangement was unsatisfactory. Though there were some separate classes for us with our own teachers mostly we were shared round among the Wycombe Abbey classes, but wearing our own uniforms. Once a week we had our own Assembly: otherwise we hardly saw our own teachers or the high mistress. The Wycombists resented the invasion of an alien host and despised us 'billetees', as, we felt, did their staff. Most of us hated our time at the school and our own teachers did not hide their dislike of the situation from us. Miss Pasmore, our senior art teacher, who had been given a shed in the grounds as her studio, let me spend as much time there as I could, colluding with my evasion of hockey. Despite my lack of talent she encouraged and helped me to take up oil painting. The arrangement at my brother's school worked much better and lasted throughout the war. They kept entirely separate from the Marlborough College staff and pupils, each school using the classrooms for half the day, and the playing fields for the other half.

The Paulinas who became boarders were deeply unhappy. Used to the freedom of a day school they found themselves not only confined to the grounds but also in a very strict hierarchical structure – no one was allowed to speak to a girl older than herself unless spoken to first. Lilian, who was the second youngest in her house, spent her time almost in silence. The billeted girls fared much better. The families who took us in were all comfortably off, with room to spare for two or more girls. They were more than willing to have us. We saved them from having working-class children, who were rumoured to have lice and to wet their beds, compulsorily billeted on them, and our parents, of course, paid them a good deal more than they would have received from the government. I was placed along with two of my form, Isabel Waley and Nancy Cowen. Both were cheerful and good-natured and we got along together very well, but they did not share my interests and I had to console myself with a voluminous correspondence with Teresa. We were lodged with the Elgeys, the manager of the National Provincial Bank and his wife.

I was bitterly disappointed at losing the freedom of living at home after only a year and felt desolate when my mother left me. But with the experienced eye of an ex-boarder I quickly saw that we had been very lucky in our billet, and soon cheered up. The Elgeys were a middle-aged, childless couple who seemed totally uninterested in us and likely to leave us alone. Whilst almost all the other girls were placed in the leafy suburbs we were lodged right in the centre of the town, above the bank in the middle of the high street, where a lively market was held every Saturday. We were strictly forbidden by the school to enter any shops or use public transport or go anywhere except straight to and from school, but I thought the risk of being caught in the adjacent shops or the market was fairly low. Next door to us was a large branch of W.H. Smith, with a lending library. So with a supply of books assured, as well as salted peanuts, which were not rationed, and which I preferred to sweets, I began to relax.

The Elgeys were a very conventional, narrow minded, *Daily Telegraph*-reading couple with whom I clashed fairly often. They found the three of us irritating, especially me – Isabel remembers that I would refuse to stand up when the National Anthem was played on the radio. But totally uninterested in our welfare, they made no attempt to supervise how we spent our time, whether we did our homework or obeyed school rules, or what time we put our light out. Mrs. Elgey was French and a good cook. She supplemented the rations with a weekly roast pheasant – game was expensive but unrationed – and often gave us our favourite supper of baked beans on toast. I used to hurry back from Wycombe Abbey to their sitting room to listen to an exciting radio serial about the adventures of Paul Temple, a detective. I'm sure the school didn't know that quite soon we were joined by Mrs. Elgey's two French nephews, sent to her for safe keeping. They were older than us, fifteen or sixteen, and we thought them gauche, unattractive and dull. Teasing them in our poor French was one of our main amusements. With the egocentricity of adolescents we didn't consider their plight, separated from parents, friends and country, hardly able to speak the local language. Later, I came across them when they had joined the Free French Forces and found them much more self confident and relaxed.

Isabel and I shared a double bed, Nancy had a camp bed at its foot. My mother was with her school in Somerset and could not visit me, nor could Nancy's parents. But even though petrol was rationed to three gallons a week Isabel's parents managed to drive down by car on some Sundays. They generously entertained all three of us, taking us out to tea and to see the surrounding country, which we were otherwise forbidden to visit. Between visits Isabel's father frequently sent her, and sometimes me, postcards of art works. He was the only person I've known to be consistently witty on a postcard. In October, identity cards were issued and supposed to be carried at all times. I took what seemed to me a splendid opportunity to change my middle name, Patricia, which I'd always disliked, to Anne, without consulting anybody. Later, the discrepancy with my birth certificate led to endless bureaucratic hassles, even in adult life, so I would advise anyone against that particular blow for freedom.

The most significant aspect of my stay in High Wycombe was that I began an involvement with the Communist Party. There were two reasons for this. No sooner had I arrived at the Elgeys than I started to receive a copy of the *Daily Worker* by post each day, with no indication of who had sent it. I was enormously puzzled and intrigued by this and decided that the sender must be my father, the missing member of the family about whom I was still intensely curious. This attribution was a huge mistake on two counts – my father, like the rest of my family, was very opposed to the Communist Party, and moreover after his unsuccessful 'kidnapping' attempt he never displayed any curiosity or interest in me. After a couple of months I discovered that the newspaper was being sent by G.T.C. Giles, a friend of my mother's, who was on the Executive Committee of both the National Union of Teachers and the Communist Party. I wrote to thank him, whilst pointing out that I was not a communist. He replied, 'It means quite a lot to people like me to know that young people are interested in thinking intelligently about politics.' There followed three foolscap sides in which he 'explained' why the dictatorship of the proletariat differed from other dictatorships, and why Russia was right to have signed the non aggression pact with Germany. He did not mention that the Communist Party had initially supported the war until instructed by Moscow not to do so. Much flattered that Giles should bother with a schoolgirl I diligently read my *Daily Worker*s, to the disgust of the bank manager. I even offered to post them on to Teresa, a suggestion she hurriedly declined, as likely to prove compromising at her boarding school.

It is difficult to see how I could have read the *Daily Worker* with pleasure. I recently found a copy amongst my papers, dated December 6th 1939. Its four pages are devoted to crudely slanted pro-Soviet and anti-war propaganda – 'the war means ruin for small shopkeepers', and reports of opposition to the war in trade union and Labour Party branches. Looking at it now it seems almost comic in its solemnity. The only light relief is a pools forecast by a football correspondent. A list of recommendations for books to give at Christmas is headed by the 'History of the Communist Party of the Soviet Union.' and 'World Affairs and the U.S.S.R.' In later years some excellent journalists much improved the paper.

A second reason for my involvement with the Communist Party was that every Saturday it had a stall in the market opposite the bank, run by a middle-aged English woman, Elizabeth Taylor and an older, lugubrious Austrian refugee, Julius Fried. It was difficult for them to recruit support in a very middle class area at a time when the party opposed the war, and the Soviet Union had not only signed a non-aggression pact with Germany but invaded Finland. This was probably why the stall workers put most of their effort into trying to sell Marxist classics. I used to chat to them and help give out leaflets to passers-by, and I spent much of my pocket money on fairly incomprehensible publications of the Little Lenin Library and a hard back edition of the even more unintelligible *Das Capital*. Only the *Communist Manifesto*, written by Marx and Engels in 1848, proved to be both straightforward and inspiring. Intrigued I suppose by her thirteen year old supporter, Mrs. Taylor – children did not address adult acquaintances by their first names then – invited me to tea several times. She had first to get written permission from the school. Any opportunity to get away from the school and the billet was a welcome break. I was surprised to find that she lived in a beautiful modern house, the like of which I'd never seen before. It had been designed by her architect husband, and they were obviously well off. Until then, it had not occurred to me that people like the Taylors would be communists.

I had very little understanding of Marxism or of the ins and outs of current policy. I think that the Communist Party attracted me partly because it was about the only way I could rebel against my very anti-establishment but anti-communist family. But probably the major attraction was its romantic appeal. It seemed to represent a heroic, idealistic stance, far removed from the compromises of the Labour Party. The widespread, hysterical opposition to the Communist Party in the 1920s had been replaced during the 1930s by a more sympathetic attitude amongst intellectuals, including the younger poets, Auden, Spender, Isherwood and distinguished scientists like J.B.S. Haldane and J.D. Bernal. This was mainly because communists throughout Europe had taken the lead in opposing fascism, many dying in fascist prisons and concentration camps and in the Spanish civil war. In Britain the Communist Party led the opposition to the Blackshirts, a group of British fascists whose marches through the East End were violently anti-semitic in intent. Heroic young communists like John Cornford were killed in the International Brigade in support of the Spanish republic. As to the Soviet Union, it seemed at the time an egalitarian, just society, held back only by the plots and hostility of capitalist nations. I believed the Soviet assurance that those executed after the Moscow trials of 1936-38 were involved in a Nazi conspiracy to assassinate Stalin, and that the accusations that Stalin had instituted a reign of terror were capitalist inventions.

Nonetheless, since a major appeal of the Communist Party was that it was the only party to oppose fascism unambiguously from the beginning I found, like most sympathisers, that the Nazi-Soviet pact in September, followed by the party's sudden switch from supporting to opposing the war, was embarrassingly puzzling. The Communist Party did not disclose the fact that this change was the result of a directive from Moscow but argued that the war we had embarked on was not in fact against fascism. It was a war between different capitalist powers, all of whom were primarily interested in defeating the Soviet Union. As evidence they pointed out correctly that most of the British Cabinet in this pre-Churchill government were 'Guilty Men' because of their pre-war sympathy for Nazi Germany and their strong anti-Soviet attitudes, and that the French government had declared the Communist Party illegal at the onset of war. They argued that these pro-German sympathies of the Allied leaders explained why it was a 'phoney war' – why, although war had been declared, there were no air raids, and no fighting, apart from some attacks on shipping. In fact, Chamberlain's strategy at the time was to starve Germany into submission by an economic blockade, rather than launch air attacks, which he believed would only bring reprisals. He expected the war to be over by the spring.

I could not go along with the Communist Party's opposition to the war. But it was not such an unpopular policy on the left as might nowadays be thought, and in fact the party increased in membership, mainly amongst trade unionists, during the 'phoney war'. It tends to be forgotten that at the outset of the war many British people had little enthusiasm for it. On the day before war was declared, *Mass Observation* reported that one person in three thought that 'anything would be better than war.' There was no repetition of the jingoism and enthusiasm that had marked the start of the First World War. A minority of left-wing and non-political people still held pacifist views. The left-wing of the Labour Party, led by Stafford Cripps and Aneuran Bevan, argued for a struggle on two fronts, against Hitler and against the government of Chamberlain.

But the support for the Communist Party amongst working people was due to the militancy of those of its members who were shop stewards, and its campaign for deep public air raid shelters. Time was to prove the party right on this. Whilst Germany had provided such shelters in its cities the British government had not done so (except for the likes of royalty and the Cabinet) on the ground that people would acquire a 'shelter mentality' and be reluctant to leave them. Instead, they offered Anderson shelters, quite a superficial protection, to those with gardens. They cost £7 or were free for those with incomes below £250 p.a. – my grandparents, of course, qualified on this count. Only the materials were provided – curved sheets of corrugated iron panels four feet six wide and six feet six long, and two end panels. They had to be buried four feet in the earth so that a large pit had first to be dug. The roof then had to be covered with at least fifteen inches of soil, on which vegetables could be grown. A bench could be put along each side, so six people could sit down but only two could lie down. The shelters were damp, cold and in some areas waterlogged. People were reluctant to sleep in them, my grandparents never did, but they did offer protection from debris and flying glass.

The majority of Londoners in central London and the East End did not have a garden and those public shelters that had been built, each housing about fifty people, were not adequately deep. They were built of brick with a thick slab of concrete for a roof, and were cold, dark and damp. When air raids began East Enders, often led by Communist Party members, took matters into their own hands by occupying the underground stations. They took along bedding and vacuum flasks, bought platform tickets and refused to leave. After a while the government accepted the fait accompli, and at 10.30p.m. trains were stopped, the electric current in the rails switched off, and the lights dimmed. Not all stations were deep enough to survive a direct hit and some terrible disasters occurred, notably at Balham. Despite the subsequent fame of these shelters a census in late 1940 found that only four per cent of people in central London used them, whilst nine per cent slept in the street shelters and twenty-seven per cent in Anderson shelters. The majority of Londoners were either doing night work, or fire watching, or like my family remained inside their homes.

Sometime during our second term at Wycombe Abbey I learnt with enormous delight that St. Paul's would re-open in London in the summer term. I recently discovered that the main reason was financial. St. Paul's had to give the school fees we paid them to Wycombe Abbey, whilst they still had to pay the salaries of their own staff and also the cost of keeping the buildings in Hammersmith in order. They would soon be bankrupted. The parents of the girls at High Wycombe were asked whether they would be willing to let their daughters return to London and assured that a good air raid shelter with gas proof rooms had been built in the basement. Since the expected air raids had not materialised the majority of parents said that they would. In April 1940 the school reopened in London with 153 Paulinas. We were not alone in making this decision. By January 1940 forty per cent of the children evacuated through the government scheme had returned to London. Many, unhappy away from their homes, had begun to drift back after a few weeks and in the absence of schools were roaming the streets. My mother, who was herself unhappy in Somerset, had come back to London in December 1939 to open Ashburton School, in the Victoria Docks, for returned evacuees.

Chapter 7

Living in London during the Battle of Britain and the Blitz

I returned home at Easter 1940 to find, to my amazement and delight, that without telling Michael or me my mother had moved out of her parents' house into a flat at the other end of London, in Chelsea. Soon after Christmas she had found the flat in *Dalton's Weekly*. Because of the evacuation of the civil service and large firms a lot of property was available to rent quite cheaply. Our flat was 117 Beaufort Mansions, Beaufort Street, which runs from Battersea Bridge to the King's Road. Chelsea was then still a socially mixed area. Although wealthy people lived around Sloane Square, parts of Chelsea, especially where we lived near the World's End, were distinctly shabby. Our flat was not at all attractive but I was thrilled that at last we had a home of our own, and in an interesting area. It had a living room overlooking Beaufort Street, which was a noisy bus route, three bedrooms, and a dark kitchen overlooking the inner well of the flats. A little lift outside the kitchen window brought up coal and took down rubbish.

The King's Road, today mainly boutiques and restaurants, was then full of small butchers, bakers and grocery shops, some of which sold exotica I'd never seen before, such as honeycombs. There were florists with marble floors and buckets full of English country flowers such as larkspur, greengrocers who sold field mushrooms picked that morning and small second hand bookshops. To get to school I had only to walk about ten minutes through some elegant streets to South Kensington underground station, from where it was four stops to Hammersmith. I felt very independent and grown-up as I went to meet Michael at Paddington on his return from Marlborough for Easter. I was almost fourteen.

Alas, the family idyll darkened. After Michael returned to school Billy Spikes, my mother's friend for a number of years, moved in with us. This, I immediately realised, was why she had left her parents' house and put a considerable distance between her new home and West Ham, where she had spent the first forty-two years of her life. Not only would her mother have been deeply shocked by what she would regard as scandalous conduct, but so would the education world in West Ham. Spikes was the head of the local grammar school, my mother was one of the school's governors, and they were both members of the West Ham Education Committee. I had thought for some time that Spikes was a serious admirer of my mother's. He sometimes came round at weekends and once went on holiday with us, sharing a room with Michael. On one occasion he said to me, 'You have arms just like your mother's', and I thought it strange that he noticed my mother's arms, and perhaps that meant he was in love with her. This did not worry me, a lot of people admired my mother and Spikes was undoubtedly an interesting man. Tall and heavily built, he had the judicious measured manner of someone secure and confident in his authority. He talked interestingly and was very charming when he chose. But for him suddenly to move in with us was another matter. My mother had given us no warning of what was to happen. One day he stayed the night, and never left, and nothing was said to us then or subsequently. I was outraged, as was Michael, though at the time we did not speak of it together.

I think my outrage was mainly due to jealousy at Spikes' intrusion and to what I saw as my mother's deception in telling us that we would now have a home of our own. Perhaps I was uneasy at the thought of my mother having a sex life. I was also outraged because I was suddenly sure that the considerable charm that Spikes had extended towards me had been a calculated ploy to get me on his side. He had paid much less attention to Michael, who was always cold towards him. Probably he realised from the start that he had little chance of winning Michael over. My liking for Spikes changed instantly to hatred. I immediately decided I would be taken in by his charm no longer and would be as unpleasant and rude to him as possible. I also decided that adults who appeared to be friendly to me probably had an ulterior motive and could not be trusted. I tried not to behave unpleasantly to my mother, it would have been too threatening to criticise the one person who had always loved me and whom I idealised.

But I must have realised at some level that my hostility to Spikes would also punish her, spoiling her pleasure in her new life. After school each day I was often alone with Spikes whilst she was at some committee and Michael was back in Marlborough. Initially Spikes offered to read aloud to me at this time from Willa Cather's *Death Comes to the Archbishop*. He read extremely well and I listened with pleasure, but I refused to admit this or relent in my hostility to him. After a while he abandoned the reading sessions and we ignored each other after school. When the three of us were together I would be consistently and deliberately bad tempered, dragging behind them if we went out, objecting to every suggestion.

Although I was angry and behaved atrociously to Spikes, on my own or with just my mother I was very happy. Having escaped from the oppression of Wycombe Abbey I felt wonderfully free. I loved wandering down the King's Road, spending my pocket money on second-hand books. For the first time I acquired a book, *Mansfield Park*, because it was a pleasure to hold. It was gilt-edged, with coloured illustrations by C.E. Brock. Sometimes I spent part of my pocket money on field mushrooms, freshly picked that morning, which I had a passion for, and cooked for my tea. I loved helping my mother with housekeeping and was very proud of the responsibilities she gave me, aged just fourteen. During the week I bought the food we needed in little local shops, and when she was late coming home I cooked supper – we had switched, though the matter was not discussed, from a working-class bread and butter tea to a cooked meal, presumably at the wish of Spikes. With no experience and no one to teach me some of my meals were dire – I was particularly prone to burn the vegetables. At the weekend my mother and I did some sketchy housework. Spikes never took part in any domestic activity, much to my relief, as I enjoyed sharing it with my mother. When Michael was at home he was conscripted to wash the kitchen and bathroom floors, which he did without protest, but ineffectively. I can see him now, languidly pushing a mop, still dressed in pyjamas and a red rayon dressing gown. My mother was usually at meetings for all or part of Saturday, but on Sundays we would walk in Battersea Park or go to a park further afield, sometimes listening to the speakers at Hyde Park Corner.

One weekend the three of us went to visit Michael in Marlborough where his school spent the war sharing the facilities of Marlborough College. A number of famous writers had attended this public school, including William Morris, MacNeice, Sassoon and Betjeman, and they must have been moved by the beauty of the surrounding Downs. We stayed a few miles from Marlborough in the Red Lion, a four-hundred-year-old pub. It was built, as was the village of Avebury, inside great Neolithic circles, much larger and more impressive than Stonehenge. Nearby is the three-thousand-year-old Silbury Hill, a huge man made mound whose purpose is still unknown, and Windmill Hill, with its extensive barrows. Anyone with an historical imagination must be awed by the area, and it was quite magical to wake up in the morning and realise that you were in the middle of the stone circles. In 1940 there were few other visitors but when I rashly tried to repeat the experience twenty years ago, staying in the same, but now modernised pub, mass tourism had arrived and the magic had gone.

Alas, the interlude in Chelsea was short lived. As St. Paul's returned to London the Germans invaded Denmark and Norway. In May the German offensive against France and the Netherlands began and Churchill became Prime Minister. On June 4th Dunkirk fell and on June 17th France surrendered. German forces and troop barges were assembled on the French coast poised to invade Britain. By this time the majority of the 153 girls who had returned to St. Paul's, including Isabel and Nancy who had shared my billet, had been sent by their parents to boarding school. I don't think I knew how near we were to invasion, and, just as when war was declared, I didn't feel frightened. This must have been partly because my mother and the staff at school were calm and did not appear to be alarmed. But in any case the threat of invasion, which was very real, was downplayed in the media and not generally understood. A Gallup poll in May 1940 found, incredibly, that only three per cent of people believed that we might lose the war.

Before invading, the Germans first had to defeat British air power to prevent it bombing their invasion force. In July the Battle of Britain began with German attempts to destroy the R.A.F., their airfields and the aircraft industry. Most of the air battles took place over the sea and over south east England. The enormous losses suffered by the R.A.F. – over 1500 planes with their crew between July and September – were not revealed at the time, nor was the fact that we came near to defeat. Perhaps with the deliberate aim of maintaining morale the air battles were bizarrely reported in newspaper posters and headlines as though they were cricket matches -'100 to 30, England not out'. The number of German planes destroyed was greatly exaggerated and the number we had lost always understated. Nonetheless, I was very aware as I walked home from school, looking at the cloudless blue skies – it was a beautiful summer – that young men were up there, killing each other, only fifty miles away.

As the Battle of Britain continued we spent most of the summer holiday in Chelsea, although Michael who was now fifteen went to a forestry camp. At the end of August this terrible battle, in which the two air forces tried to destroy each other, came to an end. Each side had inflicted very heavy damage on the other's air force, but since the British air force was smaller it is now believed that the Germans would have established air supremacy if they had continued the battle a little longer. Instead they launched an air attack on London. This, it emerged after the war, happened because on the night of August 24th a German pilot mistook his target and unintentionally dropped a bomb in the London area. In retaliation the British bombed Berlin and a furious Hitler then ordered his air force to switch from attacking our air force to destroying London. His invasion plans were postponed and on Saturday September 7th the 'Blitz' on London began, with heavy raids for seventy-six consecutive nights. On the first night 300 bombers attacked, supported by 600 fighters, killing 430 Londoners and badly injuring 1600. Large numbers of children who had returned to London were evacuated again.

By chance we were away that first weekend. The National Union of Teachers had at the beginning of the war moved its headquarters to an enormous Victorian Gothic country house in the Cotswolds, Toddington Manor. It is now owned by Damien Hirst. Once a fortnight my mother drove down for weekend meetings taking me, and Michael during school holidays, with her. The house was immensely grand. It had huge Gothic windows, gargoyles, wood carvings, cloisters and a massively wide main staircase. Whilst my mother was in meetings Michael and I would wander around the house and extensive grounds, admire the gardens and go into the empty and unused chapel, pretending to preach in the pulpit. We were at Toddington Manor on September 7th. My mother, who must have had her plans ready, dispatched Michael and me next day by a circuitous train route to Barnstaple, in Devonshire. There we found our grandmother and my cousin Kathleen already installed in the home of my grandmother's sister, Auntie Francie, and her daughter, Vera. It was ten years since I had spent an unhappy convalescence with them.

They had left Shoeburyness because Vera, who was a shop assistant in a grocery store, began an affair with the owner, Fred, a married man. To escape the scandal that resulted he bought a business at the other end of the country and settled there, living above the shop with Vera and her mother, who was to act as housekeeper and lend respectability to the household. Fred was a kind man and put up uncomplainingly with Auntie Francie's gloom and bad temper, which I remembered of old. She was scandalised by the relationship and lived in a state of permanent disapproval, barely speaking to them, although now that she no longer had to take in washing her life was very much easier. I had known none of this before my arrival and only learned the situation gradually from Vera. Vera was a cheerful, kindly young woman, who coped uncomplainingly with four extra people crammed into their flat – I had to share a bed with my grandmother.

On their half day – all shops then closed on Wednesday or Thursday afternoons – and on Sundays Vera and Fred took us children to the coast in their van for walks along the sand dunes with their dog, a huge and good-tempered chow. Initially my grandmother, who like her sister would hardly even talk to the couple, tried to stop us from going out with them. She wanted us to have as little as possible to do with such an immoral couple, despite the fact that they were sheltering all of us. Vera refused to take this seriously. Vera, who was rather like my mother even in appearance, usually found a way of doing what she wanted with as little upset as possible. She was in effect head of the household. I'm not sure what housekeeping her mother did, she certainly didn't cook, nobody did. After the shop was closed and on Sundays Vera would simply take food from the counters for us to eat upstairs- they sold all kinds of food except fresh meat and fish. It seemed a delightfully easy way of housekeeping to me.

Sometimes Vera would let me help in the shop and she was always willing to let me take food and try out recipes from women's magazines for our supper upstairs. I would have been happy enough if it hadn't been for the gloomy, disapproving presence of Auntie Francie and my grandmother. I can see now that it must have been very difficult for such an active person as my grandmother, who had never had a holiday in her life, to be marooned with nothing to do in the house of people she would have preferred to have had no contact with, worrying about her home and her hens in London. It was hardly surprising that she was depressed and bad tempered. Years later I learned that the grocery business subsequently prospered and that Vera and Fred, eventually happily married, bought separate houses in Barnstable for themselves and Auntie Francie.

Michael only stayed about a week before returning to Marlborough. A week or so later I returned to London in time for the start of the autumn term, though the bombing of London continued remorselessly until the following May. The docklands and adjacent areas were the worst hit, but soon the West End and the inner suburbs were also attacked, as well as other cities, especially Coventry, Merseyside and Clydeside. Whilst I was away Beaufort Mansions had been bombed. Our flat was not directly hit, but damaged, and since there had been other raids on Chelsea my mother decided we had better move.

She was working to the limit of her capacity. Parts of West Ham were so devastated by bombing that after a while the infantry used them as a training ground for street fighting. Her school, Ashburton Road, was in one of the most bombed areas in London, Custom House, by the Victoria Dock. Not only was my mother running her school but she was also responsible for the adjacent rest centre. A rest centre was a temporary reception centre for bombed-out local families who would arrive distraught. The provisions for them were totally inadequate, with minimal washing facilities, little bedding and few chairs, because the government's intention was that families should rest there for only a few hours. They argued that if people were made too comfortable they would be tempted to stay. But no alternative accommodation was provided for them to go to. Whilst better off families like mine could leave the area to stay with relatives and friends or could rent furnished accommodation, or wealthy families could move into hotels or go to houses they owned in the country, many families with no resources to fall back on remained for weeks. My mother worked with local voluntary organisations to make their stay tolerable, by providing free meals, blankets, and mattresses.

The docks were one of the main German targets, but somehow my mother's school and rest centre escaped, as did my mother, although the air raid wardens' post opposite received a direct hit, killing eight wardens. My mother decided that if she was to function effectively she needed to sleep somewhere relatively quiet. She found a house to rent, White Lyons, at 17 Coptfold Road, Brentwood. Brentwood was then a small country town in Essex about twenty miles north east of London. With little traffic about she and Spikes could quite quickly drive in to West Ham every day. Petrol was rationed and from 1942 was entirely disallowed for private use, and the manufacture of cars was stopped. My mother, though, always managed because of her work and her union and government committees to get enough for her needs. I think I've already made it clear that she generally managed to get most things she needed.

But for me a daily journey to Hammersmith would have been impracticable, since it would have taken at least two hours. I was sent instead to stay with Mrs. Boyd, the mother of a Paulina, who lived in a big house almost opposite St. Paul's, and had offered to take in four girls as lodgers. I saw at once with a sinking heart that the situation was vastly inferior to the billet in High Wycombe. Mrs. Boyd, the widow of a colonial official, was another *Daily Telegraph* reader with whom I inevitably clashed. But unlike Mrs. Elgey she kept a close eye on us, saw that we did our homework and did not allow us out on our own at all. In effect she ran a miniature boarding school, and as her daughter Beth was at school with us we could not even grumble amongst ourselves about her mother. Every evening after supper we would wash and put on our pyjamas and then our 'siren suits'. These were rather like babygro suits, all-in-one garments with sleeves and legs, much used in public shelters and tremendously liberating. Before the war very few women or girls, certainly none I knew, wore trousers. Then we would cross the road to spend the night at school.

The ceiling of part of the school's basement had been reinforced, and massive pillars built to support steel girders. There were four separate, supposedly gas-proof rooms, where we had lessons during the day when the air raid sirens sounded. One room had been turned into a large bunk room where we slept, as did the cook and some of the waitresses and some teachers, who took it in turns to fire watch at night. Twenty-eight fire bombs were dropped on the school one night that term, and put out by the staff before too much damage was done. We had to take our gas masks with us. Since the beginning of the war it was compulsory to take them everywhere, but in 1940 only thirty per cent of adults did so, since people no longer believed that gas attacks would occur. The sinister appearance of the masks could be concealed by turning the cases into fashion accessories – a variety of attractive cases were sold. For me they became a great trial, as I kept absentmindedly leaving mine in trains and buses and having to go to the Lost Property Office at Baker Street to retrieve them. I can't remember when we no longer had to bring them to school, but at first we had to take them wherever we went inside the school. In the morning we would return to wash and dress at Mrs. Boyd's and have breakfast, then return to school for lessons.

I do not remember then, or at any time until the rocket attacks in 1944, feeling afraid. This was partly perhaps because the number of casualties was kept from us – I only learned recently that 60,000 civilians were killed in air raids in Britain, half of these in London, and two thirds in the blitz of 1940-41. London was throughout the war the main target and bombed continuously over a longer period than any other city. But this was still a war fought mainly between armed forces – more than five times as many British armed forces and merchant seamen were killed as civilians. The government could conceal the extent of the casualties but not the massive destruction of buildings – one Londoner in every six was made homeless by the end of May 1941. The city, the docks and the East End were most often targeted in the 1940-41 blitz, but most parts of London received some damage. As I was never outside during the night raids I did not see the terrible fires which raged to the east. Every night the air raid sirens wailed, the bombers could be heard overhead, then there were explosions, the AA guns blasted, and eventually there was the steady note on the siren that meant 'All Clear'. Daytime raids were shorter and were seen by most of us Paulinas as a welcome break from lessons, though they continued after a fashion when we had settled down in the shelter.

I don't think I ever considered the possibility that we would get a direct hit and adults often remarked on how brave I was. But a brave person is one who overcomes their fear and I was not consciously afraid. I think, though, that fear operated within me at a deeper level. Throughout the war I had a recurrent dream of being chased, terrified, through endless underground tunnels by people whom on waking I identified as SS troops. A few years ago, meeting with several school friends I discovered that, perhaps more imaginative than me, they had been very afraid during the air raids. Lilian, for example, lived on the second floor of a seven-storey block of flats which had basement shelters. Her family decided they would not survive under seven floors of rubble and might as well stay in their flat. Lilian kept moving her mattress to parts of the flat she thought might be the safest, under the dining room table, by the front door, and eventually back to her room. None of my friends discussed their fears at the time.

Hitler had assumed that his massive bombardment would lead Londoners to demand that their government sue for peace. The first great air raid on September 7th did result in chaos in the East End and anger about the lack of adequate shelters, but Londoners soon adapted to the extraordinary situation with stoicism. The 'bulldog spirit' attributed to them was in part a collective identity constructed by Churchill and reinforced by the government media as a necessity for survival. Londoners were constantly presented with the image of themselves as people who never panic and who endure the hardships of war stoically, good humouredly and with determination. Most people more or less consciously tried to live up to this image. But the same qualities were shown by Berliners during the earlier years of the war, according to Christabel Bielenberg, an Englishwoman married to a German, who was in Berlin at that time. Like us, they responded with jokes and 'a dogged determination to survive, and if possible to help others survive'. Many Londoners took comfort in a camaraderie which they later looked back on nostalgically. Even we Paulinas, hurrying together with our teachers into a fairly comfortable shelter, experienced a feeling of interconnectedness that did not survive the ending of the raids. In London, suicides, mental breakdowns and drunkenness all declined, the latter perhaps because beer was heavily watered and spirits almost unobtainable.

The determination was not necessarily matched by wholehearted support for the war, especially during the blitz. My mother, seeing each day the terrible destruction and suffering in the East End, sometimes questioned whether this misery would eventually be proved worthwhile. It is hard to know how prevalent such 'defeatist' views were since they would only be expressed within the privacy of the family. I had the impression that younger people were more enthusiastic about the war than their parents, who had lived through the last war, and men more than women. But I think it's significant that the most popular songs on the home front during the war were not about heroism or defiance or Hitler, they were about separation, for example, 'The white cliffs of Dover', and 'We'll meet again, don't know when, don't know where'. They were repeatedly played on the Forces radio programme, which was relayed continuously in factories and service canteens. It had been started at the outbreak of war to broadcast popular songs and humorous programmes, whilst the Home Service, the only one until that time, continued to broadcast news, talks and classical music. Most of the popular songs were intensely sentimental and nostalgic. Nostalgia has been defined as 'memory with the pain removed' and it is interesting that the popular songs among the troops, as opposed to civilians, were not nostalgic, but bawdy. But perhaps the most popular song among the troops in several countries was one suffused with pain. It was 'Lily Marlene', a wonderfully moving German song about a soldier who is eventually killed, and whose sweetheart replaced him by another man after he left to go to the war.

Two aspects of my stay with Mrs. Boyd illustrate the very different levels at which as a fourteen year old I was living. The daughter of the house, Beth, had a number of Chalet School books, stories set in a Swiss girls' boarding school which I had not come across before, and I spent all my spare time reading them with intense fascination. Soon after I left their house Beth told me that her mother had received a visit from the plain clothes police, inquiring about the young communist they understood was living with her. Naturally, I was hugely flattered. Presumably I had attracted police attention at the High Wycombe stall or perhaps as the recipient of the posted *Daily Worker*. At that time the Communist Party, which continued to oppose the war until Germany invaded the Soviet Union, was regarded as dangerously subversive and the *Daily Worker* was in fact banned a couple of months later, in January 1941.

To my great relief, after some weeks with Mrs. Boyd my mother, who could not afford her rather high boarding fees any longer, told me that a friend of hers, G.T.C. Giles, (called 'Giles' by everyone) had suggested that I should stay with him. It was Giles who had posted the *Daily Worker* to me. He was a member of the executive committee of both the National Union of Teachers and the Communist Party. Although my mother was implacably anti- communist, on educational issues she and Giles were allies and friends. So in October 1940 I went to live with him and his wife Betsy, a journalist, a member of the Communist Party and very active in the National Union of Journalists. They were also giving a home to Margaret Clarke, an old friend of theirs, another party member. Like Giles she was a head teacher, and she had recently been bombed out of her home. Later, in 1943, she was badly injured by a bomb blast whilst leading her school into a shelter. Also living with them was a fourth communist, Tom, the housekeeper. He was a Welsh ex-miner, very small, thin and frail. Their home was a big detached double fronted house, The Chestnuts, 29 Burlington Road, Chiswick, only four stops on the underground from Hammersmith. A ground floor passage had been turned into a bunk room shelter with a reinforced ceiling, where I generally slept. Although from the summer of 1941 raids became much less frequent I thought it was easier always to sleep downstairs rather than sometimes getting up in the night. I kept my clothes, and occasionally slept, in a tiny bedroom, the dressing room leading off the Giles' bedroom.

There was a large dining room on the ground floor, never used as such, where I did my homework, and a large sitting room where, when they were at home, Giles, Betsy, Margaret and I spent much of the evening reading – in their case, invariably left-wing political papers or detective stories. At that time detective stories seemed the almost universal recreational reading of intellectuals, especially left-wing intellectuals. These stories were not violent, like crime fiction today, but concerned with detection in the genre of Agatha Christie. Tom, the housekeeper, always reserved and quiet, would retreat to his own room. I don't know whether this was because he did not feel it 'his place' to sit with the others – though he was never in any way treated as a servant- or because he preferred his own company. Meals were eaten, and there was much sitting around and talking, in the 'breakfast room', which led off the kitchen. The kitchen was Tom's territory. He did all the cooking and the rest of us rarely entered it, though Betsy used to make her packed lunch there whilst he washed up in the evening. I don't think any of us ever helped in the house – Tom cooked, washed up, did the shopping and light housework, a cleaner did the heavier housework and a jobbing gardener looked after the sizeable garden.

Giles, Betsy, and Margaret were all tall and large framed, though certainly not overweight. The two women were quite plain, I thought, but Giles was definitely handsome, with an open, friendly, though very firm expression. All three were middle-aged and grey haired, and the Giles' were apparently without vanity – their clothes seemed to me drab and unobtrusive. Tom, the housekeeper, was even more drably dressed. He had a terrible cough, and spent the afternoons lying under an ultra violet lamp, trying to improve his health. I don't ever remember him smiling, and I think now he was depressed. But I was too young and self-centred to think about his loneliness and social isolation, so far from his mining village, of which he never spoke. Now I wonder how he came to be the Giles' housekeeper, but then I didn't ask.

The house was quite shabbily, though comfortably enough furnished, the decoration, all in neutral beiges and browns on a par with the Giles' clothes, had not been renewed for many years. Neither of the Giles', I decided, noticed the way things looked. There was nothing that anyone might think beautiful in the house and they rivalled my grandmother in their lack of interest in consumer and leisure expenditure. But whilst my mother would have enjoyed more of the good things in life if she could have afforded them, and my grandmother disapproved of them on principle, the Giles' could have afforded them, did not disapprove of them, but seemed indifferent to them. Like Quakers, or even nuns, their lives were entirely focussed on their beliefs and they seemed to me very good and selfless people.

I stayed with them for two years until after my School Certificate exams (equivalent to GCSEs). They were the most trouble free, relaxed years of my childhood, perhaps of my life. It was a very calm household. There seemed to be no tension, voices were never raised, quarrels never occurred. Giles and Betsy were cool and detached, Margaret, I felt, had the potential to be explosive but was restrained by their influence. Once she told me that, helping her sister prepare for a dance, she had picked up the iron and ran it over her sister's dress whilst her sister was wearing it – so she ended up in hospital, not at the dance. Margaret recounted this to me as an example of her absent-mindedness, but even to a fourteen year old this seemed an unlikely explanation.

Margaret was different from the Giles' in many ways. I think that her personality was subdued in their presence. She did not have their aura of what I thought of as disinterested nobility, she seemed much more ordinary. She showed a certain amount of interest in clothes and as I discovered when I visited her in later years, she owned some lovely china and furniture. She took less interest in me than the Giles' did and didn't often talk to me, but the whole household were extraordinarily kind to me and treated me, at fourteen, as an adult. There was not even a hint that there were rules to be followed, Betsy only occasionally mildly suggesting it was perhaps time that I should stop reading at night. For the first time in my life I was always agreeable and well behaved. My mother was incredulous when Giles told her I was a pleasure to have around. Not only was I still being consistently nasty to Spikes at home, but she was well aware that never before had anyone found me easy and pleasant to live with.

In the Giles' household no one made any emotional demands on me or asked what I was doing at school or talked to me about their lives, or offered to see or look at my homework. Their conversation with me, as amongst themselves, was almost entirely about political and union issues. But although they were detached and never physically affectionate, the Giles' treated me seriously, gave me a lot of attention, and I knew they were concerned for me. This concern was demonstrated on one desperately embarrassing occasion. I had come back from my mother's one Sunday evening and was in tears for some reason I have forgotten. Rather than admit to the reason, when they asked me what was the matter I said I had toothache. Giles at once started phoning around the local dentists, none of whom would see me on a Sunday evening. Finally he took me in his car to one of them, knocked him up and absolutely insisted that he treat me. The denouement of this scene, when the dentist discovered there was nothing wrong with my teeth, I have thankfully forgotten.

I would dally home from school after standing for some time talking with my friends at Hammersmith Broadway, make myself some tea and try to chat to Tom, who was remarkably unforthcoming, though never hostile. He would be preparing the evening meal; he was an excellent and adventurous cook, and tended to make dishes I'd never had before, including delicious vegetable casseroles. No one in the household was a vegetarian but this was a good way to eke out the rationed food. The Giles had a cookery book called *Recipes of all Nations*, with separate chapters for each European country, the U.S.A., the Far East, and the Middle East. I read it with interest, having had no knowledge before of these cuisines – at that time foreign restaurants were hardly ever found outside Soho.

Before or after doing my homework in the dining room I would phone at great length the school friends I'd recently left. I knew that the Giles' phone was tapped so my friends and I decided to keep the security forces busy by pretending to be Russian spies, discussing our plans and code words, amidst much giggling. In retrospect this seems absurdly irresponsible, given that spy mania was then at its height, the *Daily Worker* was banned and the Cabinet was debating whether to make the Communist Party illegal and intern its leading members. But Giles tolerated our foolery with amazing good humour. This was even more surprising because as an open communist his job as head of a grammar school was then seriously under threat from the local authority and a group of parents. I did not know this at the time. Such threats became even more serious in 1948, during the Cold War, when his job and his union position were again in question. A campaign against communist teachers led to candidates for election to any position in the N.U.T. having to state whether or not they were members of the Communist Party. He lost his seat on the Executive committee then for several years.

After supper, whenever he was at home Giles would talk to me at length about politics, explaining the events of the day and the Communist Party 'line' on them. Until the Soviet Union was invaded in June 1941 they argued that the British people were suffering in an imperialist cause. With the imminent threat of invasion they did make it clear that they were not in favour of surrendering to the Germans, after all, they would be the first to be shot, but they wanted a 'People's Government' formed, which would arm the workers and bring in socialism. Giles told me that this would end the war by encouraging German workers to rebel against Hitler, as they had against the Kaiser in 1918. It seems now extraordinary that the communist leaders could so misread both the national and international situation. It seems even more extraordinary and very sad that their members, many of whom were selfless and devoted people like the Giles', lived and died for the belief that their first priority must be to defend the Soviet Union, which they saw as the only state struggling to build socialism.

Giles was a remarkable man. Educated at Eton and Kings College Cambridge where he got a first class degree in Classics, he fought in the First World War, and was invalided out of the army in 1917. Thereafter he taught in public schools at home and abroad, including Eton, until in 1926, the year of the General Strike, he joined the Communist Party and applied successfully for the headship of Acton County (Grammar) school. He never explained what had led to his political conversion, and this was typical of his reticence about personal issues. Like my mother he was a passionate advocate of multilateral schools and campaigned for the best possible education for all children, not just those from privileged families. Like my mother he believed that higher pay for teachers was essential both to improve their status and the quality of state education. Unlike my mother he was too quiet and unemotional to be a very effective platform speaker, but he was firm and persuasive in individual discussion. He was so very courteous and charming and had such striking and obvious integrity and selflessness that people found it hard to believe he was a leading communist.

I used to wonder why he should devote so much time to me and was so consistently kind. Perhaps for a while I took the place of the daughter he never had. Betsy was his second wife, and they had no children together, but Giles had two sons by his first wife whom he rarely saw. Margaret gave me this information, Giles himself never spoke of his personal affairs. She told me that his sons did not want to see him because they were angry with him for sending them to a local grammar school instead of to his own old school, Eton. Presumably he didn't in any case have that kind of money, but I think he must have had some inherited wealth. Although the Giles lived in most ways puritanically they had a big house and plenty of domestic help. I admired him tremendously and I was a little in love with him. But at the back of my mind I kept wondering whether his kindness was a ploy to win favour and influence with my mother, especially since he refused to take any money for having me. This was of course absurd, since my mother, although personally friendly to him, was a lifelong opponent of the Communist Party, hardly likely to change because of kindness to her daughter. Nor did the theory accord with my own feeling that Giles had a striking nobility of character. Perhaps my suspicion arose only because of my experience with Spikes or perhaps it reflected a longer lasting belief that adults couldn't possibly like me for my own sake.

As I got older Giles sometimes took me to meetings with him in the evenings. After the German invasion of the Soviet Union in June 1941, which by the diversion of forces to the east meant that Britain was finally safe from the threat of invasion, the Soviet Union became, almost over night immensely popular. Within a week the Communist Party reversed its policy, declared its support for Churchill and began a campaign to increase productivity and open a second front in Europe. British attitudes not only to the Soviet Union but also to the Communist Party changed dramatically. The heroic resistance of the Russians seemed to vindicate the Soviet system and party membership increased fivefold within a year. In this new sympathetic climate the party organised 'select' social meetings with wine and food and informal speeches to raise support and funds from sympathetic intellectuals, actors, etc. They were encouraged to join the party or at least be 'fellow travellers', and Giles was usually one of the speakers on these occasions. Despite the fact that he was not an outstanding speaker his tall good looks, air of quiet reasonableness and suave charm must have made him a great asset. I found it very exciting to mix with these well known people, especially since, now that the Communist Party supported the war, I had lost my earlier reservations about its policy. Before the meetings Giles sometimes took me to a Turkish restaurant in Soho – he did appreciate good food – which made me feel very grown-up. For the first time I had yoghurt, then almost unknown in England. It was quite sharp and fresh, unlike modern commercial yoghurt.

If my mother had an evening committee in central London she would occasionally meet me for a meal. I treasured these occasions when I had her all to myself. We would meet at a Lyons Corner House. The Corner Houses were huge buildings in the West End with a variety of restaurants on four or five levels, where the relatively poor could eat reasonably well in an opulent setting. Rather like the Odeon cinemas at the time there were marble pillars and thick carpets, large gilt mirrors and comfortable chairs, staffed by 'Nippies', speedy and attractive waitresses in black and white uniforms. They were open twenty-four hours a day – musicians from night clubs would go there to eat at 4 a.m. – and in the different restaurants you could have just a cup of tea or a snack, or a three course meal. During and especially after the war there were usually queues for each restaurant, but once at a table you could relax in comfort.

On Fridays after school I would go to Brentwood for the weekend, taking the underground to Aldgate East and then a 'Green line' bus, which went deep into Essex. The house would be empty when I arrived, as my mother and Spikes were at meetings, but I never minded that. The kitchen was warm from the coke boiler and I used to happily make myself baked beans on toast and read. It was an interesting and attractive house, long and low, made of two old cottages knocked together, with two staircases, oak beams and a large open fireplace. We rented it furnished and I was very impressed by the thick fitted pink carpet throughout the house – I'd never lived in such a house before. The kitchen, which I thought ideal had, besides the boiler, which heated both the water and the room, a gas stove, a table where we ate and a glass door leading on to the garden, with big windows on either side. This made the room very light and meant that you could sit at the table and watch the birds and flowers. A stone-floored unheated scullery, desperately cold in winter, with a sink, larder, and food cupboards, led out of the kitchen and also overlooked the garden. German bombers sometimes unloaded their bombs in the area on their way home, so we slept on the ground floor and rarely went into the bedrooms.

The house was just behind the high street where there were attractive little food shops, a bookshop and a cinema. On Saturday mornings my mother usually had to return to London for a meeting, and I would change her books in the local library and do some food shopping. I was very good at selecting the kind of books she liked. Reading was her only leisure activity, in such little leisure as she had. She read what the librarian called 'high class contemporary fiction'- she did not read non-fiction of any kind, modernist novels, or classics, crime fiction or popular romances. Sundays we would spend the morning together, cooking and doing a minimal amount of housework, just vacuum cleaning where absolutely necessary and washing the kitchen floor. Every Sunday my mother made a Victoria sponge, the only cake she ever made, and of course the Sunday roast meat, two vegetables and a fruit pie. I used to enjoy helping her cook. I would prepare the vegetables and make the pastry and a supply of oatcakes, using unrationed oatmeal and a little lard. On Sunday afternoons I had to do my homework, which throughout my adolescence cast a pall over Sundays. I don't think we ever went out, my mother must have been too weary to do so, although she never complained. Sometimes I returned to the Giles' on Sunday evening, but more often I left for school very early on Monday mornings, getting a train from Brentwood to Liverpool Street and then the underground to Hammersmith. I never minded the long journey, but I hated setting out in the dark.

These Sundays largely spent cooking and cleaning must have added to my mother's chronic exhaustion from the enormous amount of work and travelling she did, and the trauma of the air raids. I wrote to a friend in March 1941 that on Wednesday the East End had its worst air raid since September, with 350 families in the area of my mother's school made homeless, and several of her pupils killed. The week before she had left London three times on behalf of the N.U.T. to Glasgow, Beaconsfield and Cheltenham, using trains that were overcrowded and, in the evenings, unlit. The constant strain she was under lowered her resistance – every winter she suffered from a succession of very heavy colds. She should have spent at least part of Sunday in bed but I never knew her even to get up late. Yet she didn't ask Spikes for any help at the weekends and he didn't ever suggest that we should go out for Sunday dinner. I suppose that both she and Spikes assumed that however hard she worked outside the home it was her responsibility, as a woman, to make a good job of feeding and looking after her family. Perhaps she saw it as a challenge which she could meet.

She was at this time very worried about Michael's future. He was now sixteen and had joined the school Air Training Corps to prepare for service in the R.A.F. Perhaps as a concession to her exhaustion, in the summer of 1941 the four of us had a family holiday, our first since 1938 and as it turned out, our last together. Most of the coast in southern England and East Anglia was occupied by the army, to defend against invasion, so we drove to west Wales and spent two weeks in a hotel near St. David's in Pembrokeshire. I thought it the most beautiful place I had ever seen and determined to return as an adult, as, indeed, I did.

The Giles' kept my ration book during the term time, but food rationing was never a serious problem in our family. This was partly because we all had school dinners – meals were 'off the ration' in the canteens of schools, colleges, factories, large firms, and in restaurants. The government had set up a chain of 'British Restaurants' for those who could not afford ordinary restaurants, cafeterias where substantial meals could be bought very cheaply, patronised each day by half a million customers. A typical dinner was roast beef and two vegetables, treacle pudding, bread and margarine and a cup of tea, for eleven pence. Moreover, my always resourceful mother negotiated exchanges of rationed food. You had to register with a particular butcher, milkman and grocer for the basic rations. The amounts varied slightly from one year to another but typically included, per person per week, 12-16 oz of meat, 4 oz of ham or bacon, 8 oz of fat, of which only 2 oz could be butter, and 4 oz had to be margarine, the rest cooking fat, 2 oz of tea, 2-4 oz of cheese, 4 oz of sugar, 3 oz of chocolate or sweets and 2-3 pints of milk. Eggs were very scarce, not more than thirty in a year, though packets of dried eggs, which could be used in cakes and puddings or made into a kind of omelette, began to arrive from the U.S.A. in 1942. My mother found people who were more than happy to take most of our tea and sugar ration in exchange for cheese and sometimes bacon. We ate little sugar and were quite happy to drink coffee, then so unpopular that it wasn't rationed. Nescafe, which later led to the widespread use of coffee, had only just reached Britain, in 1939. Other people would gladly give us their 2 oz of butter in exchange for 4 oz of our margarine. Moreover, we 'registered' for eggs with my grandmother so that we usually had some, though not many, eggs.

These basic rations were supplemented by an ingenious 'points system' for other foods which were not always available. Everyone had a number of points each month, which could be spent on any of a variety of foods, each of which had a points value fixed by the government according to supply. Food 'on points' included tinned fish and meat (Spam, a spiced ham product imported from the U.S.A. was very popular, though some preferred corned beef) tinned fruit and vegetables, rice, dried fruit, breakfast cereals and porridge oats, biscuits, jam, marmalade, syrup and honey. Home-grown fruit and vegetables were never rationed and bread was only rationed after the war ended. However, white bread disappeared in 1942 to be replaced by the 'National loaf', which used nearly all the wheat, including the husk, with added calcium carbonate, bran, and oats. It was darker then white bread, and rougher, but without the flavour of proper wholemeal bread, and was generally disliked. Foods that were very scarce but price controlled, notably fish and oranges, were not rationed. Instead people formed long queues outside any shops that had them. Although queuing, for example to get into football matches or cinemas, occurred before the war, shortages led to it becoming almost a way of life for many women. My mother and I preferred to go without rather than join the food queues, especially as the goods often ran out before you reached the top of the queue. Sausages, mainly made of bread, were not at first rationed, nor was offal, which most working-class people wouldn't eat, though we cooked liver or kidneys once a week. Other unrationed foods that the government tried to encourage people to eat, for example horsemeat, rabbit and whale meat, were very unpopular – we sometimes bought rabbit, we tried whale meat and thought it horrible and could not bring ourselves to even try horsemeat.

Pregnant women, children under six and heavy manual and agricultural workers all had special rations. There was no need for anyone to be actually hungry, in the sense that bread, potatoes, and vegetables were cheap, unrationed and always available, but many people complained that they felt 'unsatisfied', probably due to the lack of meat and fat in the diet. A degree of time, planning and especially flexibility in eating habits was required to make palatable meals and in practice many people were reluctant to change their food habits. The government publicised widely in the press and on the radio the virtues of unrationed vegetables, especially potatoes and carrots, and recipes of dishes to make with them. Perfectly good recipes were promoted under ridiculous names– for example a baked dish of potatoes, apples, sage and cheese was called 'Mock Goose', croquettes made of minced cabbage and boiled potatoes, shaped like small sausages, were called 'Mock sausages'. However, *Mass Observation* reported in 1943 that very few people tried any of these recipe suggestions. Inevitably, though, people ate more bread, potatoes and vegetables than before the war, and less sugar and fat.

Of course, as always, wealthy people did best. They could afford to eat in restaurants as often as they wished and although the government controlled the price of restaurant meals, with a top price of five shillings, expensive restaurants served better meals by adding a large 'cover charge' and by marking up the price of wine. Those who could afford it could also supplement their diet with expensive foods that were scarce but not rationed or price controlled, for example grapes, game, fresh salmon, lobster and oysters. Nevertheless most people thought that the system was on the whole equitable. The degree of control which people accepted, almost without question during the war, is remarkable. On this restricted diet the health of the nation improved, children grew taller, heavier and had better teeth, probably not only because of their improved diet, but also because a large section of the working-class were better off, with full employment and increased wages.

At school in London during the Blitz 1940-42

The St. Paul's that reopened in September 1940 was dramatically reduced in size. Most of the girls who had initially returned from Wycombe Abbey had been sent to boarding school when the Blitz began. In the country as a whole almost as many people left the cities that autumn as at the outbreak of war. Only sixty-five of the original 450 Paulinas came back in September, though by January the number rose to ninety-six. All but nine of the staff of thirty-two, including the art teachers, were dismissed and the number of forms was reduced from twenty to eight. The science block was at first closed and the swimming pool was closed throughout the war. Gradually numbers crept up and the dismissed staff were re-employed – there were 117 Paulinas in July 1942 and 300 in September 1943, but the pre-war number was not regained till after the war.

The autumn term of 1940 was the start of our two years preparation for G.C.S.E.s, or School Certificate as it was then called. Our education undoubtedly suffered during the war. The first year of the war was disrupted by evacuation, the second by the constant interruption of air raids. There was then a lull from the summer of 1941 to the spring of 1942, when a year of minor sporadic air raids was followed by another lull before the rocket attacks in the summer of 1944. After-school activities such as clubs and drama disappeared from the start of the war. The teachers were overworked and tired from fire watching at night. It was the younger, livelier teachers who, in the main, had been dismissed and the remaining, older teachers probably lacked the energy to do more than present the material they were familiar with. They were kindly, middle-aged, dowdy, unmarried and we thought, very different from us. Most had taught in the school for decades, and most remained there till they retired. Only the history teacher, Miss Patrick, sarcastic, and a fierce disciplinarian -'Eyes on me or on your books, girls!' she would cry – tried to provoke us to think by attacking any opinion we advanced and making us defend it.

All the teachers sensibly saved themselves a good deal of marking by starting lessons with a test to see what we remembered of the previous lesson, and then getting us to mark each others' answers. Essays were returned with just a grade and a single word comment at the bottom. The curriculum was old fashioned by today's standards – we learnt to parse (analyse sentences into their grammatical parts) and to spell, we learned the capital cities, principal rivers and products of foreign countries and we learnt passages of Shakespeare by heart- all useful skills and knowledge, which I'm glad we were taught. We read several Shakespearean plays, with much emphasis on studying the footnotes, but we never acted a play, or saw one acted. The rest of the English curriculum was extraordinarily inappropriate for our age – the De Coverley papers and Addison's essays stand out in my memory. The staff concentrated almost entirely on preparing us for public exams. There were no projects and few opportunities for individual work. We learnt nothing of art history, or literature outside the set books, there was no music appreciation or debate about current events. In all these respects our education seemed unenterprising and limited in comparison with my brother's, and with the pre-war St Paul's as I remembered it, but it is possible that a broader education was offered to the non-scientists in the sixth form.

Because the numbers were so small we all had to take the same subjects for School Certificate – English, Maths, French, German, Latin, History and Geography. The native French and German teachers had left and these subjects were taught almost like dead languages. Art and scripture were taught as non-examination subjects but instead of the two pre-war art teachers there was only Miss Pasmore, the senior teacher, employed for two days a week. Throughout the war there were no clubs or extra curricular activities other than music and sport. Currently there are about twenty-five clubs at St. Paul's, ranging from chess, philosophy and photography to yoga, as well as a great variety of sports. When I commented to some ex-Paulinas recently that I thought our education had been narrow and boring they didn't agree, and argued that it had been the foundation for my own successful career. In fact, I think much of my education took place outside the school, from my reading, contacts with adults and involvement in semi-political activities.

Our English teacher Miss Jenkinson, much the youngest of the staff, she was perhaps thirty, encouraged us to read about classical Greek culture. But she made no reference to any twentieth-century literature. I used to buy and learn by heart the works of contemporary poets, especially Spender and MacNeice, but in the fourth and fifth forms at school we read no poetry. Probably because I was a nuisance during lessons, with too many questions and comments, Miss Jenkinson sent me off to do projects on my own in the school library. These usually involved reading books of Shakespearian criticism and writing essays on them, and I was more than happy with this arrangement. One summer weekend after we had finished our School Certificate exams she took several of us to Oxford for the day. She showed us round some colleges including her old college, Lady Margaret Hall, and punted us on the river. I decided then and there that I would go to Oxford, it seemed quite magically beautiful.

The high mistress, Miss Strudwick, was a classicist who had previously been a Latin lecturer at Bedford College. But her special love was Greek, which even before the war was not a popular subject. She was determined to keep its torch burning through the war years, so every year she chose one fourteen year old to receive private tuition for the School Certificate exam. In my year her choice, to my dismay, fell on me. Twice a week she would sweep into an empty classroom and seat herself behind the teacher's high desk on a platform, motioning me to sit at the pupil's desk immediately below her. She made no concessions to the one-to -one situation but behaved exactly as though she was teaching a class, nor did she lessen the rigour of her demands by talking about Greek civilisation and culture. We simply worked through an old-fashioned grammar book. I'm afraid my lack of enthusiasm must have been obvious, as was my slow progress, and I had the impression I was yet another of the many girls who in one way or another had disappointed her hopes of keeping the classics alive. My lessons were stopped at the end of the year.

Miss Strudwick was even then a figure from a bygone age. She was in her late fifties, very tall, quite thin and bony, with a horse-like face and large, projecting front teeth. She dressed eccentrically in flowing dark robes, a style that must have been influenced by her father, who had been a successful pre-Raphaelite artist. To our amusement her slip often dipped below the hem of her dress. She had a beautiful mellow speaking voice but her mind, we thought, was fixed on the glories of the Ancient World so that she barely seemed to attend to the present. She urged us to work hard and, with a total lack of realism, to acquire a love of the classics. There was not during her regime, which lasted till the early fifties, the competitive atmosphere or pressure to win Oxbridge awards that later generations at St. Paul's complained of. She somehow imbued the school with a high moral tone, perhaps by not believing that we would act unworthily, and she often told us that not only were we to do well academically but we must go on to contribute to society. It was difficult to imagine her attending to the minutiae of running a school and although she inspired awe and respect she was definitely not a role model. No one wanted to be like her, or indeed like any of the staff.

By the time I was fifteen I had assumed the role of a political 'red' and school rebel, as well as being clever and a useful source of help with homework. I was seen by my class mates as an eccentric, but they were prepared to support me – my days of being unpopular at school were behind me. During the war because of clothes rationing we could wear our own clothes to school, instead of the regulation navy 'gym tunics' and white blouses, though we still had to wear the school hat and coat, and the gym and games kit. These were universally hated, especially the shapeless beige aertex tunics, known as 'sacks', required for gym, and the hard bowler shaped navy hats, expensively made for us by Scotts in the Burlington Arcade. On one occasion I came to school in a red dress, which the staff thought was going too far and I was told not to wear it again. My class mates were indignant and decided that next day everyone would turn up wearing something red. Wisely the staff decided to ignore this, and having made my point I kept the red dress for home. When I recently met some old Paulinas who had been in my class the 'red dress day', a collective act of transgression, stood out in their memory of school life.

Discipline in the school was remarkably mild. By modern standards we were very well behaved. The games staff were always roaming the school looking through the internal windows for anyone slumped at their desk, who received a 'position mark'. Apart from this the usual punishment was to incur the disapproval of the head mistress, Miss Strudwick. For minor misdemeanours one was sent to sit for the rest of the lesson on a bench outside her room. There was a chance that she would not appear during that period, when you could return to your class scot-free, but if she did, she would give one a pained look or make a few reproachful remarks. Since we were all in awe of her this was punishment enough. For more serious crimes an appointment was made to see her and we knew that she would express severe disapproval. My crimes during those two years were plentiful, trying to evade the gym and daily games classes, but especially being rude to teachers. I wrote in a letter to Isabel in December 1941, when I was fifteen, that Miss Strudwick had accused me of 'irradiating an intangible atmosphere of veiled insolence.' I took a particular dislike to the German teacher, who after a while refused to have me in her class, so that from then on I had to study German on my own for School Certificate. I regarded this as a privilege – and achieved a credit in the exam.

There was, I think now, a distinct change in the social composition of the school at this time – the wealthier families had sent their daughters to boarding school. For the rest of my time at St. Paul's my friends came from homes not very different from mine, since my home situation had changed quite dramatically since 1940. There was no longer the threat that visitors would meet a drunken grandfather and I now lived in a series of middle class areas – Chelsea, Chiswick, Brentwood and later

Blackheath – in houses that I could feel comfortable about inviting my friends to. I did, in fact, invite Teresa and Isabel, as well as some friends from my Bedford High School days with whom I still corresponded, to Brentwood, but none of them came. Brentwood was not seen as a safe enough area and most parents, though not my mother, didn't want their daughters travelling alone in wartime conditions.

In any case the passionate friendship with Teresa was coming to an end. At the outbreak of war she was sent to a small exclusive boarding school where shooting and riding were on the curriculum. She sent me long and desperate letters at least once a week. They were in effect love letters, I thought, looking through them again recently. They began 'Very dearest' and ended 'Goodbye, my sweet love, write soon.' 'Please, please, please, do go on writing very, very, often, please, darling'. 'Oh, God, will I ever be so happy as I was in those days.' There were comments on the war from a left-wing pacifist stand, 'What is the point of war? When this is over I doubt if it will have been won by anyone.' Most letters also included comments on poetry and novels by authors such as Sassoon, Flecker, Yeats, Sinclair Lewis and J.B. Priestley as well as references to our shared hero, the actor Emlyn Williams.

Meantime Teresa had discovered more about her father by the method I had used – looking through her mother's drawers. 'I hastily took the wallet and its contents and went to the lavatory and locked the door' she wrote. 'The wallet included a photo of a man with his initials in the corner and on the back the name of a hotel and the date. He looks the most fascinating man... It gave me quite a shock to see just how like him I am. I also found the most charming letters I have ever read from him to Mummy. I felt horrible guilty reading her private letters, but I do think I have the right to know something about my own father. Please don't breathe a word of this to anyone, you are the only person I can confide in'. Somehow she discovered the identity of her father, who turned out to be a public figure I had heard of, he occasionally gave talks on the radio. As a married man he had decided to end the brief relationship with Teresa's mother.

Teresa was much more open about her emotions than me. Some months after the discovery of her father she wrote in horror that her mother was proposing to marry a widower with two teenage children.

After the marriage she expressed the same distaste with the happy couple as I had felt but never talked about. 'I haven't had a father for fourteen years, and I don't want one now, unless I could have my own. Besides, Mummy is quite awful. They sit about and hold hands (which is disgusting at their age, though I suppose it will wear off)... It's going to be hellish in the holidays as his children will be here... I have to exercise great self control to stop myself going out and slamming the door whenever he and Mummy come in'. Later, she wrote, 'Rather an awful thing has happened. I'm beginning rather to dislike Mummy. It isn't only since her marriage, it started before. It's dreadful really, I try hard to conquer it, and I don't think I've let her see it yet'.

Because Toddington Manor, the National Union of Teachers' wartime headquarters, was fairly near Teresa's new home, a beautiful Elizabethan house in Broad Campden, we met on several occasions in the school holidays. Somehow we seemed rather distant, not close as in the letters, partly no doubt because others were always present. But reading her letters now it looks as though she wanted to keep me only as a correspondent. She gave many not very plausible explanations of why she could not invite me to stay and, more plausibly, that she could not come to stay with me in Brentwood because of the air raids. The relationship ended in 1941 when one weekend my mother took me from Toddington Manor to Teresa's house to meet her as arranged. I found she was out, visiting someone else. I had to sit with 'the Lady' and wait for several hours, feeling agonisingly miserable and humiliated, until my mother fetched me. I think Teresa must have made another close friend and decided to jilt me. I had been aware all along that although her mother was polite enough to me she saw me as unacceptably of a different social class, and preferred Teresa to develop friendships with the daughters of her friends. I felt desperately hurt and mortified by the rejection.

When I was seventeen and planning to travel near Broad Campden I wrote to Teresa suggesting that we met. Her reply was a brush off, 'It was nice of you to write. I would have liked to meet for tea but unfortunately I am usually away most of the holidays and am in fact going up to London tomorrow and then on to stay with some friends.' It had been such a very close relationship that I always had it in mind that one day I would meet her and try to find out what had happened. When, in my fifties, I met Isabel I learned that Teresa had refused to go to the university, had moved to New York, married a wealthy night club owner and died of cancer at the age of forty-seven. Her brother had been killed in the army near the end of the war. I felt shaken, as one does at that age, to learn that a contemporary has died, and enormously frustrated that my intention to effect a closure on the episode of our relationship had been so irrevocably thwarted.

But if Teresa abandoned me Isabel was still eager to have me as a friend, although she was now at boarding school and never returned to St. Paul's. I'm afraid I patronised her but I did appreciate her sunny nature and her sense of humour. Like most of my friends, she would ask me to recommend books to her. There was no teenage fiction then, and I would suggest novels I thought she would like by Vicki Baum and Somerset Maugham. Teresa told me that Isabel wrote to her, ' I have a lot of quarrels with Barbara about politics, with Barbara always in the right.' Isabel was the first friend of my age to become seriously interested in boys – to the horror of her mother she started to hang around with the village boys when she was fourteen. I stayed with her several times in 1941 and 1942 in the house in the Wiltshire countryside which her family had bought to escape the blitz. Her mother seemed to find life difficult and depressing without her pre-war servants and only a daily help.

The journey there, like all train journeys during the war, was an ordeal, but also an adventure. Trains were usually late, often delayed by a bomb on the line or the priority given to troop trains. They were always over-crowded, the corridors crammed with servicemen on leave, and there were no buffet or refreshment cars. It was hard to know when to get off since platforms were not lit and the boards with the names of railway stations had been replaced by miniature signs, the letters not more than three inches high. At night the carriages had no black-out and were lit only by a very dim blue light, so that it was not possible to read. I feel no nostalgia for steam trains – the compartments were dirty and you arrived at your destination with smudges of soot on your face. Road travel, though more comfortable, was even more adventurous, since from 1940-43, to confuse invaders, signposts and street names were removed altogether. Even the milestones were defaced, whilst street lighting was removed or greatly dimmed, and car lights had to be masked to let out only a thin slit of light.

Isabel and I lost touch when we were about seventeen. In middle age she phoned me and we met. She did not go to the university, married very young, and then lived in South America and Tanganyika. She returned at twenty-eight, a widow with two young children, to live near her parents in Wiltshire. The only friend from before the war who, like me, returned to face the bombs in the autumn of 1940 was Lilian, the girl with Middle Eastern Jewish parents. She had gone to Wycombe Abbey as a boarder, hated it, thankfully returned to London with St. Paul's, and remained there, as I did, all through the war. I'm afraid I patronised her too. She wrote, 'I am very glad you recommended some suitable books for me to read, as I have read only four books lately, and I don't think I'd better mention their names in case you don't approve of them'. Sometimes in the holidays we would meet to go to the cinema with one of her brothers. She seemed to have no opinions or interests of her own. But years later she told me I had been very important to her, not only as someone with a much more extensive knowledge and ideas about politics, religion, and the position of women than the other girls, but as someone who had been very kind to her and given her the first Christmas present she had ever had. I have already mentioned her metamorphosis after her marriage. She phoned me occasionally over the years about various psychological problems of her relatives, hoping I could offer good advice. In middle age she took a course in jewellery making, and subsequently sold, exhibited and won prizes for her beautiful work. At last, she had gained confidence in her abilities.

Nancy, who was billeted with Isabel and myself at High Wycombe, was sent to boarding school when the blitz started, but returned to St. Paul's the following year. She was rather like Isabel, cheerful and unintellectual. Her father owned a big garage in Twickenham and her mother was an extremely warm, hospitable woman who was always inviting me to their house in Richmond. She would discuss books very seriously with me, seeking my opinion as though I were an adult. I used to help Nancy with her homework in the school dinner hour. She later told me that St. Paul's had been the wrong school for her, with too high academic standards, undermining her confidence. On leaving school she went into the forces and later became a photographer. She phoned and occasionally visited me over the years. She never married and until recently still lived in the house where I used to visit her from school.

Lilian, Isabel and Nancy were Jewish, and I asked them in adult life whether they had experienced anti-semitism in any form at St. Paul's. Isabel and Nancy insisted that they had not, Nancy contrasting this with her experience in her previous school. Lilian said that in the junior St. Paul's (for girls under 11) she had been ostracised, not only for being Jewish but for her dark skin. Over seventy years later, whenever she remembers this experience she still feels hurt inside. She did not experience anti-semitism from other girls in the main school, but she remained intensely self-conscious about her colour, and believed that the other Jewish girls, who were of Ashkenazi (European) origin looked down on her. And she found the effect of having a separate Jewish assembly, scripture lessons and *Kosher* food was to make her feel an outsider, and excluded. She also knew, as the others did not, that the school limited the proportion of Jewish girls admitted.

At this time I made new friends whom I had not known before the return to London, because they had been in a parallel form, Vivienne Tanner, Gillian Staynes, and Angela Frost. Angela was an extremely pretty, blond, blue eyed non-academic girl who seemed more mature physically and emotionally than the rest of us fourteen to fifteen year olds. By this I mean she was quite curvaceous, had her hair coiffured like a film star, and wore makeup out of school. Whilst not in the least presenting herself as sophisticated or sexually knowing, she probably was. A touch of tragedy marked her as she was always worrying about her brother, who was in the Merchant Navy, and who was drowned later in the war. I think the only connection between the four of us was that we wanted a life beyond the stereotypical schoolgirl concerns with school marks, team games and film stars. Our friendship was emotionally quite superficial, very unlike my deep attachment to Teresa. We did not confide in each other and were certainly not physically affectionate. Girls at that time did not embrace each other -indeed at school we were forbidden to touch each other, even linking arms brought a rebuke.

St. Paul's drew its pupils from all parts of London but none of my friends lived near me, so I rarely saw them at weekends or during the holidays, and 'sleepovers' were then unknown. I had no neighbourhood friends, since because of the secrecy of my mother's private life we did no more than nod to neighbours. However, my friends and I wrote to each other quite frequently during the holidays and Isabel wrote to me often from her boarding school. I don't know why we wrote, rather than chatted on the phone, perhaps phone calls were expensive, or it may have been simply that letters were then the customary way to communicate with absent friends. All my friends, including Isabel and Lilian, would write asking for book recommendations. Vivienne, for example, wrote at Christmas 1941, 'I hope you are pleased with me, I am reading *Scoop* by Evelyn Waugh. Would you suggest a few more improving books, or just give me a list of good authors.' We borrowed our books from public libraries and to this day I have a feeling of deep satisfaction when I return home with several library books, though now I have a strong preference for new, clean copies.

Vivienne and Gillian were academically bright, high spirited girls, who, though not in the least interested in politics themselves, developed an elaborate, rather surrealist pretence, sustained over a couple of years, that we were a band of communist conspirators or at other times a group of Russian spies. Angela did not join in the game, which she considered childish. Vivienne took the leading part, writing spoof letters to us during the holidays. She addressed us as 'Comrade', though I was often called 'Proffy' – at fifteen I was already typecast as an academic. We would walk together after school to Hammersmith Broadway where our routes diverged, and stand talking, reluctant to part. When we got home Vivienne made long phone calls to me, discussing the details of our supposed plot. The high point of the game was to play it in situations, for example on buses or tube trains, where someone might take us seriously and be alarmed.

I don't think our families were aware of this bizarre game, which could have had dangerous consequences, since I was living with communists who probably were, in fact, suspected of being Russian spies. This group of friends belonged exclusively to the period when I was living with the Giles'. I abandoned the game, which therefore collapsed, in 1942, when I became involved in real political activity. We were all carefree in those two years leading up to School Certificate. We enjoyed fooling around and had relatively little homework, I certainly finished mine within an hour. I don't remember feeling at all stressed by the School Certificate exams in the summer, perhaps because nothing turned on the results. Soon afterwards we entered the sixth form, and the light-hearted period of our lives ended. Our interests diverged, we studied different subjects, formed new friends and we no longer had much to do with each other.

Before this though, Vivienne, Angela and I went on holiday together at the beginning of the summer holiday in 1941. We were all fifteen. The plan was to start at Maidenhead and walk to Cookham and then Henley, Weston, and along the Thames valley, staying in youth hostels. We intended to walk ten to twelve miles a day and be away for about nine days, calling at the Post Offices in these towns for any messages from home. Whilst my mother was used to my travelling on my own I was amazed that the parents of the other girls agreed. Perhaps a youth hostelling, walking holiday sounded healthy and safe.

Youth hostels were generally sited in lovely parts of the country or on the outskirts of small country towns. They were extremely cheap, a shilling a night, and were intended to encourage walking and a simple, outdoor way of life. You had to arrive on foot – cyclists and motorists were not admitted. The accommodation was very basic. There were large separate-sex dormitories with bunks, and cold showers. Blankets were provided but you had to bring your own sheet sleeping bag. There was a living-dining room and a kitchen where you cooked your own meals, although some hostels provided a cooked meal very cheaply. In the morning to help the Warden, but also to encourage social responsibility, everyone was given a cleaning job to do. This was inspected before you could leave, which had to be not later than 10a.m. You were not allowed to return or check in before 5p.m., whatever the weather. This daytime exclusion from the hostel was intended to prevent people idling indoors when they should be out walking. The lights were put out by the Warden at 10p.m. and smoking and drinking alcohol were not allowed.

All this would be unacceptable today – now you are allowed to drive to Youth hostels and family rooms are available for couples with children. But for us youth hostelling was wonderfully liberating. We were not bothered by the austerity and strict rules, which we were used to, and for the first time we were away from the authority and oversight of parents, parent substitutes and teachers. The other youth hostellers were always friendly and we would spend the evenings exchanging experiences or playing cards or table tennis with them. However, we soon abandoned walking for hitchhiking. One afternoon it began to rain heavily, no bus was due, and I remembered the hitch hiking skills I'd learnt with the Dienes' (find a good place on the edge of, or just outside of a town, before the traffic increases speed, but not on a bend, smile, etc.) The others had never hitchhiked but were keen to try. There was very little civilian traffic around in 1941 and it's difficult to hitch a lift for three people, but I suppose that fifteen-year-old girls were likely to be lucky, and so we were. After that there was no going back. We enjoyed the diversity of people we met and the holiday turned into a hitch hiking one. I don't think it ever occurred to us that this might be dangerous, although we did not tell our parents, whom we knew would not approve of the change in our plans.

Usually we got lifts in lorries but once two men in a large car stopped. Vivienne decided to play the spy game so, sitting in the back she started to discuss with us our local 'contacts' and the next move in our supposed plot. At the height of the invasion scare this was perhaps somewhat foolish. To our alarm the car pulled up at a police station and the driver told us to get out. Then he explained, smiling at our discomfiture, that he wasn't going any further, they were police officers and he asked to see our identity cards. He left it at that but we decided to be more careful with our spy game in future.

Not only had we fallen from grace by hitchhiking but we also ventured into a pub one evening, a new and transgressive experience for Vivienne and me. It came about because we got chatting with a soldier, they were omnipresent during the war, who pressed us to meet him and his friends in the evening in a pub not too far from the hostel. This was distinctly challenging since Vivienne and I must have looked, as we were, not old enough to be admitted to pubs. In fact the publican did not query our age, but we felt uneasy with the soldiers' very limited sexual advances, the pub scene, and the shandies we were bought. Angela, who could have passed for seventeen, seemed quite comfortable but we didn't repeat the experience. I think this was the most carefree holiday I ever had, before the pressures of exams, politics and boyfriends entered my life.

The following summer, 1942, when I was sixteen, this period of my life ended. I took School Certificate and left the care of the Giles' to live with my mother, who had moved to Blackheath.

Chapter 8

A London sixth form. Life, love, and political activities 1942–44

In the summer of 1942 when I was sixteen another chapter of my life opened. The air raids had eased and my mother decided to move from Brentwood to Blackheath. This would be a much shorter journey to work for both her and Spikes, via the Blackwall tunnel. The house would be the ninth I had lived in, not counting boarding schools and billets. I didn't mind the moves, especially because recently each one had led to some improvement in my life. I immediately liked Blackheath, which at that time was much nearer its 'village' appellation than it later became. It was then very quiet, the centre a high street lined with small food shops, a haberdasher's, a cobbler's and a bank, with residential streets of Georgian or early to mid Victorian houses leading off each end. Southern railway trains to central London ran every twenty or thirty minutes. I could get to St. Paul's in about an hour, via the train to Charing Cross, and then the District underground line to Hammersmith.

Apart from the summer of 1940 this was the first time I had lived with my mother during both term time and holidays since I was six. Michael never did so – he remained in Marlborough until he left school and went to Cambridge. Although I had been very happy with the Giles' I was excited at the idea of living at home and left them without a backward glance. Thereafter I visited them infrequently and I fear now that they must have thought me ungrateful. This I certainly wasn't, but with the thoughtlessness of childhood as my life moved on I shed friends, made new ones and rarely looked back.

Rental property, often belonging to evacuated civil servants, was still plentiful and cheap. We found a semi-detached, white-stuccoed Georgian house, 14 Eliot Place, on the edge of the heath, with a long garden winding down hill. I thought everything about it was beautiful except the basement kitchen, which was below ground level, cold and dark. But it opened into a large living room where we ate and spent most of our time in the winter, as the rest of the house was unheated. This room was very light with big windows and a glass panelled door opening on to the garden, a big dresser, a large walk-in larder lined with shelves, and a coal fire place where we lit a fire every evening. Stairs winding out of the room to the ground floor made the room look, I thought, like a stage set. There were still intermittent air raids, when at first we sheltered under the stairs, but later we acquired a 'Morrison' indoor shelter. This was six feet long and four feet wide, about table height, with a steel top and removable wire mesh sides. You could use it as a large table, which we did, and put the sides on and crawl under it with some discomfort during an air raid. On the ground floor was the dining room, almost never used, and a very light sitting room overhanging the garden. The first floor had two bedrooms and a bathroom, the second floor two small attic-like bedrooms. The house was unfurnished, so my mother was able to move in her furniture, bought for the Chelsea flat, which had been in storage for two years.

The period from September 1942 to 1944 when I was in the sixth form at school were years of great debate in England about post war British society. The debate was started in the summer of 1940 by J.B. Priestley, a popular leftist novelist. He had insisted, in a series of persuasive radio talks, listened to by a third of the population, that this was a citizens' war and must result in a more just and truly democratic society. His eloquence, combined with his Bradford accent and his portly, pipe smoking, avuncular persona gave his message widespread appeal. Eventually his contract with the BBC was not renewed because he was judged too left-wing, but he had started, or perhaps reflected, a widespread feeling that we should discuss our war aims. How could it be acceptable for the young men who were defending us against Hitler to return to unemployment and slum life? People had not forgotten how politicians had betrayed their promise of 'a land fit for heroes' after the First World War. The question gained impetus from the second half of 1941 with the entry of the Soviet Union and then the United States into the war. Although people were aware that much suffering lay ahead, eventual victory began to seem inevitable. A new Adjutant General set up the Army's Bureau of Current Affairs, with the unprecedented aim of informing all soldiers about the progress of the war and what they were fighting for. Exhibitions, wall newspapers and lectures about current issues were organised for the forces with civilian lecturers, who often held left-wing views. A general drift towards the left became evident. Conservative candidates lost by-elections and the *Daily Mirror*, the soldiers' favourite paper, called for social change. Even *The Times* in1941 argued that the government must promise to create social justice when the war ended and in 1942 the Beveridge Report set out measures to show how this could be done.

There were no echoes of these discussions in St.Paul's, where at that time nothing new or lively happened, but there were in other schools. In January 1942 the Council for Education in World Citizenship (C.E.W.C.) founded in 1939 'to provide opportunities for young people to debate international issues and to encourage them to be active citizens' began a series of conferences for sixth formers. Michael and three of his best friends planned to go to the first of these, and although I was only fifteen and not yet a sixth former I managed to get a place, and persuaded Angela to come with me. Angela had no knowledge of, or interest in, international affairs but was attracted by the prospect of meeting boys. This was probably a significant part of the motivation of all of us. At that time there were few co-educational schools, and opportunities for middle class adolescents to meet the opposite sex were rare, and contacts were often discouraged. Pamela Mason, who, aged seventeen, became my brother's first girlfriend, told me that at boarding school a collection of short stories by Somerset Maugham which Michael sent her was confiscated and the matter reported to her parents.

The conferences were residential and held in public schools. The first was at Leighton Park, a Quaker boys' boarding school, and lasted for four or five days. Boys and girls were lodged in separate houses. We girls were shocked to find that the showers were communal and the toilets had no doors. There were lectures and 'commissions' of about twenty young people who met once or twice a day. Each commission discussed a different issue, such as 'The Atlantic Charter' and 'Social and Economic Reconstruction'. We divided into mixed sex work groups for domestic tasks – setting and clearing tables, washing up. Michael, who had a great disinclination for such work, skilfully and with his usual good humour managed to be appointed the work organiser.

These conferences, held every year, with between times shorter London meetings, became a very important part of my life until I went to Oxford. For the first time I was not a lone eccentric with an interest in politics and left-wing views, but surrounded by contemporaries just as knowledgeable and just as involved as myself. Michael and I formed a new bond, three of his friends spent a weekend with us in Brentwood and I began to meet them in the school holidays. At the end of the first conference we formed a Schools India Committee to campaign for school children to sign our 'Free India' petition. I was the secretary-cum-treasurer, Wolf Mankowitz was the chairman, and the committee included Michael and two of his friends. We went round Fleet Street trying to get publicity from newspapers and weeklies and we visited the elegant Krishna Menon, an Indian Congress leader who had lived in England for some years. He was then secretary of the India League and after independence became Indian High Commissioner to the U.K. At that time he was glad to welcome help even from school children and gave us a small room in the League's headquarters at 165 The Strand to use as an office. We went on to organise regional petitions and a one day conference, with advice and a small grant obtained for us by the parliamentary private secretary of Stafford Cripps, who was then in the War Cabinet and a supporter of Indian independence.

These were heady times for me. After the next conference we set up an Inter Schools Committee, elected annually at the residential conferences, which subsequently took place in Sherborne and Queenswood schools. We acted as an advisory committee to Monica Luffman, the secretary-organiser of C.E.W.C. My brother and I were both on the committee, as were, in different years, Wolf Mankowitz, who later became a playwright and screen writer and Karel Reisz, who became a film director. In fact, all the people who worked on the committee and many of those who attended our conferences were later distinguished in the media, the universities or the professions. We had our own Inter Schools Committee notepaper printed, and twelve sixth formers in different parts of the country arranged local conferences with the help of Monica. She was both remarkably efficient and diplomatic, managing to encourage our activities whilst tactfully restraining our inflated idea of our importance and trying to prevent us from presenting too left-wing an image. I suspect her own views were very left-wing but she never disclosed them. She was probably in her mid-thirties, but perhaps in part because her hair was prematurely grey and certainly because of her firm though discreet authority and excellent organising ability, she seemed to us part of the older generation.

Monica encouraged the committee to produce and distribute a termly journal for school pupils which we called 'Phoenix'. It included short articles, many by committee members including Michael and myself, with such titles as 'The Crisis of Western Faith', 'The Later Work of T.S. Eliot' and 'School Democratisation'. Hilary Rubinstein, who became a well-known literary agent, was at one time the editor. One issue had a poem by Karel Reisz, which on re- reading recently I still thought rather good. I began an extensive correspondence with the other committee members and my former correspondence with my school friends came to an end. Indeed, from that time on, although I continued to have girlfriends at school and university, my closest friends were always boys. I'm not sure why this was. There was always a mild degree of flirtation involved, but they were not usually 'boyfriends.' I believed at the time it was because boys were more interested in politics and ideas, less interested in gossip, than most girls, but re-reading recently some of the letters Michael's friends wrote me I saw that they were in fact full of gossip.

After the first conference at Leighton Park two of Michael's friends, Guy Williams-Ashman and Malcolm Pines, began writing to me. Predictably, they had been smitten by the lovely Angela, but finding that she was not interested in remaining in touch with them, she thought them too young, switched their attention to me. Their tactics to explain this switch were disarmingly unconvincing. Guy, for instance, wrote, 'I was attracted very much by your very charming personality while I was at Reading, and very touched by all the help you gave me with my speech. I asked you for Angela's address, not to write to her, but hoping to start a correspondence with you, to strengthen our relationship.' Malcolm wrote, 'Angela seems such a spineless creature, sexually very attractive, but intellectually worthless. I should like to meet you on Saturday, and explain this more.'

Guy took me to classical concerts, a new experience for me, and I found it a strain to sit still for so long listening to Bach in reverential silence. There were not many places for young people with limited pocket money to go – coffee bars were as yet almost unknown. Usually

I would meet one or other of them at Leicester Square tube station and we would stroll up and down Charing Cross Road. It was then a fascinating place for anyone with a passion for reading, lined with second-hand bookshops where a huge variety of books could be bought very cheaply. Our relationships were not emotionally highly charged. We had little, if any, experience of the other sex, and I think we were trying out how to relate to each other and how the others' minds operated, as well as establishing status for ourselves by going out with a boy/girl.

This was a period before teenage culture had been invented – even the term 'teenager' was not in general use in Britain until later in the forties. The idea that adolescents should have their own characteristic teenage fashions, hairstyles, music, magazines or books was a product of post war consumerism. It was imported in the late forties and fifties from the U.S. where this new mass market was already being exploited. Before then girls changed at some point in adolescence from reading school girl magazines to women's magazines, from children's books to adult books, from straight bobbed hair with a fringe to a permanent wave and hair set like an adult's. Aspiring to an adult-like appearance was a problem during the war for school girls with very limited pocket money, at a time of stringent clothes rationing. Some girls could borrow clothes from their older sisters or mothers, but I was too small for this to be a possibility and had to be content with making the most of the few clothes I had. I did have a 'perm', so that my incorrigibly fine, straight blonde hair could be set in the then fashionable 'pageboy' style of film star Veronica Lake – straight, but with the ends curled under. None of us had money to spend on alcohol, and alcohol was not offered at the infrequent mixed age parties held in the circles in which I moved.

In the autumn of 1942 Guy, Malcolm and Michael went up to Cambridge. At that point in the war it was possible for students to defer war service for a year. This course was recommended by their school because it would secure them a university place when war ended and competition for places would be greater. I began to go out with newer members of the Inter Schools Committee, especially Tom Elkins and Martin Wigg. Tom was as impoverished as myself, but Martin seemed to have substantial amounts of money. He, or perhaps his father, was a member of the Arts Theatre Club in Soho, where he would often take me to lunch.

On arriving in Cambridge Michael threw himself into student political activities and gradually drifted away from his school friends, who had other interests. Malcolm later became a well-known psychiatrist and psychoanalyst, Guy a distinguished cancer researcher and Professor of Biochemistry in the University of Chicago. From the outset Michael hoped to hold office in the Labour Club and the Cambridge Union, the historic student debating society. These positions were the traditional stepping stones to a high powered career in politics, which I think must then have been his ambition. He quickly made new friends. Malcolm wrote to me a term later that, 'Mike is very prominent politically, knows everyone, is liked by most and has a small circle of fairly close friends, all very active politically.' As he had hoped, he was elected Secretary of the Cambridge Union in that year, and Vice Chairman of the Labour Club, and referred to as 'the blue eyed darling of West Ham'. Michael's connection with West Ham was decidedly historic by this time, but he made the most of it – which was, I think, preferable to forgetting it. He and I had become quite close in the past two years, and he wrote to me several times that year from Cambridge, sympathising with my dislike of school, advising me not to join the Communist Party and issuing pressing invitations to visit him – "This is crazy, but could you come for next Monday? I would like you to be here for this debate, I feel I may do rather well. When I'm busy there are lots of people who will look after you. I'm proposing the motion, 'That the house urges His Majesty's Government to implement the Beveridge Report without delay'. I must make a good speech, if possible my best in Cambridge."

My mother, of course, didn't allow me to accept this invitation. I was now in the sixth form, with for the first time a heavy workload. Since I had decided that I wanted to be a doctor I had to study for four science 'Highers' (A levels). The only science I had done before was a year when I was twelve. I had a lot of ground to cover, especially since I had set my heart on going to Oxford or Cambridge and this would only be possible if I won a science scholarship. In the autumn of 1942 when I entered the sixth form St. Paul's numbers rose to 165. This was because since the summer of 1941 when the Germans invaded the Soviet Union air raids on London had become sporadic. Several very bright girls entered the sixth form, including Jean Ginsburg, later a distinguished endocrinologist, like me intent on an Oxbridge scholarship, and like me interested in politics. Several of us read the *New Statesman* regularly, though I was the only one to read *Tribune*, a more left-wing weekly, whose literary editor and columnist from 1943 was George Orwell. There were other brilliant periodicals at the time discussing serious issues, all with left-wing editors, notably *Picture Post* and *Lilliput*. At the school lunch table political arguments were now common, since one of the newcomers, Pat Hutchinson, was a well-informed Conservative. After Oxford she went into the Foreign Office, never married, and eventually became British ambassador in Uruguay.

We now led a more-or-less normal family life. I was usually the first home in the evening and got on with my homework. I didn't, as in Chelsea, have to cook or shop as my mother bought the food in little shops round her school. She operated a pared down, distinctly eccentric cooking regime, geared to the fact that she was often out in the evenings. From her butcher, whose children had attended her school, every Friday she bought unrationed sausages and liver and a large joint of meat, much bigger than her ration entitlement. Shop keepers always had a little largesse to distribute because, for example, people who were 'registered' with them might be away or have recently died, so small-scale favouritism – no money was involved – was probably widespread. My mother would cook the sausages and liver on Friday and Saturday evenings and roast the joint for Sunday lunch. What was left was kept in the fridge (a new purchase, our first ever) drying up further each day. We would eat the meat cold every evening from Monday to Thursday, usually with bread and butter or if whoever was home bothered to cook, with boiled potatoes, and salad in the summer, tinned peas in the winter. Frozen vegetables were not introduced in Britain till the late forties.

If the joint was finished too soon we would have baked beans on toast and if my mother was home for Saturday lunch she would cook eggs and chips. I helped her prepare the traditional Sunday dinner with roast potatoes, and sprouts in the winter, fresh peas or runner beans in the summer, and a fruit pie. My mother also cooked a Victoria sponge every Sunday, with an egg from the small supply we got from my grandmother, and this, too, lasted several days. Unlike her own mother she was not a great cook and was not interested in cooking. Her roast meat tended to be overcooked, her pastry and cakes heavy and her food was so often slightly burnt that for years I tended to find food that wasn't at all burnt rather tasteless. We had cereals for breakfast and we all had school dinners during term time, so we were adequately, if not elegantly, fed.

In the winter fruit was very scarce, oranges and lemons rarely available, bananas not at all, but we had more fruit than most families. We bought boxes of apples in the autumn and spread them out on the floor of one of the attic rooms. With frequent checking, and discarding any that went rotten, they would last till spring. In the autumn we sliced and dried cooking apples. Spikes never attempted to cook or do housework but he proved to be a passionate gardener. He turned the second section of the garden, screened from the house by trees, into a large fruit and vegetable plot where he grew salads, tomatoes, runner beans and peas and soft fruit – gooseberries, black currants and raspberries. We had so many raspberries that we had large bowls of them for breakfast, a luxury I've never experienced since. At the weekends I helped my mother, who never stopped working, to bottle our fruit and tomatoes and make jam. We also bought and bottled plums. You could exchange your jam ration for sugar for jam making, and in any case we did not use all of our ordinary sugar ration. Whatever her deficiencies as a cook my mother was an excellent jam maker and fruit bottler. It was very satisfying to see the fruits of her labour lined up in the cupboard under the stairs.

For the first time my mother employed a cleaner, who came one morning a week with her two small children, for whom sweets were left. With the chocolate and sweets ration at two or three ounces a week this was a welcome gift. My mother had stopped taking her washing and ironing for her mother to do and sent most things to a laundry, the usual recourse for middle class families until washing machines came into widespread use. After the end of the war she did acquire a washing machine, a cumbersome object. It had to be filled and drained with a hose-pipe then refilled with clean water to rinse the clothes, which were then put through a wringer. The sheets and Spikes' shirts continued to be sent to the laundry – my mother was no great ironer. Her Saturday mornings were still often spent at meetings at the N.U.T. headquarters, now back in London, and she usually had meetings after school. By now Spikes, who usually came straight home after work, was noticeably jealous of the men she met in these meetings. Often he would silently sulk when she returned or would make snide remarks about the 'other two Billys' with whom she spent a lot of time, Billy Griffiths, on the N.U.T. executive, and Billy Cove, an N.U.T. supported Labour MP. I used to watch with admiration as she quietly ignored these remarks and sulks, coaxing him into a better mood by telling him amusing anecdotes about her day. I admired almost everything about my mother. I would watch her with a scarf tied round her hair, gypsy wise, as she dusted the room, and think how pretty she looked, much prettier, I thought, than after she applied powder and lipstick – at that time eye make-up was rarely used – before setting off to work. Few professional women would leave home at that time without makeup and, until well into the 1950s, without a hat.

I remember only three occasions in my childhood when my mother upset me. When I was about fourteen she took me to a West End cinema to see the premiere of a film for which she had been given tickets – the only time I ever went to the cinema with her. Before the film started she noticed that H.G. Wells was sitting nearby, and having met him a couple of times she insisted on taking me at the end to be introduced to the great man. I was extremely reluctant to go. Why on earth, I argued, would he want to meet me, and sure enough he looked irritated and bored by the intrusion. I wasn't sure that he even recognised my mother. I suppose that everyone's parents embarrass them at some time in their adolescence, and this was the only occasion when she embarrassed me, on her behalf as well as mine – but I don't think she was at all put out. And once, when I was about fifteen, while she was washing up I started to confide in her about a problem I was having with a friend at school. Suddenly I realised that she had not been listening at all and I was so surprised and hurt that I determined I would never again confide in her, and I never did. It seems a very unfair over-reaction, especially since I was critical of my friends' mothers who seemed overly concerned with their daughters' lives, but I suppose it is by such trivial events that close parent-child ties gradually loosen.

The only other occasion when my mother upset me happened when I was about eight and refused to do my piano practice one day during the school holidays. My mother, exasperated, and probably thinking how much my piano lessons cost her, bent down and slapped my legs. I was much more hurt and astonished that my beloved mother had done this than hurt by the blow, and I never forgot the incident.

We still had very few visitors because of the secrecy of the relationship between my mother and Spikes. There was then enormous hypocrisy about sexual relationships and a woman's reputation would be ruined if she was known to have an extra-marital relationship. When my grandmother or aunt came to visit, without anything being said my mother would conceal all traces of Spikes' residence, though I'm sure my aunt, at least, was not deceived. We did have one quite frequent visitor who was welcomed by Spikes, even though he was clearly another admirer of my mother. This was her G.P., Harry Boyd, who had an almost entirely working- class practice very near her school in the docks area. He was an early advocate of preventative medicine and healthy lifestyles, though to his despair his patients rarely followed his advice, partly because many could not afford to do so. A great and lively talker, he was active in the Labour Party and the conversation, very boring to me, would be mainly concerned with West Ham Labour politics. He was unhappily married and I think our home was an escape from his own. He planned to emigrate after the war with his five children to Australia, so that they could all have free university education. In the event, alas, he died before this could happen.

After we moved to Blackheath I discovered that it was Spikes' home territory. He owned a big house about twenty minutes walk from ours, in Lee Park, where he had lived with his wife and five children. His two daughters, Helen, who was about to start at Cambridge, and Diana, who had graduated, were still living there with Diana's husband Peter Hewett. The youngest son lived elsewhere with his mother, and two other sons had grown up and left home. Peter Hewett was an English teacher at Spikes' school, and he and Diana had been at Cambridge together. They were so close, and shared so much experience, that if they were on opposite sides in the games, such as charades, that we sometimes played in mixed aged parties, they had an unfair advantage – they could always guess what was in the other's mind.

Peter played an important role in the family conspiracy of silence. Spikes could not give people the same address as my mother and always pretended that he still lived in his former house. Correspondence for him was brought to school each day by Peter and surreptiously handed over. We saw Spikes' children quite often, especially Peter and Diana, although there was always a certain tension between my mother and the daughters, who naturally identified with their deserted mother. When I met Diana some years after my mother's death she told me how much she had resented my mother breaking up her parents' marriage through her 'womanly wiles'. I was puzzled by this phrase but decided that she was referring to what most people saw as my mother's charm. Diana's husband, Peter Hewett, was very suave, beautifully mannered, and had an extensive knowledge of literature. Later, he published his poetry and became senior English master at Ipswich Grammar School, living in a converted windmill. After his death some well-known writers whom he had taught paid tribute to his inspiring teaching.

Both Peter and Diana talked often and nostalgically about their student days, reinforcing my ambition to get an Oxbridge scholarship. They told me, as none of the staff at my school had, that to achieve this it was not enough to know a great deal about your subject as taught in school, you must show that you have ideas and knowledge around it and in other areas. This was a relief to me, it sounded as though I might be able to compensate for my hastily acquired, and necessarily less than considerable, knowledge of the four sciences. I would be competing against girls some of whom would have a passion for at least one of the sciences, naturalists, perhaps, whilst I was much more interested in contemporary events and in books by J.B.S. Haldane and H.G. Wells about the history of science and scientific ideas.

My general education occurred out of school in my own reading, at C.E.W.C. conferences, listening to Peter and Diana's conversation, as formerly I had listened to Giles', and even listening to the 'Brains Trust'. This was a weekly radio quiz programme, on Sunday afternoons, with a regular panel of Cyril Joad, a philosopher, Julian Huxley, a zoologist, both brilliant educators and Commander Campbell, supposedly representing the man in the street. He was a retired naval officer, a source of excellent, implausible anecdotes, notoriously starting, 'When I was in Patagonia…'. Each week they were joined by two or three knowledgeable guests. Unlike contemporary question programmes and quizzes the questions were not about politics, or questions of fact to which there was a right or wrong answer, but about serious scientific or philosophical issues. Joad was famous for his opening gambit, 'It depends what you mean by', which introduced the nation to philosophical thinking. The programme succeeded in being both educational and entertaining and was hugely popular, with an audience of ten to twelve million. I listened to it throughout my sixth form years.

During those two years I was busy with the Inter Schools Committee, of which I was chair, sometimes looking for speakers amongst the many foreign groups then in London. This was when I came across the French boys from our High Wycombe billet, now in the Free French forces. Polish men from the Free Polish Forces were very popular amongst women, they were considered romantic, but I found them not much interested in issues that didn't concern Poland. U.S. soldiers, GIs, were the most numerous – in 1944 over a million were stationed in the U.K. They were definitely not romantic, they tended to make the nature of their interest in women very clear. British attitudes to them were mixed. They were much better paid, dressed, and fed than British soldiers, very friendly and generous with their sweets, cigarettes, and even sometimes nylon stockings. These were newly invented and not on sale in the U.K. till after the war. We still had only lisle, woollen, artificial silk, or if you were rich, silk stockings, all of which, especially in a time of clothes rationing, needed frequent mending. (Tights were not introduced till the early 1960s and only became popular in 1964, with the introduction of the miniskirt.) British men often resented GIs, notoriously regarding them as ' overpaid, oversexed and over here.' But the attraction of the GIs, apart from their generosity, was that they seemed to bring with them the glamorous world of U.S. films, with their American accents and casual references to drug stores and ice-cream parlours. On the other hand a lot of us found the apartheid they imposed on black GIs shocking, and some were critical of the tardiness of the U.S. entry into the war.

Amongst my foreign contacts I was most impressed by a German Jewish refugee, Mr. Siebert. (At that time adults were always addressed as Mr., Mrs., or Miss, unless they were personal friends.) He was a communist who had spent several years in a concentration camp for his political views. Whenever you met him he was ready with an erudite Marxist analysis of the current situation. He was a man of extreme austerity and sternness, who seemed detached from personal relationships, totally absorbed in attempting to advance the class struggle, fanatical in his defence of the Soviet Union. Today I would find such a person chilling, but then I greatly admired his dedication.

These activities made school seem very boring, especially since I found it difficult to be interested in the science syllabus I had to study. I was really much more interested in English and history but since I wanted to do medicine I had to grit my teeth and get on with the course. It seemed to bear very little relationship to the fascinating popular science books I was reading, such as H.G. Wells' *The Science of Life*. Our teachers stuck closely to old-fashioned text books and made no attempt to explain the importance or excitement of the topics we were studying, or what their application might be. The subjects were presented mainly as tasks involving huge amounts of memorising. This was less true of physics, which, however, I found difficult, and zoology, which I thought the most interesting subject, though the practical work, dissecting animals, called for a certain degree of manual dexterity, never my strong point.

Besides my Inter School Committee activities I had a social life centred on school. My main friends were Jean Ginsburg and Elizabeth Zaiman, who both lived in Golders Green. Both, like most of my school friends, were Jewish, both were *New Statesman* readers and lovers of classical music, and both planned to study medicine. Elizabeth's mother's life seemed to be entirely centred on her daughter, whose every move she watched protectively, feeding her all the right things, but controlling her intake of them (for the first time I heard the threat 'once on the lips, twice on the hips') and ensuring that she worked hard at her homework so that she would get an Oxbridge scholarship. Mrs. Zaiman didn't have a job, of course, none of my friends' mothers did, and Elizabeth filled her life. All my girlfriends were intent on a career. But we also expected to marry and have children and we would have long discussions about the qualities we would want in a husband. Intelligence, generosity, and a sense of humour tended to top the list. I don't think we considered the issue of how we would combine a career and a family, there were so few women who attempted this at the time that the difficulties involved had hardly emerged. My own mother was so atypical, and a single mother, that I hardly thought of her in this connection as a role model.

Most weekends Jean, Elizabeth and I, with several others from school, watched the Sadler's Wells Ballet perform at the New Theatre in St. Martins Lane. (After the war it became the Royal Ballet Company, and moved to Covent Garden). We would take it in turns to be at the theatre on Saturday mornings at 10am to book the first stools that were put out in the street, which would ensure that we would get places on the bench in the front row of the gallery. The bench was hard and narrow, the gallery at a great and precipitate height, but we were watching some magnificent dancers at an early stage in their careers – the supreme Margot Fonteyn, and Beryl Grey, Moira Shearer and Robert Helpman. They performed classical ballets, *Swan Lake*, *Coppelia* and *Les Sylphides*, and modern ballets, including *Hamlet* and *Comus*, and I thought the combination of music and dancing breathtakingly beautiful. Later I had friends whose son was in the Royal Ballet Company, and learned that the price of that beauty for the dancers was terrible daily pain, competitiveness, jealousy, and an extraordinarily narrow life.

Miss Strudwick, the high mistress, did not approve of our passion for ballet, probably because she suspected that it involved schoolgirl 'crushes' which teachers at girls' schools then did their best to prevent. Some of the girls, especially Elizabeth, did indeed have a 'crush' on one or other of the dancers and would rush round to the stage door after the performance to wait for them to come out. I was never tempted to join them having given up 'crushes' by the time I was thirteen. 'Crushes', a mild form of contemporary pop fan fever, were quite common among schoolgirls then. One girl in our class developed a 'crush' on Bebe Daniels and Ben Lyons, an American couple who spent much of the war in London. Their radio show 'Hi Gang' was, after 'Itma,' the most popular radio comedy in Britain. She found out where they lived and haunted the pavement outside their house, waiting for glimpses of them. After she left school she did a secretarial course and subsequently managed to get a job working for them. Alas, her illusions were soon shattered, and after Ben made a particularly crude pass at her she hurriedly left. It was the dream she wanted, not the reality.

Nowadays, entry to Oxford and Cambridge is on the basis of A level results and interviews. In my time there were special entrance exams in March and those who did best were then interviewed for scholarships. It was usual for Oxbridge candidates to spend three years in the sixth form, taking Highers (A levels) after two years and the Oxbridge entrance/ scholarship exams in the spring of the third year. I felt that I could not bear to stay so long at school and pleaded to be allowed to take the exams in the second year. Michael, who understood how boring school could be, persuaded our mother to support this decision. He himself after a year in Cambridge was called up in July 1943. Bravely, he opted to be a pilot in the R.A.F., but because his eyesight was not perfect he was instead trained for the even more dangerous job of rear air gunner. Our mother was of course terrified for him.

In the event he was sent to South Africa for his training, where he met his future wife, Molly. He survived a spell of service in Europe, before spending some time in a relaxed posting in the Cayman Islands, acquiring a taste for Pimms. After he was demobbed he returned to Cambridge for two years to complete his law degree. During his first months in the R.A.F. Michael wrote frequently to me, his 'precocious kid sister', long letters raising fundamental objections to the Communist Party. He argued for the sanctity of human rights, even for fascists like Mosley, and insisted that if ends are used to justify wrong means, the ends are unlikely ever to be achieved. The latter argument, though very strong, seemed inappropriate for someone engaged in bombing raids, but I came to agree with his view.

Fortunately the school agreed to let me try the Oxford scholarship exam a year early. Perhaps they were pleased to do so. I heard later that an ex-Paulina at Oxford had described me before I arrived there as 'the most unmanageable girl they ever had at St. Paul's.' This was surely a gross exaggeration, but in any case it was certainly not true of my behaviour in the sixth form. For one thing I did not have to keep breaking rules, since it was now much easier to get out of both gym and the hated school games and we were allowed to stay inside during the dinner hour and morning 'break.' But, more important, I made a deliberate decision to avoid antagonising the teachers. I knew that if I were excluded from classes as I had been in the previous two years I could not cover the syllabus, which required access to the labs. The zoology teacher particularly disliked me for some reason and seemed almost disappointed when I suddenly became very meek, and responded to her attacks on me with polite apologies. I think, though, that this tactic of lowering the flag of independence and, so to speak, collaborating with the enemy, damaged my self-esteem.

Mastering the four subjects in four and a half terms, starting as I did from scratch, was a formidable task, and for the first time ever I had to work hard. It was made possible because I had a very good visual memory at the time. It was not a photographic memory, I could not revisualise details, but I relied on my technique for organising notes, a topic for each page, with subtopics down the page headed in different colours. I could then summon up a coloured visual image of the appropriate page, with its subheadings, when usually the points under each subheading would come to mind. At the suggestion of a friend of my mother's I spent two weeks of the Christmas holiday in a famous tutorial school, Gabbitas and Thring, which provided intensive coaching in exam techniques. I don't remember how helpful the experience was or anything about it, except that the building was a warren of small dark rooms, up and down narrow staircases, very different from the large light spaces of St. Paul's.

What my classmates remembered most about that period, years later, apart from our visits to the ballet, was our production of a play, *The Barretts of Wimpole Street*, in the summer of our first year in the sixth form. I still have the programme. There had been no school drama since the war started so we decided to put on a play ourselves, without the assistance of the staff. There were five acts, and a cast of fifteen, including all my friends. I was the director, and many rehearsals were required. Amateurish it certainly was, but we enjoyed the experience hugely. I can't think how I found the time to do this, whilst working for exams and acting as chair of the Inter Schools Committee, but I don't remember ever feeling overwhelmed. In the summer terms I was at last given a role in the school games which I positively enjoyed – it was a sedentary one, official school scorer at cricket matches. This involved sitting at a table under the shade of a tree, recording the scores on a large sheet of paper as the umpire called them out. The players wore white, no masks were used and only shin pads, and cricket was then a very slow game. I found it a rather dreamy, restful experience to listen to the thud of the ball, the ritual cries of the players, and watch the white shapes moving on the green field.

In the summer holidays after our first year in the sixth form I went with a group from my class to work in an agricultural camp, helping Land Army girls with the potato harvest. It was an appalling experience. We had backache all the time, constantly bent down, hurrying to keep up with the tractors which were turning up the potatoes. Usually I collapsed in my tent in the evening but sometimes I went with other girls to the nearest pub, to be stood drinks and ward off the amorous attentions of the U.S. soldiers stationed nearby. In the end we all came down with dysentery, said to have been caused by some pork we had eaten. Lilian, the worst afflicted, was taken to hospital. She regarded her illness as a punishment for breaking the rule of her religion by eating pork, for the first and last time in her life. This potato harvesting was my only contribution to the war effort and contrasted sharply with what was expected of boys of the same age, who had to put their careers on hold and risk their lives.

During my second year in the sixth form I acquired my first serious boyfriend, Anthony Ryle. I had been going out with various boys who were members of the Inter Schools Committee, especially Tom Elkins and Martin Wigg, and although Tom in particular was a good friend the relationships remained at that level. I met Anthony at a C.E.W.C. sixth formers' conference at Sherborne in January 1944. We were immediately attracted to each other. We were both seventeen. Anthony was at a boarding school, Greshams, which Auden, Spender and Benjamin Britten had attended and he shared my passion for poetry. He spent his holidays in his parents' homes in Oxford and Sussex so our relationship was initially developed by correspondence. He was tall and very good looking, with thick brown hair, which flopped over his face, very blue eyes, a diffident manner and a charming smile. He had the strong healthy appearance of someone who came from a long line of well-nourished ancestors. We were both planning to study medicine at Oxford and we shared an interest in the Communist Party, as well as poetry, both of which formed the main subjects of our early correspondence.

Anthony had never been happy at boarding school despite his athletic prowess – he was captain of rugby. He missed his family and at that time had no close friends who shared his interests. He said he was only happy at school when listening to classical music and going for long walks and cycle rides – boys at boarding school were given enormously more freedom than girls. He had become interested in contemporary poetry in the past few years and more recently, through his sister Margaret, who was a member of the Oxford student Communist Party, in communism. Neither interest was shared initially by any one else in his school, although soon he made a political convert and friend. Unlike Anthony I had a lot of left-wing friends but none of them since my friendship with Teresa five years earlier were interested in poetry, and none of them had Anthony's passionate interest in communism. We felt we had at last discovered a soul mate. Both of us admired the contemporary left-wing poets, Auden, Spender, MacNiece and Day Lewis and we copied out passages of their poems that we liked to send to each other. Anthony wrote poetry himself which he sent to me for comment – a tricky assignment, since they really were not very good.

He read and discussed at length in his letters a great deal of Marxist writing. He agonised over whether it was possible to combine being a member of the Communist Party, which he was contemplating, with living a happy personal life and whether it was right to study medicine when his contemporaries were being killed in the forces. We both thought that a painful conflict would arise in the future of wanting to live in the country whilst as doctors our work would be most needed in cities. Anthony often felt guilty about his privileged, secure life. To my amusement his mother insisted on him returning to Oxford for the holidays on a circuitous route, to avoid going through London. He planned to go to India or Africa after he qualified, to help alleviate suffering.

A new 'little blitz' had been launched with thirteen major air raids on London between January and March 1944 but I continued doggedly preparing for the Oxford exams in March. I had decided to try for Oxford rather than Cambridge because it was known to give credit to ideas and knowledge outside science and in fact had a 'general' paper to assess this aspect of the candidates' knowledge. I put Somerville as my preferred college because it had the reputation of being the most intellectual women's college. But as soon as I saw the Zoology practical examination paper I feared the worst. We were required to dissect a worm and display and draw its reproductive system. I had never dissected anything as small as a worm, and knew little about its reproductive system (which was not on the A level syllabus) and, despairing, suspected that I had dissected out bits of connective tissue instead.

However I sailed through the 'general' paper and was short-listed and invited to Somerville for a scholarship interview. I was glad that other girls from my school went too. The event, which involved staying in the college overnight, would have been much more intimidating for someone on their own. We had dinner in the great Hall, the Fellows seated on a platform at one end and we Paulinas then spent the evening together happily discussing the books we had enjoyed as children. At the interview I was confronted by all the Fellows of the college in their long black gowns seated each side of a very long table, the Principal of the college at one end and myself at the other. A number of Fellows fired questions at me but fortunately there were no tricky questions about science. The only question I can remember was a request to describe and comment on the white paper on a proposed National Health Service, published in the previous month, with which I was luckily familiar. In April I was offered a scholarship at Somerville.

In April, too, I was invited by Anthony, with five other members of the Inter Schools Committee, to spend a week at his home in West Sussex. Three boys were invited, Karel Reisz, Tom Elkins and Martin Wigg, and three girls, Elisabeth Zaiman who was in my class at school, Pamela Mason a recent girlfriend of my brother's, and myself. All three girls were intending to study medicine and Pamela and Elizabeth both became psychiatrists. We brought emergency ration cards which Mrs. Ryle would need in order to feed us. Their house, Glatting, was set in a remote part of the South Downs, quite far from a village. As soon as I saw it I was stunned by the beauty of the house and surrounding countryside. The farmhouse was very old, part of it fourteenth century, with thick walls and heavy oak timbers inside. It was surrounded by an acre of orchard and kitchen garden and it was very large – it could accommodate six guests easily. The house was their country retreat, where they could walk, and it was near enough to the sea for them to sail. The furniture was old and the large kitchen had an Aga cooker, which I'd never seen before, a long wooden table where we ate and an old brick floor. There was no electricity or running hot water, only oil lamps, and candles in the bedrooms.

I immediately fell in love with the Ryle family as well as their house. All the men were tall and handsome and all were deeply committed to some serious purpose. Anthony's father, John, had formerly been a Guys Hospital consultant with a Harley Street practice and had then taken a large drop in income to become Regius Professor of Medicine at Cambridge. An early advocate of social medicine, he became convinced of the devastating role that poverty, poor housing and occupational hazards had on health, factors ignored by most clinicians. He had recently moved on to become the first Professor of Social Medicine at Oxford. He seemed old to us – he was about fifty-five – kindly, and somehow emanating an air of nobility. I think we all felt in awe of him. He spent most of the time in his study, emerging only for meals and to listen to classical music, though one evening he explained his research to us with the aid of large diagrams.

The oldest son John was also a doctor, serving in the navy. The second son Martin, then aged twenty-six, was a physicist. Later he was appointed to a new chair of Radio Astronomy in Cambridge, became Astronomer Royal, was knighted and won a Nobel prize. When we arrived at Glatting he was taking a brief respite from his secret war work, which he could not discuss. He was obviously exhausted both physically and mentally. We had, of course, no inkling of the importance of this work or of the distinctions that would later come to him. There was a daughter, Margaret, who was not at Glatting, in her final year of zoology at Oxford where she took a first class degree. Anthony was their youngest and clearly most beloved child. Other Ryles were distinguished establishment figures. John's brother Gilbert was a well-known Oxford philosopher and their father had been a bishop. They seemed an unusually close family, spending a lot of time together, apparently never quarrelling, apparently living on a higher moral plane than the rest of us. How could I not fall in love with them!

I did not, however, fall in love with Anthony's mother, Miriam. She was like the others tall, though more heavily built, and had a manner that was both forceful and queenly. Like the men she was high minded and serious, but as a full-time mother and wife this mainly took the form of enforcing a puritanical life style. Nobody was allowed to smoke or drink alcohol in the house and sexual activity of any kind outside marriage was not countenanced. Mrs. Ryle strongly disapproved of vanity in women, including such manifestations of it as make-up, permanent waves and high heels. Years later Anthony told me that it was not until she was fifty that his sister Margaret was able to break from her mother's influence enough to have her ears pierced. Mrs. Ryle's influence on all her sons, including their choice of wives, turned out to be very strong. She gave the impression of wanting to live in an earlier rural society. The family lived as far as possible on local produce, including honey from their beehives and Anthony helped on the farm above Glatting, especially at harvest time. Mrs. Ryle both spun and wove the wool from their sheep and used it to make her far from fashionable clothes. In my first year at Oxford she came to have tea with me, and on another occasion when my mother was visiting for the day, with both of us. I felt extremely uncomfortable under her scrutiny, and angry with her for, as I thought, patronising my mother, who for once was not at her ease.

I kept a diary of our week at Glatting which is mainly a record what we did each day – long country walks, lying in the sun, listening to classical music, reading poetry aloud, playing table tennis, talking round the fire in the evening, taking it in turn to wash up. Martin Ryle, much older than us, usually kept us company. He was a Hamlet like figure, melancholic, tense, with occasional outbursts of anger. I learned after the war that the work he had been involved in was the development of radar and that he was at the time developing the radar counter measures for D Day. He and his colleagues worked ten to twelve hours a day seven days a week, sometimes flying on bombing raids to check how their equipment functioned in action. That week at Glatting he was exhausted and withdrawn, rarely speaking, and when he did talk he often seemed cynical and bitter. I told him he was like a ghost. He replied that he felt emotionally empty and that this was essential for him to remain focussed on his work.

After the war, wanting nothing more to do with the military, he turned to astronomy and developed a powerful radio telescope, with which he could observe the most distant of the known galaxies. His observations provided important empirical support for the theory that the universe is expanding, and hence for the 'big bang' theory of its origin. He was appointed the first Professor of Radio Astronomy at Cambridge and received a Nobel Prize. But he became very bitter when the new techniques he had developed were immediately used by the military to improve their radar and sonar systems. He began to believe that fundamental science contains a greater potential for evil than good. Towards the end of his life he wrote, 'I am left at the end of my scientific life with the feeling that it would have been better to have become a farmer in 1946.... Our cleverness has grown prodigiously – but not our wisdom'.

I was surprised, reading the diary I kept at Glatting, to find very little mention of my fellow guests. I seemed to have been almost entirely interested in the Ryle family and my own feelings about them. I did already know the other guests very well, except for Karel Reisz, whom I had known for a year or so as an active member of the Inter Schools Committee, but who had always seemed inscrutable. At Glatting he was polite and joined in all the activities, but he remained quiet and reserved. It was impossible to know whether he was preoccupied with the fate of his family left behind in Czechoslovakia, or was bored or for some other reason uninvolved. I was even more surprised that my diary failed to mention an aspect of the week that had a deep and permanent influence on me. This was the experience of long walks in the South Downs. I cherished this memory and when, years later, we could afford to do so, we bought a house in this part of Sussex. After the week at Glatting my relationship with Anthony intensified and we fell seriously in love, and Anthony began to write me very moving love letters.

My last term at school, in the summer of 1944, was severely disrupted by the 'Flying Bomb' onslaught on London, which began in June, and continued night and day, but especially in the daytime, until September. These V1s were pilot-less jet propelled planes each carrying a ton of explosives which detonated on impact. You first heard a distant hum, which increased to a rattle as they drew nearer. When they ran out of fuel they crashed to the ground and exploded, causing damage over a radius of half a mile. The sudden silence when the motor cut out was the moment to run for cover. Sirens warned of their approach but since they came throughout the day, on average seventy four a day, it was hardly possible to shelter from them unless you were prepared to spend all day in a shelter, so casualties were high. Over 5000 people were killed in these raids and over 15,000 seriously injured. Our defence forces, it emerged later, destroyed many V1s at sea but there was no defence against those which reached built up areas, since artillery fire would have detonated them in the air. They tended to fall short of the centre of London, in south and east London and outer southern suburbs such as Croydon. I used to walk home after school up the hill and across Blackheath, watching a V1 flying overhead, waiting for the ominous silence. Over a million people left London, schools were once more evacuated and most people slept in some form of shelter. Half of the pupils at St. Paul's left but lessons and public exams went on all day in the school shelters. These raids somewhat diverted Londoners' attention from the battles in Europe, which had begun on D Day, on June 6th.

For the first time I felt afraid, and ashamed of this fear. Years later I read in a *Mass Observation* study that many people found the 'Blitz' spirit hard or impossible to recapture, which they tended to attribute to war weariness. This may well have been a factor, but in retrospect I think it was also a combination of the impracticality of sheltering from the V1 attacks, which were mainly in the daytime, the fact that we knew that no defence was put up against them, and perhaps in a strange way their robotic character. Instead of the familiar routine of the Blitz – the siren warning at dusk, hurrying with others to take shelter, going to sleep listening to the ack ack batteries attacking the planes and eventually by the morning the 'all clear' sounding – you were on your own, watching the sky, waiting for the silence that portended death. The V2 attacks that started in September of that year and continued at intervals till March 1945 were even more unnerving. The V2s were precursors of the rocket that went to the moon. They travelled higher than planes could fly and faster than sound – they took only four minutes from being launched to reaching their target. There was no warning, no action you or any defence force could take since they were silent and unseen, suddenly dropping death. A V2, landing on Woolworth's in Lewisham, just down the hill from us one

November lunch hour killed 160 shoppers. The only rational attitude to the danger was the fatalistic Cockney acceptance, 'If your number is on it, you've had it.'

I did not discuss my fears with anyone and my mother calmly went to work as usual, but Spikes and his school were evacuated. I longed for a respite from London, and there was no reason why I should continue at school. Having won my scholarship I did not need to take 'highers' (A levels) in the summer term, so I joined Spikes' school at Corton, on the coast near Lowestoft. They were staying in a pre-war holiday camp, a kind of downmarket Butlins, made up of small chalets. It had been taken over by the army at the beginning of the war, but now that the danger of invasion was past it had been handed over to the education authorities. The beach, however, was still mined. Since I had left school I was in an intermediate social position there, neither staff nor pupil, but I was lucky enough to become friendly with one of the younger women teachers, who taught me to ride her bicycle. I knew that this was an almost essential skill for Oxford students, so though I repeatedly fell off and was covered with grazes I eventually learned to stay on.

I also learned that there was a big social class difference in the sexual maturity (not a term I knew then) of young people. Almost on the first day I was approached by David, a boy who was about to leave Spikes' school, and was like me going on to study medicine. After a few walks and a visit to the local cinema he seemed to assume that we would move on to passionate kissing. A sixth form party, from which I fled, involved turning out the lights for what was then called 'heavy petting.' Though David was cheerful and intelligent he alarmed me. I found the notion of casual sex without emotional attachment very unappealing. I finally extricated myself by showing him one of Anthony's love letters.

In the summer holidays I spent a week at Glatting with Anthony and one of his school friends, and on two separate occasions a week with the Ryles in Oxford. They had a flat in Kybald Street, behind University College, just off the High Street. We were woken every morning by the bells of the many neighbouring churches. Martin and Anthony were both there and I think the three of us were always together, probably Mrs. Ryle didn't want Anthony and I to be alone together. Both brothers looked very elegant as one or the other punted us down the Cherwell. They taught me how to play Pooh sticks and we went to the cinema. Martin seemed much more relaxed and even cheerful, probably because D Day, in which his work played a crucial role, had been successfully accomplished. It was, however, very clear that their mother did not approve of me, with my make-up, permanent wave and high heels. I'm sure she was the only person ever to consider me frivolous.

I felt very lucky that I was coming back in the autumn to Oxford. I knew Cambridge from visiting my brother, and most people probably regard it as a more beautiful town with its 'Backs' and matchless Kings College and Trinity College and its compact university district. But Oxford as it was in 1944, with no tourists, little traffic, much more dominated by the university than it is now and without the present ugly pedestrianised town centre, seemed to me to have the greater charm The rest of the summer I earned a little money doing clerical work in Marx House in Clerkenwell Green. This was a Marxist educational centre and memorial library, set up in 1933 with the support of Lawrence and Wishart, the communist publishers. No classes were going on, and I had time to read what still seemed the impenetrable, but I assumed essential, works of Marx and Lenin.

At the end of August Tom Elkins came to see me in Blackheath. We had been very good friends, and I think he was a little in love with me, but he knew about my relationship with Anthony. We used to talk about politics and Inter Schools Committee people and business, and I gave him advice about his relations with girls. He was depressed since although, like me, he had a university place for the next term, he had to delay this and was due to enrol as a soldier in a few days time. Tom was very sensitive, introverted, and lacking in confidence and he was fearful, not of being killed, but of the army life that lay ahead. He had volunteered to work in the coal mines, which was then an alternative, but was rejected as not being sufficiently strong. Two years later, still in the army as part of the occupation force in Germany, he was not reconciled to it. I quote from a letter he wrote after meeting me when he was home on leave because it gives an idea of the difficulty that someone as introverted and sensitive as Tom had with army life. It also suggests why some soldiers were glad to return to their units – it was too painful to experience civilian life again, knowing it was for such a short period.

'I have allowed myself to emerge for once from that convenient private cell of mine, and my heart is aching because I have permitted myself to see, for once, that I do not belong here any more. It is all right while I am alone in London, I can play a game of make believe up and down the streets, in the bookshops, galleries, theatres; I can pretend that I am merely on an afternoon out, and that tomorrow I shall be going in to a lecture, talking about work over coffee. But when I meet someone who really matters to me, one of the few people for whom I still exist, it is all finished. Then I know that I shall never be happy till I am doing the work I want. I want to belong. I want to slip through the crowd, knowing some of them, and knowing that some of them know me. I go to meet you and find that there is still sympathy, fineness, understanding, left – and I wish I were back in Germany. I can deal with any emergency there, but I cannot deal with this.'

He went on to say of his leaving me, just before he enrolled, 'It was a wet day, and you had a new red coat. I felt then as the train left, and you were walking back up the platform, that I had said goodbye to all my life, all my friends, all my aspirations. Suffice to say that you have this amazing power of moving me to think of what I have lost, of standing for everything worth while.'

Re-reading this recently, I felt surprised and humbled to have aroused these thoughts. After Tom was finally released from the army he went to the university as he had passionately wished to do, and later became Professor of Geography at Sussex University. We lost touch long ago, and I recently heard that he had died.

Chapter 9

Oxford: Student life and loves 1944-48

When I went up to Oxford in October 1944 the war was moving away from the home front. Some V1 and V2 attacks on London continued until the following March but the black-out was no longer enforced, street lighting reappeared and the Home Guard had been disbanded. However, stringent food and clothes rationing continued. In Europe the Red army was advancing westward, the British and U.S. armies eastward. Everyone longed for the war to end and I longed to start at the university.

I was one of a very small and fortunate minority. Today over a third of eighteen year olds enter university and more than half of these are women. But until the early 1950s only a tiny proportion, three per cent, of eighteen to twenty-one year olds, became full-time university students. Most of these were men. At Oxford only sixteen per cent of undergraduates were women. I don't remember ever thinking about this gender disparity except when faced with the large, and I thought obnoxious, majority of men in the medical school. Perhaps this was partly because I was used to it – boys had predominated in the C.E.W.C. conferences and on the Inter Schools Committee. And among the Oxford student communists, with whom I mainly mixed, a larger proportion, about a third, were women, including some very assertive leaders.

Financially I was in a much better position than students are today. I had three separate student grants, none of which are given nowadays: an entrance scholarship from Somerville, a school leaving exhibition from St.Paul's, then awarded each year to the girls going up to the university who were considered the highest achievers, and a 'topping up' grant from the London education authority. All of this amounted to quite enough money to pay my fees and college maintenance with a reasonable amount over for books, fares, etc. It would not have stretched to the expense of frequent drinking or foreign travel but none of my student friends could run to that kind of expenditure, and nobody I knew left the university in debt. Stringent clothes rationing meant that clothes were not much of an expense. It never occurred to me or anyone I knew to get a job during term time, which would not, I think, have been allowed though it's possible that some students worked during the long summer vacations. At that time very few Oxford students came from state schools, but although some came from definitely wealthy families most of my friends did not. We just accepted that as students we didn't have much money. I was delighted that at last my mother didn't have to spend her so hard-earned money on me, though of course I usually stayed with her during the vacations.

Going to the university was a great liberation for girls of my generation. We were no longer under the close supervision of our parents or teachers, and arts students could choose how to organise their day. At Oxford our time was more structured than in many universities since everyone had to attend one or sometimes two tutorials a week, and write essays for them. This meant that it was difficult to fall seriously behind with your work. Attendance at lectures was optional for arts students but science and medical students had much less freedom. They were expected to attend lectures and also laboratory sessions, which took up most of each day. There was no requirement on students to eat in college – if you could afford to you could always eat elsewhere. In some colleges you were expected to attend chapel, but not at Somerville. When the college was founded in 1879 its regulations stated that students should not be subject to religious tests or obligations. We had to return to college by 11.15p.m. though some brave spirits, more athletic than I, climbed in over the walls after this time. The women's colleges still had a strict rule about male visitors, who were only allowed between 2–7p.m. One or two students were rumoured to keep men in their rooms overnight but it was difficult to see how they smuggled them out in the morning.

All new students had a room in college but we had to stay in approved lodgings near the college in either our second or third year. Our rooms were cleaned by 'scouts,' who were only cleaners, not as in the men's colleges personal servants who brought meals etc. to their rooms. The accommodation was very lacking in amenities compared with most universities today. I recently revisited Somerville, and found that there are now showers, washing machines and small, shared kitchens, but the hygienic arrangements have not improved. There are still no washing facilities in the students' rooms, and often the lavatories are still at one end of the corridor, with all the bathrooms and wash basins at the other end. In my time there were no cooking facilities for students other than kettles in a tiny maids' service room, though we could make toast over our small electric or gas fires, the only form of heating. However, strangely for wartime, there was usually hot water and for the first time in my life I had daily baths. We were always cold in the winter, but that was also the case in most people's homes. Later we experienced real discomfort. January 1947 was the coldest month in England for fifty years, when water froze in many people's pipes. Coal was strictly rationed, the gas pressure was very low and electricity was cut off for long spells. The government asked people not to use electric fires in the mornings. We students were told that four people should share a one bar fire and we would huddle round it, wearing our coats, trying to work.

But I arrived at Oxford with no very high expectations of comfort and happily set about arranging my books and hanging a picture I had bought, a reproduction of a painting of a vase of irises. Neither I nor any of my friends knew much about art, which had been totally neglected at my school, except in the form of painting classes in the lower years. I had never been to an art gallery or exhibition. I did buy postcards of famous paintings, and I had bought this print because it was of flowers, my lifelong passion.

I had assumed, without actually remembering, that I had no problems settling into this new environment, until I found a letter from Anthony written to me during my first week at Somerville, sympathising with my gloom. Like most students I initially complained of feeling friendless although I was much luckier than most. Several other girls from St. Paul's started at Somerville with me, including Pat Hutchinson, my Tory friend. But Elizabeth Zaiman and Jean Ginsburg, my closest friends, who were also intending to read medicine had stayed at school for a third year in the sixth form. I soon discovered that there were a number of 'sets' amongst the students at Somerville which cut across disciplines – on the whole, people mixed almost entirely with students in their set. For example, there were 'swats' who seemed to do little but study, socialites whose main interest was in dances and parties, others whose main interest was in sport, or in one of the political clubs.

The most notable figure in the Somerville Conservative group was Margaret Roberts (Thatcher) who was studying chemistry in the year above me. I mainly remember her as an energetic recruiter for the Conservative club, always bustling about organising people, leaping up and down during meal times. It was said of her at the time that her main ambition was to marry a rich man and/or an aristocrat and no one I knew, including my friend Pauline Cowan, who shared digs with her one year, had any inkling of the role she would play in history. A friend who had been at grammar school with her said she was known there as 'What's your percentage Margaret'. Apparently each girl was given an overall percentage for their school work at the end of term, and Margaret would rush around asking all the other girls what their percentage was, intent on telling them how well she had done, and anxious that no one should have done better.

In my first week I wrote to Anthony that undergraduates were 'self-centred, unconscious of privilege, irresponsible'. But I very soon began to make friends in the Oxford student Communist Party with people who were definitely socially conscious and aware of their privilege. I had never committed myself before this time to joining the party or felt any desire to join the Young Communist League but now the Communist Party became a major part of my life. Indeed, having joined there was little choice about this – a party member was expected to spend a large part of their time, second only to their university studies, which were always given priority, on 'party work'. This might involve taking a specific responsibility – at some point I was Membership Organiser – but all members were supposed to undertake general duties such as leafleting and attending 'education classes', where the works of Marx and Lenin were studied. The leading members were very able people, well organised and immensely knowledgeable about these sacred texts. I quickly became particularly friendly with one of them, Martin Milligan, who was my best friend, but not a boyfriend, during my first three years at Oxford.

Martin was one of the cleverest and most eloquent people I have ever known. He talked brilliantly, if rather too much. He had been blind since the age of eighteen months but was astonishingly independent, refusing to use a stick, making his way confidently round Oxford with his hands in his pockets. He was guided in part by echolocation – he usually whistled as he walked to increase the echoes. He could also 'hear' potential obstacles such as lampposts, as atmosphere-thickening occupants of space, probably because they absorb sound waves. And he was aware of objects at head height because they slightly affected the air currents reaching his face. He was always cheerful and took a matter of fact attitude to his blindness. He was a Glaswegian, three years older than me, who had already taken a first in Psychology and German in Edinburgh and was now studying PPE (philosophy, politics, and economics) on a scholarship at Balliol. A few of the books he needed were available in Braille but mostly he relied on a posse of volunteer women students who took it in turn to read to him in the afternoons while he made notes in shorthand on a Braille machine. His speeds in shorthand and typing were professional. Although he was able to read far fewer books than sighted students he more than compensated for this by remembering and thinking more effectively about those that he did read.

Martin was a fanatical communist, austere in the sense that he didn't smoke or drink, had no interest in money or possessions and didn't mind what he ate. Personally he was warm and friendly although some of his tutors considered him arrogant and aggressive, as perhaps he was when they attacked his Marxist beliefs. Studying and political activity absorbed most of his time but early in my first term he took me round the colleges, confidently pointing out the architectural features of each. I did not know then that he was also a talented pianist. Later he got a starred first class degree and should have been set for a brilliant academic career. But he was not even interviewed for any of the university posts he applied for – as the Balliol archives show, his references all stated that he was a fervent Marxist and communist. Hobsbawm wrote in his autobiography that no known communists were appointed to university posts during the cold war, from 1948-58, and that was the case with Martin. He was finally appointed to a lectureship in philosophy in 1959 in Leeds, where he later became head of department and dean of the faculty of arts. Before then, at times despairing, he supported himself by working as a shorthand typist and doing some adult education lecturing, whilst translating early Marxist manuscripts. Soon after he left Oxford I organised a collection amongst his many friends to pay for a guide dog for him.

Although he always seemed tremendously confident, whistling his way around Oxford, refusing to use a stick, I thought that this imposed a strain on him and that a guide dog would be a blessing.

Many years later, after he had finally left the Communist Party in the 1970s, Martin threw his energy into campaigning for the greater social integration of blind people, whose handicap he argued is grossly exaggerated by the sighted. (By this time he had given up having a guide dog.) After his death in 1993 the philosopher Bryan Magee published a fascinating correspondence between them, 'Sight Unseen', in which Martin describes and analyses what vision and its absence mean to blind people, and argues with Bryan about the difference that sight or its absence makes to our understanding of the world.

I had some serious problems during my first year at Oxford. I soon became very disaffected with the medical course. This could really have been predicted – after all, I had been bored by the sciences I studied in the sixth form. But becoming a doctor had been my career aim since I was about 11, inspired by books, such as *Microbe Hunters* by Paul de Kruif, about great microbiologists and pioneering doctors. The fantasy of healing people was so strong I had not taken into account that in reality I found the sixth form science lessons boring and had been horrified by my first experience of watching an operation. This was before I went up to Oxford, when a rather sadistic surgeon my mother knew, who disapproved of women doctors, suggested that I should spend a day watching him work. I'm sure he saved up his most alarming looking operations for that day and I had to do much gritting of teeth to sit through the oceans of blood involved in the hysterectomies. However at the time I reassured myself that I would not have to be a surgeon.

During the first two years of medicine at Oxford we studied for an initial degree in anatomy, organic chemistry and physiology, then taught as basic sciences, almost entirely without reference to patients and their diseases. At the end of that period we moved to a hospital. I found the chemistry uninteresting, but the real stumbling block was the practical work in both anatomy and physiology. The physiology lab work involved killing and experimenting with frogs, in what seemed to amount to torture, which I found almost impossible to do. Anatomy involved dissecting human corpses laid out on tables in the dissecting room. We worked in pairs, each pair being given one part of 'their' corpse to dissect at a time – a leg, an arm, the head and neck, the thorax or the abdomen. The terrible sight of these gradually dismembered corpses and the disgusting smell of the fat layers preserved in formalin permeated our hands, overalls, and textbooks, and remained in my mind for some years.

I never overcame my revulsion to cutting a person up, which I think disturbed to a varying extent all the students, if only for a while. They dealt with this in different ways, the men usually by joking and hurling body parts at each other. They were almost all, I thought, ostentatiously upper class, boastful, rowdy and immature – they seemed like a strange and undesirable species, very different from my brother's friends and the boys I had met through the Inter Schools Committee. At that time there were very few women medical students, in my year perhaps six. I only remember two, both of whom coped much better with the situation than I did. Ruth Lister was the other medical student from Somerville. She had been in my class at St. Paul's, though not a particular friend. She was stout and comfortable-looking, with pink cheeks and a thick blonde plait, always cheerful, hardworking, placid and determined. She just ignored the men's antics and got on with what had to be done. The other woman was in her early twenties, recently widowed, her husband had been a pilot. She was vivacious and fashionably dressed, much more self-assured than other students, with very different, adult preoccupations. She had a baby whom her parents were looking after and her mind was full of practical problems, including her need to qualify, repay her loans and maintain her child. As a war widow everyone, including the obnoxious male students, respected her but in any case she regarded them rather indulgently, as tiresome younger brothers.

Medical students no longer have to dissect dead bodies. This is done by their lecturers, and the dissection is displayed to them. They also no longer have to learn anatomy in the extraordinary detail that was formerly the case. My non-verbal memory turned out to be mediocre. Anatomy involves three dimensional spatial learning – everything had to be visualised and remembered in relation to the layers of structures above, below and to each side of it. Once a week the lecturer, Alice Carleton, called students together, a group at a time, and fired questions about the anatomy we should have learnt during the week's dissection. She was a sharp-tongued woman who seemed to delight in holding up to ridicule anyone who gave a wrong answer. But whilst she could be indulgent to the men's errors she gave the women a particularly hard time, gleefully humiliating us in front of the group. I dreaded these occasions – today, I think she would be reported to the university for bullying. Histology, a branch of anatomy, held no terrors of this kind. It involved peering down a microscope attempting to identify the cells displayed, most of which looked very similar to me, and attending slide shows of them in afternoon lectures. These occupied long stretches of time in a darkened hall, during which I struggled to keep my eyes open. I was used to finding learning easy and being top of the class, now I found some of the course quite difficult and I thought my achievements were distinctly average.

For physiology and chemistry we had the same tutorial system as arts students. That is, in each subject you had a tutor, usually on the staff of your college, for whom you wrote a weekly essay, which you read aloud and discussed at the weekly hour-long tutorial. Traditionally, this is a one-to-one encounter, but the women's colleges were less wealthy than the men's, and two students usually shared a tutorial, unless your tutor was from one of the men's colleges. One of your college tutors was also your 'moral tutor' who in theory had an overall care for your welfare and progress. The tutorial system is the pride of Oxford and Cambridge and one of the main reasons that they are so expensive to run but I don't think the cost can be justified. The justification is said to be that the system allows the tutor to draw out knowledge from each student rather than spoon it in, and that it requires students to adopt an intellectual position and defend it against the tutor's criticisms in a one-to-one encounter. But I suspect that this Socratic encounter may be quite rare. In my experience many tutors lacked Socratic skills or did not bother to exercise them or were impatient with students, some of whom found tutorials a terrifying experience. In a larger group, of, say five or six students, discussion might well be livelier and such tutorials could be supplemented with much larger seminars and lectures. Equally important, the tutorial system is very wasteful of the time of gifted researchers who are often not particularly good at, or interested in, teaching undergraduates.

An excellent example was my moral tutor and chemistry tutor, Dorothy Hodgkin. As a fellow of Somerville she was responsible for the teaching of chemistry in the college and must have had to spend a sizeable proportion of her time eating meals at the high table (a requirement for fellows) attending committees and supervising students. She was at that time doing research on the structure of penicillin for which, with her research on the structure of vitamin B12, she was later awarded a Nobel prize. She was thirty-four, married to an historian, Thomas Hodgkin, and had three young children. Thomas was a member of the Communist Party and Dorothy was a sympathiser and later very active in the international peace movement. She was a gentle, kind, diffident woman, but despite her genius she was not gifted at making chemistry interesting or clear to beginners, and indeed, seemed hardly to know what to do during tutorials. There would be long stretches of silence while we waited for her to say something. As a moral tutor she seemed so otherworldly and abstracted that it was impossible to imagine anyone confiding their problems in her. Even then I knew that she was doing very important research and it seemed to me absurd that her time should be wasted on undergraduates.

My career as a medical student was not made easier by the problems that developed in my relationship with Anthony. During my first term he was still at boarding school writing me beautiful and eloquent love letters. He was supposed to remain at school another year, but there were anxieties that he might be developing tuberculosis. His father decided, to our delight, that he would prefer him to start as soon as possible at Oxford, where he could keep an eye on his health. So after Christmas Anthony started at University College as a medical student and in the small medical school we were constantly, though publicly, together, as we were in the student Communist Party. We were very much in love and planned to get married when we moved to a hospital. His parents, who lived a stone's throw from his rooms, became alarmed. During the summer term they sent for me and told me that our relationship was 'unhealthy' and much too intense. Together with our political activities it was preventing us both (though it was undoubtedly their son they were thinking about) from taking part in 'healthier' activities (though Anthony was, in fact, playing rugby for his college and sailing) and making other friends. I suspect now that they feared I might get pregnant, though in fact Anthony had assimilated their prohibition on premarital sex.

We were not exceptional in our chastity. When I discussed this issue recently with Pamela Mason, my brother's first girlfriend, subsequently a psychiatrist, she said that none of the boyfriends she had in her teens had even kissed her and she thought that amongst middle class young people at that time any sexual activity during the teenage years was very unusual. This may have been in part because of the girls' fear of pregnancy. Contraception was difficult to obtain unless you were married – clinics only accepted married women. Abortion was illegal and generally considered too shocking to even talk about. A novel by the Bohemian, leftist, Rosamund Lehman, published in 1936, depicts the unmarried heroine becoming pregnant and having an abortion without explicitly naming either event in the text. A fellow student told me under oath of secrecy that during the vacation she had had an abortion, illegally, from a doctor. She had been distraught, on her own trying in great secrecy to find a doctor who would do it and someone who would lend her the large sum of money required, and terrified by the procedure itself.

The Ryles decreed that contact between Anthony and myself must be reduced to a minimum during the next year with no contact at all between us during the vacations, and Professor Ryle wrote to my mother to enlist her support for this decision. It is difficult to imagine students' parents intervening in their lives in this way today and to be fair to my mother she did not do so. If we had wanted to get married she would have been alarmed, but boyfriends did not worry her. I think she would have been baffled by the notion of an unhealthy relationship, especially since she had taken a liking to Anthony when he spent a weekend with us in Blackheath. I don't know how she answered their letter, which she never mentioned to me and I only found in her papers after her death. But the Ryle parents kept up a relentless pressure and my relationship with Anthony became very fraught. He was the beloved youngest son, very close to both his parents, and he had never opposed their wishes or rebelled against them in any way. I felt that he was not putting up an adequate opposition to his parents and was too prepared to compromise. I thought he was too young and too totally dependent on them to fight them. We were both so continually emotionally disturbed that I found life intolerable and decided to end our relationship. We did not talk the crisis through properly and I learned many years later that Anthony did not even know that his parents had sent for me and written to my mother, and he had not understood why I was rejecting him. He concluded I had rejected him for another man, which was far from the truth.

I felt I had been very cruel to him and I felt guilty and distressed. In some sense the episode left a lifelong mark on us both. My girlfriends thought I was crazy to abandon the best looking man in Oxford but I never thought of him in that way. We were both too young and too emotionally immature to cope with the situation and I ran away from it. Anthony gave up attending Communist Party meetings though he continued to be a party member and a year later he moved to University College Hospital in London. We met once, very briefly, a few years later, or so he remembers – I had forgotten – when I consulted him about my mother's illness, and then not again for nearly sixty years. After qualifying Anthony did not go to India or Africa but worked as a G.P. in Kentish Town, north London. Later, be became a psychotherapist and developed a new form of time limited therapy he called Cognitive Analytic Therapy (CAT), which now has over 800 practitioners.

The separation decreed by Anthony's parents had tipped the scales for me. I now felt I must give up medicine – it would be impossibly difficult and painful for us to meet in the labs each day. For me, the impetus to becoming a doctor had always been the belief that it would be the best way of 'doing good' but by this time I did realise that one could contribute to society in other ways. Many of my friends, including Martin Milligan, were studying Philosophy, Politics and Economics (PPE) and these sounded excitingly new studies, with the added bonus of giving one a great deal more freedom than the all day grind of the medical course. However, in order to change courses there were formidable obstacles to overcome. I had to persuade Somerville to allow me to make the change and keep my scholarship, which had been in science. Moreover I had to persuade St.Paul's and the London education authority to do the same. Finally, I had to persuade my mother that this was the right decision for me to make. This proved to be the hardest part. The college authorities decided that because I had done very well in the 'general' scholarship paper my scholarship could be transferred to PPE, provided that I start again at the beginning and the other funding bodies accepted their recommendation.

My mother, however, was deeply upset. She had worked extremely hard for years to give Michael and myself an education that would allow us to have successful professional careers. She was sceptical about whether PPE would lead to a career which would be as socially important, well paid, and secure as medicine, and she thought I was throwing away the opportunity for inadequate reasons. A measure of her distress is that she wrote to Giles and accused him of having been a bad influence on me, although I hadn't been in touch with him for a while and certainly hadn't discussed the issue with him. I didn't explain to her that my decision had been influenced by my changed relationship with Anthony since I never confided in her about my relationships. She couldn't understand why I did not make up my mind to put up with another year of the course, after which I would be in a hospital and everything would be different. She was right, and I was reacting quite irrationally, desperate to remove myself from a situation that was distressing for so many reasons. I would not give way or convincingly refute her arguments and this caused the first breach we had ever had in our relationship. She remained very angry with me, but I have never regretted my decision. As a research psychologist I made some contribution to knowledge and to society in an interesting, reasonably well-paid and secure job. But this, because of her early death, she was never to know.

Before these emotional crises developed the war in Europe had ended. On May 8th, VE day, a two days' national holiday was declared. Crowds poured into the streets in Oxford, church bells rang out, there was dancing in the streets round Carfax and we all felt ecstatically happy, unaware, though older people probably had forebodings, of the formidable problems that lay ahead for the country and the world. On May 23rd Churchill announced that polling for a general election would take place on July 5th. Whilst most of the press assumed that Churchill, the war hero, would be swept back to power, in the Communist Party we were convinced, as were most people on the left, that the war had radicalised people. Rationing, for example, had been accepted by most people just because it was based on the principle of fair shares for all – entirely at variance with the principle underlying pre-war society. Discussions in the forces through ABCA, (the Army Bureau of Current Affairs) and throughout the public media had encouraged the idea that post-war society would be more equitable than before, and there was a widespread feeling that Churchill was not the man to make these social changes. Most of the student Communist Party branch remained in Oxford after term ended to help in the campaign of Jack Dunman, the nearest communist candidate, in North Berkshire.

Enthused by local party officials we worked long hours each day, often sleeping on the floor of the offices we were using, expecting, if not a victory, at least a very large vote for our candidate. We had dispersed by the time the results were announced three weeks later – the delay was due to the collection of the overseas forces' votes. I was excited by the Labour victory, but shattered by the fact that our candidate had only achieved a few hundred votes. I suspected that the party officials, who had kept assuring us that if we all worked just a bit harder our candidate would be elected, had knowingly deceived us and this was the first small crack in my allegiance to them.

I had no money for holidays and travel abroad was as yet impossible, so I spent the long summer vacation staying with friends, but mostly at home in Blackheath. After the election campaign I hitchhiked up to Scotland with Martin Milligan to stay with his family. They lived in Strathaven, near Glasgow, above their small sweet and tobacco shop. His parents seemed ordinary enough, kindly people, politically conservative and also religious, but they had produced two exceptionally able left-wing sons. Their younger son, Jimmy, who was then seventeen, was like Martin high spirited, eloquent and a communist. Later he too became an academic, an urban planner, and campaigned for a Scottish parliament. I understood how Martin had become so independent when I saw the matter of fact way in which his brother and parents behaved to him. When he lost his sight at eighteen months his parents determined not to be over protective and to treat him as far as possible as though he were sighted. They sent him to pioneering primary and secondary schools in Glasgow which provided integrated education for blind and sighted children, with the result that he grew up accustomed to coping on his own in a fairly rough sighted world.

I left them to stay for some days in Edinburgh with Pauline Cowan, a fellow student at Somerville and Communist Party member, later a Professor of Biochemistry at Sheffield University. Accompanied by a boy of fifteen, a friend of her parents, we set out to hitchhike up the west coast of Scotland staying at youth hostels. These were situated in beautiful areas of the Highlands and in the summer of 1945 had hardly any visitors. A few were unstaffed – we had to fetch the key from someone in the local village. As we went north lifts became increasingly scarce. Once we walked all day without seeing a car or lorry but we were picked up shortly before it became dark.

I was back in London for VJ day, marking the end of the war with Japan on August 15th. It was a week after atom bombs had been dropped on Hiroshima and Nagasaki and the enormity of these events, although not yet assimilated, cast a shadow for some over the celebrations. As on VE day there was a two-day public holiday and excited crowds surged through the streets. There was a feeling of huge relief that at last the war was completely over but people seemed increasingly aware of the problems ahead. Roland Brown, who had been Michael's best friend in Cambridge, and continued to be so all their lives, was on leave in London on VJ day, and, not finding any of his friends phoned me in Blackheath and suggested we celebrate together. We milled around with the thousands in Trafalgar Square and spent the evening dancing in a club in Villiers Street, off the Strand. Later, Roland became an international lawyer and the first Attorney General in the newly independent Tanzania, where he remained until a Tanzanian was able to take over his post. I spent the rest of the vacation doing some preliminary reading for my new course.

The PPE degree was established in 1920 as more relevant in modern times than classics (Greats) for those intending to enter the higher reaches of the civil service or politics. Famous politicians who have taken PPE include Edward Heath, Harold Wilson, Imran Khan, William Hague, David Cameron, Ed Balls, Peter Mandelson, David Miliband and Aug San Suu Kyi. The course has since been changed, but in my time there were two philosophy papers, Descartes to Kant, and Ethics; two economics papers, on theory and institutions; and two politics papers, political theory and the political history of the nineteenth and twentieth century up to 1914 (no post 1914 history was then taught at Oxford). As I had expected, I very much enjoyed the new subjects which, unlike medicine, involved thinking about ideas and forming your own judgements. But once term started I realised that having to write two essays a week for tutorials in quite different subjects, say philosophy and economics, was going to be very hard work.

I was lucky enough to have tutors who were all distinguished, in some cases, famous, academics. My economics and also my 'moral' tutor, Margaret Hall, was very unlike most women academics of that period. Smartly dressed, with two young daughters, she spent part of the week in London on a succession of government committees. Her husband, Robert Hall, became the senior economic advisor to the first Labour government and her own special interest, in the distributive sector of the economy, involved a very matter of fact understanding of economics and its role in society. My other tutors were more traditional academics. As teachers, they tended to fall into two categories – those who definitely set out to teach, but expected their students to grasp very difficult concepts at once, not understanding that in tackling new and difficult ideas most students need to progress in smaller steps and at a slower pace than the tutors themselves thought necessary, and those who regarded tutorials as almost social occasions, for civilised conversation.

Phillipa Foot, the Somerville philosophy tutor, was a striking example of the former category. I was surprised to discover later that she was only six years older than me, she seemed much older because she was so immensely learned. At the time she was already developing a new theory of ethics. Her patience with ignorant students was limited, and her exposition of Kant, on whom I did a special paper, was almost unintelligible. Secondary accounts were, properly, not used or tolerated in PPE, you were expected to show that you had grappled with and understood the original texts. Luckily Martin Milligan was able to give me much clearer explanations of the philosophical positions we had to understand and in my final year I asked to be transferred to a more intelligible tutor. This was George Paul, who had been a pupil of Wittgenstein, and whose wife was a communist.

Christopher Hill, the Marxist historian, was my tutor in political history and like my other male tutors I had him to myself. He was already famous for his interpretation of the English civil war as a class revolution, in which the developing forces of capitalism threw off the last vestiges of feudal rule, making the freer development of capitalism possible. At the time I knew him he was a very agreeable, relaxed man, with a sardonic wit, who was so respected and liked by the other Balliol dons that despite being a communist he was later elected Master of Balliol. Christopher always arranged my tutorials for 12 noon. I would read my essay aloud, then he would get out the sherry and we would spend the rest of the time drinking and chatting about the subject of the essay and Oxford affairs. He was a charming and learned man, we became friends and he came to my wedding, but I don't think I was committed enough to history to make the most of the opportunity to learn from him.

Sammy Finer was my tutor in political theory. Very unlike Christopher Hill, whose father was a prosperous English solicitor and pious Methodist, Sammy's parents were Jewish immigrants from Romania who ran a greengrocer's stall in Chapel Street, Islington. He was a short man, neat, dapper, confident and charming, a passionate liberal democrat and anti-communist. Unlike Christopher who aimed to make his students talk, Sammy's love of talking usually extended the tutorial to two hours, with the sherry appearing during the second hour. He moved easily and authoritatively between history, politics and sociology. His efforts to disengage himself from his family of origin led him to present himself as a man of exquisite sensibility. Once he told me that he always pulled the blinds down when he passed through Switzerland in a train – the scenery was so vulgar. Later he invited me to his wedding to a wealthy ex-Somerville student. It was a splendid occasion, flowing with champagne, which I had never drunk before. I recently realised that all my tutors were then in their early to mid thirties – at the time I thought of them as middle-aged.

I attended very few lectures at Oxford. I generally find lectures unrewarding since having a strongly visual memory and an ability to read very quickly I can learn better from books. But good lecturers can arouse your interest and even excite you and there have always been a few academics whose dramatic talents make their lectures a popular entertainment. There were two such in my time at Oxford whose lectures I looked forward to, A.J.P. Taylor, the socialist historian and populariser, who is said to have invented the term 'the establishment' to describe his enemies, and my tutor Sammy Finer. Unlike the great majority of their fellow academics whose scholarship lay in detailed knowledge of limited periods of time or particular theories, both men ranged over great swathes of history. This was disapproved of by most Oxford academics, who may also have been envious of their gift for popularisation and their bravura, completely unscripted, public performances. Their lectures drew so many students that they were arranged early in the morning, and even then the lecture halls were seriously overcrowded.

Christopher Hill was at the other extreme of lecturing ability. He was impeded by a serious stammer, very much worse in public than private settings. This must have been a remnant of his earlier extreme social anxiety. When he had been interviewed for a scholarship, aged only sixteen, he was so nervous that he was unable to answer any questions and fled to his room. Because his written papers had been so brilliant two dons pursued him there and eventually coaxed the interesting answers from him that they expected. When I knew him he was at ease in most social situations, but his lectures were a torment to sit through. Initially as a famous historian he attracted a large audience but most students rapidly stopped coming. Since he was my tutor and anyway a very nice man I felt I must support him, and each term I was one of the few students who continued to attend.

Usually I met my communist friends – I hardly mixed with anyone not in the party – for coffee mid-morning in a workers' café in the central covered market. After another period of lectures or working in a library we would often reassemble for lunch in a British restaurant. The food and coffee we consumed must have been terrible, but at that stage in my life I had none of the discriminations about food and drink that I later developed, and which would in any case have made survival difficult in post war Britain, where even greater austerity than during the war had set in. Less than a fortnight after VJ day the U.S.A. suddenly ended Lend-Lease, the financial support that had funded us through the war and began to demand repayment. This meant that rations were further cut and bread was rationed for the first time. Bananas did begin to reappear after six years absence, but only for children. We students used to cycle along the Banbury Road once a week, first thing in the morning, to queue outside a cake factory where damaged, supposedly unmarketable cakes were sold cheaply.

In the afternoons if not working I might attend a small group to study Marxist texts or someone might punt me along the river or I might cycle along the river or into the country with John Hughes. He was a cheerful kind-hearted friend, not a boyfriend, the same age as me, like me a member of the Communist Party and studying PPE. John's father was a milkman and John presented himself as someone frank and down to earth, with no Oxford or public school airs or refinements. Later he became a trade union historian and principal of Ruskin College, which, whilst not part of the university, had been set up to give workers with no qualifications the opportunity to study in an Oxford environment. In the evenings I would go to meetings, occasionally to the cinema or to one of the socials at Ruskin College much patronised by left-wing undergraduates. There I met for the first time African students, mostly from wealthy families. Or I would work furiously on an essay which had to be ready the next day. Because of the large amount of reading I had to do for my two weekly essays, whilst the rest of my time was crammed with social activities, during the terms I read fewer novels than at any period of my life, almost none, in fact, and no poetry at all.

That year, from the autumn of 1945, the student Communist Party branch was swollen by the arrival of returning ex-servicemen, some married with children. Their wives struck a new note in our social life. They were not usually graduates and had no more money than us, but by their greater skill in presenting themselves they made us women students look dowdy. Most of the communist ex-servicemen had been army officers, some had been majors and colonels. They seemed immensely grown up, intent on studying, with little taste for student life but with strong political convictions. It may be difficult for a younger generation to understand the attraction that the Communist Party held for many students, including battle hardened ex-servicemen. To do so, you must imagine yourself living in the very different world of our childhood and youth. Britain in the thirties was a society where capitalism seemed to have failed with disastrous consequences for the workers, many of whom were out of work for years. It was a society where there were hunger marches, mostly organised by the communist led National Unemployment Workers Movement, many people lived in slums, many were unable to afford adequate health care and infant mortality was high. It seemed intolerable that post-war society should revert to these conditions.

The Labour Party promised reform, but their periods in office had so far brought little change. In the thirties they had not been involved in the hunger marches or in mobilising opposition to the rise of fascism in the East End, Labour leaders had for long advocated non-intervention in the Spanish civil war and had offered no support to the young British men joining the International Brigade. From its inception the Labour Party's domestic programme had been cautious. The 1945 Labour Manifesto stated that their ultimate aim was to establish a Socialist Commonwealth (the word 'socialism' was not dropped until 1992) but that this could not be done overnight and they intended to start by nationalising basic industries. For the idealistic young more urgent and drastic action was wanted. We looked for inspiration to the Soviet Union where a revolution seemed to have established an egalitarian workers' state and had replaced a society driven by the profit motive by one with centralised planning, to provide for the needs of all. We had no inkling that this system was to fail completely, or that in the West a reinvigorated capitalism would enormously increase productivity and the general standard of living and reduce unemployment so that although pockets of great poverty remained, many British working-class people could expect to buy cars and have holidays in Spain. At the same time the British Labour government, by its introduction of the National Health Service, universal benefits, better schools and slum clearance greatly improved the security and quality of life of working-class people.

But that was for the future. What we saw in the forties was that during the Spanish civil war only the Soviet Union had supplied arms to the Republicans. Communists from many countries had fought and died in Spain and they were known to have been in the forefront of the resistance movements in every country during the Second World War. The heroism of Soviet civilians and forces in defence of their country won them widespread admiration in Britain. As a result of all these factors many people who were inclined to the left became members or sympathisers of the Communist Party. Student communists at that time, in my experience, were very idealistic, intelligent and dedicated people. Most of them later won distinction in their professions. We had powerful aspirations for a better society and to this end were prepared to study Marxist texts and accept the discipline of 'following the party line'. This 'line' was based on an apparently rational Marxist analysis of the situation, and a conviction that a small, tightly disciplined, dedicated political group had been shown by Lenin and others to be the most effective agent of change. In return for this dedication we experienced not only the satisfaction of taking part in the political struggle but also a strong feeling of fraternity – wherever you went you were welcome in the local party group and most of us formed the majority of our friendships with other party members.

The full-time party organisers and party leaders with whom I came into contact were almost all people of great integrity and selfless dedication, like the Giles', whom I knew very well and greatly admired. In my case my knowledge of them was an important ingredient in my refusal at this stage to believe the reports of repression and injustice in the Soviet Union, dismissing them as invented capitalist propaganda. There had been, after all, notorious examples of this in the past, such as the letter, now known to have been forged by M16, purporting to be from the Soviet Zinoviev, urging the British Communist Party to agitate within the armed forces. This appeared in the press four days before the 1924 general election and was believed to have led to the defeat of the Labour Party. I had faith in the communists I knew and the Soviet abuses now described seemed to me so incompatible with their high ideals as to be unbelievable, until the incontrovertible evidence of Khrushchev's speech in 1956.

Even if some communists felt uneasy about the rumours, there was a further factor that led them to put any doubts to one side. This was the fundamental importance, constantly stressed by Communist Party leaders, of defending the Soviet Union since it was the only socialist country in a hostile capitalist world. They were not alone on the left in adapting this strategy. Hobsbawm, in the *Guardian Review*, in 1997, pointed out that Victor Gollancz, who usually published George Orwell's work, refused to publish his critique of the Spanish Communist Party, *Homage to Catalonia*, 'believing, as did many people on the left, that everything should be sacrificed in order to preserve a common front against the rise of fascism.' It was not till the fifties that the consequences of such sacrifices became clear.

Amongst the new ex-service arrivals in the Oxford student Communist Party was an ex-Bevin Boy, Rufus Godson. From 1943 a randomly selected ten per cent of male service recruits between the ages of eighteen and twenty-five were directed to work in the coal mines, which were seriously short of labour. It was also possible, as some leftist young men including Rufus did, to opt for coalmining as an alternative to the armed forces. Rufus was an unlikely Bevin Boy (they were named after the Minister of Labour, Ernest Bevin). Tall, and with a definite air of a toff, he came from a public school and a well-to-do family. However, his undoubtedly close experience of mineworkers' lives and trade union activities gave him a definite cachet in the student Communist Party. I started to go out with him and to my surprise he soon produced a beautiful ring (his mother was an antique dealer) and proposed that we should become engaged. I don't know why I went along with this. I had no deep feelings for him but I needed a boyfriend, and I'm afraid on reflection one factor may have been the status it conferred on me in college – no one else in my year was engaged. But then I began to meet his mother with whom he spent a lot of time. She was a single parent with no other children and her relationship with Rufus was painful to witness. They bickered constantly and viciously but were very close to each other, like an old, unhappily married couple. This was ugly and alarming, and, never having seriously believed that the marriage would happen, I broke off the relationship during the summer term. I don't believe that Rufus had been seriously in love with me. I think now that like many of the older male students he was anxious to settle down, get married and start a family, which in fact he did the next year.

That term I went to a May ball with Ken Kirk, an ex-army major and communist. May balls were an Oxford event, suspended during the war, which I felt I should experience once. The balls, each organised by one of the men's colleges, started around 9p.m. and traditionally finished with listening to a choir singing on Magdalen bridge around dawn. Alas, I didn't manage to stay awake that long. Tickets were very expensive and in short supply and there was a strict dress code of white ties for men and ball dresses for women. Ball dresses were then unobtainable in Britain. A few girls had a dress sent from abroad, others made one from curtains, like Scarlet O'Hara in *Gone with the Wind*, or borrowed or altered the pre-war dress of a relative. My mother nobly had her only long dress altered for me. It was black lace over yellow taffeta, and it passed muster though, made by the local technical college students, it had not been very elegant in the first place.

My future husband, Jack, had arrived in England in January of that year, 1946, after five years in the army. He had a New Zealand ex-serviceman's scholarship and intended to do a doctorate in psychology in London with Cyril Burt, but Burt was not impressed with him. Jack appeared ignorant – not only was he out of touch with psychology but he appeared even more ignorant than he was, because he didn't recognise Burt's pronunciation of some psychologists' names that Jack had only read. Taking offence, Jack decided instead to do a doctorate in social history with G.D.H. Cole, a well-known social and economic Oxford historian and Fabian socialist. Cole suggested as a subject an aspect of the history of the co-operative movement in Britain and Jack moved to Oxford in the spring of 1946. He had belonged to the socialist club in his university in New Zealand and he started to attend both the Labour and Communist society meetings in Oxford, though he did not join either.

I first met Jack when we both had lunch with Martin Milligan in a British restaurant. Martin, who was enormously gregarious, played an important social role in the student left, bringing people together. Jack was tall, slim, as he remained all his life, serious looking and athletic – I used to watch in admiration as he put one hand on a five-barred gate and leapt gracefully over. At twenty-seven his hair had already retreated into his temples. His only interest in clothes was, and remained, to look, with the minimum of effort, unobtrusive within his social group. This meant at that time a uniform of a tweed or corduroy jacket, often with leather elbow patches, grey flannel trousers, a raincoat and a trilby hat. He had only recently left the army and was still shedding his feeling of being institutionalised, still feeling adrift.

Jack had volunteered for the New Zealand Field Ambulance Unit, wanting to be involved in the struggle against fascism, but unable to bring himself to kill. This meant that before every battle – and he was in Greece, North Africa, and Italy – he went with his unit ahead of the troops into dangerous territory to prepare for the casualties that would ensue in the front line. But like most ex-servicemen he almost never spoke of his battle experiences. He always said that most of the war he spent bumping around in a field ambulance, intensely bored, without books or music. The only distractions available were old copies of the *Readers Digest*, cigarettes, and, when it was available, alcohol. I admired his greater maturity – he was seven years older than me – and his anti-authoritarianism. This characteristic had led him to refuse to apply for a commission in the army and on one occasion to being put on a charge for refusing to salute an officer whom he did not respect. The 'bolshy' aspect of his character (which he later lost) appealed to me, as did his innate egalitarianism. New Zealand is a very socially egalitarian society. When I visited it I was impressed by the way a waitress would serve you, and then draw up a chair to your table and chat to you.

The elitism of Oxford repelled him, as did the loud, self-confident voices of the ex-public school boys, and he was unimpressed by its traditions and its assumption that the university, its staff and students were superior to all others. After our initial meeting we went out together at times but did not then develop a serious relationship. During that summer vacation, 1946, there was a large international students' festival in Prague, and British universities were invited to send delegates. The trip was to last a month. Somehow Jack and I managed to get included in the Oxford delegation with all our expenses paid. We were both very excited by the prospect. I had never been abroad before and travel was still very restricted. I had years of pent-up longing to see Europe.

Travelling in Europe was then very difficult. Without stopping in Paris the Oxford delegation took an overnight train to Prague. We were shocked to see the terrible destruction wrought by the allies on the German cities we passed through. Our train was extremely crowded, there were not enough seats for everyone so we students spent the journey in the corridors. We slept on the floor as people picked their way over us, or, even more uncomfortable but less often disturbed, on the swaying metal interconnection between carriages. I remember trying to sleep listening to Jack snoring nearby, and thinking I could never be interested in a man who snored. The journey seemed interminable. It certainly lasted for at least two days, since civilian trains kept being shunted off the track to give way to troop trains – there was still a lot of troop movement round Europe. We took some food with us, and supplemented it at railway stations, there were no buffets or bars on the train. After one or two inaugural days in Prague we were dispersed to different parts of Czechoslovakia. Jack and I were sent to different centres.

I was sent to Hruba Scala, in the rocky hills of what is now called 'the Bohemian Paradise', about 100kms from Prague. Hruba Scala was a fourteenth-century castle, enlarged and rebuilt in the sixteenth century, and re-Gothicised in the nineteenth century. It's now a luxury hotel. The 1945 Czech government, a coalition of communists and socialists, had recently confiscated it, complete with chandeliers, furniture and paintings, from its collaborationist owners. There were students present from many European countries. Sleeping together in single sex dormitories, which had been improvised from splendid reception rooms, we soon made friends across the nationalities. Even at that time most students except the Russians and Eastern Europeans knew some English, many spoke it quite fluently. It was very exciting to meet Yugoslav students who had until recently been partisans, and Russian students still in military uniform. Both these groups tended to stick together, and were much given to singing very stirring songs and looking out for casual sex. But the friends I made, and at first kept in touch with, were a Czech girl rather older than myself who stayed with me the next summer in London, and a young married Czech couple. Subsequently, they all stopped answering my letters. I thought perhaps they had moved, but years later I learned that after the Communist Party assumed complete control of the government in 1948 and effectively imposed a one-party system they had purged non party and some party members from government posts, imprisoning many. I feared my friends had fallen foul of the authorities, or had perhaps thought it too dangerous to maintain contacts with westerners.

At Hruba Skala there were lectures and discussions but I only remember the social side. It was a fine summer, and we often swam in the castle's open-air swimming pool. I had a bikini, given to me by Rufus' mother – bikinis had only just been introduced in the west and mine aroused much envy in the Yugoslav and Russian girls. We wandered round the lovely hills and valleys and went on trips to medieval towns.

When we had to wait for trains the Yugoslavs and Russians would break into song and start dancing along the platform, a splendid way to fill the time, impossible to imagine in England, unless people were drunk. I think we were all elated by a very real feeling of international friendship. It was the kind of world that we had longed for during the years of war. In the evenings we made our own entertainment. Sometimes we were expected to demonstrate the songs and dances of our national groups: we English would have failed miserably without the help of the Scottish and Welsh students. Even so, we must have seemed self-conscious and unenthusiastic. I embarked on a short-lived affair with the doctor who had been appointed to look after the health of the students in Hruba Skala. He was a man in his early thirties, a long time communist who, as a member of the Czech resistance, had spent much of the war in a concentration camp. He talked to me about the camp and the Czech resistance movement and I thought him a very romantic figure. His English was good, he professed a great interest in the subjects I was studying and told me that he had fallen in love with me. When the rest of the group made a short expedition to the Tatra mountains we stayed behind.

When the holiday came to an end he urged me to remain with him in Prague after the other students went home. For a reason I forget, he returned with them to Prague in the morning and left me in Hruba Skala to set out on my own in the evening for his flat. This was a scary journey, especially in the dark, involving a change of trains at a small station and a journey across Prague. Very few ordinary Czechs spoke English or French, and whilst they often knew some German, as I did, it was not safe at that time to speak German in Czechoslovakia. I managed the journey but when I arrived at his flat I discovered to my dismay that he was married and living with his wife. There was only one room, in which a double bed had been made up for all three of us to share. He expected me to spend the days with him whilst he was ostensibly at work, but horrified by his deception I fled, and with some difficulty returned to England on my own. It was over forty years before I returned to Prague.

After the summer, at the start of the second year of my PPE course, 1946-7, I began to see a lot of Jack. He played rugby for his college, as he had in New Zealand – strange that both the serious loves in my life have been keen rugby players, when my childhood was spent rebelling against the games culture. Jack still very much disliked Oxford. He could not bear the atmosphere of privilege and 'those bloody blah blah BBC voices' of the ex-public school boys who seemed to him to dominate the university landscape. He was often depressed and uncertain about his future and I think this appealed to my maternal feelings. He was very relieved when he met Karl Popper and was offered a part time post at the London School of Economics (LSE), teaching logic.

Popper was a distinguished philosopher who had fled from Vienna to New Zealand in 1937 and taught philosophy there until 1946, when he was invited to the LSE. Jack's degree had been in psychology and philosophy and Popper always said that Jack was the best student he had in New Zealand. Popper was famous for arguing that a theory could only be considered scientific if it could in principle be falsified by further evidence. He was very critical of both Marxism and psychoanalysis as not open to falsification. If contrary evidence was found, the theories were not abandoned but ad hoc additions were made to them by their adherents – and thus the theories were authoritarian rather than scientific. He distrusted all dogmatism and advocated an 'open society' of free individuals, who are able to question authority and respect each others' rights, within a protective state framework. Popper had a profound influence on Jack, who was never able to accept Marxist theory or the centralism of the Communist Party, though at that time he agreed with much of its policy.

Jack now spent half the week and the university vacations in London, where he shared a dark, damp, cold basement flat in Museum Street, just round the corner from the British Museum, with Bill Geddes, a fellow ex-serviceman and New Zealander. Bill was working for a Ph.D. in anthropology at the LSE. He was very unlike Jack, taciturn, obstinate, with a ready dry wit, and quite obsessional – they had agreed to share expenses and Bill would list every box of matches or pint of milk that he bought. But they got on very well and Bill was best man at our wedding. He lived for several years in the 1960s with the Hmong people in the mountains of northern Thailand, on the borders of Vietnam. The CIA recruited many Hmongs to fight in the Vietnamese war and after Bill became Professor of Anthropology in

Sydney the rest of his life was poisoned by persistent accusations from fellow anthropologists, including some in his own department, that he had acted as a CIA agent. Jack and I did not believe this, but Bill became increasingly paranoid, certain that we did, and that only his Maori wife, Ngaere, supported him.

Although relieved to be spending half of his time out of Oxford Jack was still quite depressed. He could not see what he was going to do with his life and talked about returning to New Zealand to teach an adult education course in one of the mining towns on the west coast of the South Island. In London he used to get up at about midday, buy the *Evening Standard* and go to the Lyons Corner House on the corner of Tottenham Court Road to eat. Neither he nor Bill had even minimal cooking or domestic skills. By Christmas we had fallen very much in love. It was hard for us to be separated, even for only part of the week.

In April, for my twenty-first birthday present my mother offered to pay for me to spend a week in Paris, where Jack could accompany me provided I was chaperoned by Michael. He was now out of the R.A.F., back in Cambridge and able to fund himself. I decided to invite as well Alison Kershaw, a Somerville friend in the year below me, with whom I could share a room. Unlike my other girlfriends she was able to afford the trip, her father had a very senior post in the Bank of England. She was an attractive girl with shoulder length black hair, in many ways both innocent and ignorant and an unlikely recent recruit to the Oxford student Communist Party. Paris was a revelation to us. In 1947 it still had its own beautiful, seedy identity – not yet touched by the creeping international consumerism that has since tended to diminish many of the differences between large European cities. It was the Paris that is preserved in the film *Les Enfants du Paradis*. The bread, the croissants, the cheeses, the coffee, the wine, the meals in little cafés, the cognac, the special smell of *Gaulloise* cigarettes, the look of the newspapers and bill boards – everything was new to us, different and exciting.

Dior had just introduced the New Look, with its court shoes, sloping shoulders, tiny waists and very full, gathered, mid calf length skirts, impossible to reproduce in Britain at a time of clothes rationing. But most Parisian women were still wearing high wedge shoes made of cork, unknown then in England and not expensive, which Alison and I bought, and tottered perilously around in. The only food rationing was by price – we were amazed to see bowls of hardboiled eggs in all the bars. We stayed in a cheap, shabby hotel in the students' quarter and fell in love with Paris. On the return journey Jack and I stayed for a night in Dieppe in a room above the little café where we had eaten. Next morning the sea was very rough and I was apprehensive – seasickness remedies were not then available for civilians. The friendly proprietor persuaded us that brandy was the best preventative. By the time we embarked I was distinctly drunk and was soon so terribly sick that I would gladly have died. Fortunately Jack, who had a very good head for alcohol, cheerfully encouraged me to survive.

During the summer term Jack saw an advertisement for a psychology lecturer at St Andrews university, and finding that the head of the department was Henry Ferguson, who had been his psychology professor in New Zealand, decided to apply. He took the Penguin *Dictionary of Psychology* to read on the train going up for his interview, claiming that he had forgotten all his psychology. But with the help of glowing references from Popper and others he was appointed to start in the autumn. He had already decided to downgrade his doctorate on the co-operative movement to a B.Litt, and he finished this during his time in St Andrews. The appointment was excellent news for Jack, it meant he had a future in Britain, but it also meant that during my final year in Oxford we would be separated. Jack was very anxious that we should get married. An initial difficulty which I had already considered was that members of the Communist Party were not supposed to marry out of the party on the grounds that this would be bound to reduce their allegiance and participation. I did not take this very seriously but I did discuss the issue with a member of the university staff communist group, Margaret Paul, whose husband, my philosophy tutor, was not a member. She assured me that unless the husband was actually hostile to the party and likely to prove obstructive she foresaw no problems. In fact, shortly thereafter Jack did join the Communist Party. That summer we went on holiday together to St. David's, in Pembrokeshire and we were so much in love that we felt that we should never ever spend a single day apart. And watching the small children play on the beach, I thought for the first time that I would like to have children.

But there were serious obstacles to our marriage. At the first mention of it my mother became even angrier with me than when I switched to PPE. It was not that she had any particular objection to Jack but that, unlike most women of her generation, she did not want to see her daughter married – there were no precedents of happy marriages in her family. And if either my brother or I were to marry, she thought it should be after we had successfully established ourselves in a profession. She feared that I would not get a good degree and that marriage so early would divert me from seriously pursuing a career. She saw my marriage intention as in some sense a betrayal of all the sacrifices she had made in order to educate me and I think she saw it as a rejection of herself. She was sure that marriage would interfere with my work and could not see why I would not wait at least until my exams were over in the summer. Faced with her fury I became very ambivalent. Didn't marriage, I objected to Jack, trap women into taking on the responsibilities of running a house, mending their husband's socks, and looking after children? At a deeper level I found it very difficult to deliberately defy my mother, receive her anger and know that I was hurting her. Because we had been separated from her for most of our lives and her presence had seemed like a visit from a charming fairy godmother, neither Michael nor I had ever had a serious quarrel or disagreement with her until I gave up medicine. I wrote to Jack that I could not write to my mother as he wished when all the time I was thinking, 'poor darling Mummy, how could I hurt her so?'

From today's vantage point it might seem reasonable for us to have agreed to her request to at least wait until the summer vacation. But Jack had two reasons for insisting otherwise. Marriage had a different significance at that time. It was not, as now, an optional alternative to living together without marrying, which was then referred to, even in student and left-wing circles as 'living in sin'. The wife of an ex-service member of our Communist Party group refused to have an unmarried couple stay for a weekend. But in my social circle it was accepted that a couple might secretly sleep together occasionally before marrying, though that was difficult to arrange. You could not book into a hotel unless the couple pretended to be married and the woman wore a wedding ring, and it would have been quite impossible for me to stay with Jack in St Andrews unless we were married. But just as important he thought it essential that I should stand up to my mother. He wrote that, 'you'll just have to realise that in her love for you there is a strong neurotic strain' and that I needed to show her that I was an independent person who could make her own decisions. I entered a state of acute anxiety, unable to sleep or eat. The doctor whom I saw in Oxford recommended that I see a psychiatrist he knew of in London. This lady's approach was very different from that of contemporary psychiatrists. She prescribed large amounts of sodium amytal, told me that my attitude to my mother was infantile, and, agreeing with Jack, said that in order to recover I must break with my mother and get married. She was, in fact, a bully, and her 'therapy' might have been counterproductive if I had been strong enough to stand up to her. She wrote to Dr. Vaughan, the principal of Somerville, that it was essential for my health that I get married, and Jack did the same.

At that time Somerville undergraduates were not allowed to marry, although exceptions had been made during the war. Dr. Janet Vaughan, the Principle, a distinguished haematologist who spent every morning in her lab., had always been kind to me. She managed to persuade the Fellows that another exception should be made in my case, helped by Christopher Hill, my history tutor, who did some private lobbying amongst the Somerville Fellows. He argued that at present I was doing no work and was so distressed that there was a serious danger of my getting a poor degree. With Jack far away in Scotland there was no reason why marriage should disrupt my work. I wrote to Jack that Dr. Vaughan told me that, 'I must cultivate ruthlessness towards my mother. She said that her family had turned her out when she married, and she had been very happy since. In any case she thought that there were far too many important things to do in life than spending energy on such personal problems.' And she invited Jack to stay with her if ever he came to Oxford.

So we went ahead with our marriage plans. We didn't get engaged, which we regarded as a bourgeois custom, and anyway Jack had no money for a ring. I was still getting angry letters from my mother, plunging me into misery. I would weep for hours after reading them. Angry letters also arrived from my grandmother, Spikes, and my brother Michael, who all wrote that I was being very selfish. Why could we not get engaged and wait till the summer? Michael came over from Cambridge to try to dissuade me in person and was almost in tears as he did so. Looking back, I think I felt the centre of a tug of war between two teams. Jack and his team won the contest, but I could not at that time feel happy about the outcome. I told Jack that I thought we should just go quietly to the registry office on our own since 'a wedding is a social, family occasion, with everyone happy. Don't lets pretend ours is a nice way to get married.' However in the end we organised a small celebration to which none of my family except Michael came. He told me that when he got back to London he found our mother on her knees in the kitchen, scrubbing the floor – something she had never been known to do before – and crying – I had never seen her cry.

Jack and me, aged 20 and 27.

We got married in the Oxford register office, on Monday, December 15th 1947. I was twenty-one, Jack was twenty-eight. This was the first possible date after Jack's term finished, but we hadn't taken into account that my friends who had graduated the previous summer and now had jobs would not be able to get away on a weekday and that most of those who were still students had already gone down for Christmas. Even Henry Collins who had become a close friend, and lived in Oxford, couldn't get off work. So almost none of my friends, including Giles, who had hoped to be present, could come. Jack sent me his clothes ration book so that I could buy a new dress for the occasion. He was anxious that I should not go home between the end of term and the wedding lest my mother dissuade me at the last minute, so I agreed to stay with his friends, the Mcbriars, Australian historians, at 9 Merton Street. The wedding party was held at their house.

Dr. Vaughan invited Jack to stay with her before the wedding but he arrived from Scotland only on the morning of the wedding day. We had lunch with the Mcbriars in an hotel. During lunch I experienced a sudden feeling of panic about the marriage, which centred on the imminent change in my name. I was overwhelmed with the fear that this would in some way result in a loss of myself. However, I was talked round, and in the afternoon the wedding ceremony, if the brief moment in the register office could be so dignified, was given its comic moment by the best man, Bill Geddes. Having missed the train from London he burst in at the very last minute, as we were sitting in front of the registrar, anxiously asking, 'Is it all over?' Later we had a small party with Jack's Australian and New Zealand friends who were living in Oxford doing postgraduate work, and, on my side, only Christopher Hill and my brother. We left by the 7.30p.m. train for London, spending the night in a fearsomely cold room in the Kings Cross Hotel, feeding coins into the tiny gas fire, and next day took the train to St Andrews. I don't think it had ever occurred to us to have a honeymoon, we wanted to start married life.

St Andrews in 1947 was a small, grey, ancient town, dominated by the university, the golf course, and by Presbyterianism. Coming from Oxford it seemed like a Siberian outpost. Jack had rented a small bungalow, Double Dykes, so cold and damp that shoes and clothes in the cupboards quickly became mouldy. Its redeeming feature was a conservatory, where you could bask in any gleams of sunshine. The atmosphere in the town was one of moral disapproval. Many of the houses had mirrors on the first floor, positioned so that the owners could watch their neighbours without being themselves seen to be watching, noting what time they took their milk in, what time they got home at night, and who visited them. No alcohol could be bought on Sundays, except by signing a register in a hotel bar and claiming to be en route between two named places. There were few if any cafés – almost the only place to have a meal out was a hotel. With the new job, Jack's confidence rapidly increased. At first he was very happy because, he wrote, ' the two things I've wanted from life are coming true, someone to love and be loved by, and a job which I feel is worth doing.'

The psychology department then consisted only of its head, Henry Ferguson, and Jack, with some sessions from a psychiatrist in Dundee, John Uytman, a communist sympathiser. At that time, immediately after the war, at least one or two Communist Party members or sympathisers could be found on the staff of any U.K. university. Jack wrote that, 'few of the university staff do any work to speak of. They play golf and drink, have a good time in a genteel sort of way, and do a minimum of reading.' He was shocked to find that the students were only expected to read the prescribed books, whilst in his opinion the professors had fossilised and were uninterested in anything new. However, he set about teaching his courses with enthusiasm, working very hard at night to revise and update his knowledge. A young physicist offered to coach him in statistics and he almost immediately made friends with a young philosophy lecturer, Tony Lloyd, from Balliol, who later became Professor of Philosophy in Liverpool. Tony was a left-wing social democrat, very witty, and, Jack wrote, 'he is very much the Londoner, with a certain unconscious or half conscious air of superiority. I am always surprised that you didn't fall in love with someone like him, amusing, highly civilised, cultured, rather than someone so homespun as myself.' But it was just Jack's 'homespun' qualities that appealed to me.

During that year Tony and Jack were almost constantly in each other's company when not teaching. Nothing ever happened in St Andrews in the evenings, so they would have a drink together in a pub, go back to Jack's house (Tony lived in a university hostel) make some kind of meal, drink coffee, and talk endlessly till Jack threw Tony out and set about preparing his lectures. Jack, as had been his custom in London, often worked until 3a.m. I think both of them were lonely and very much needed each other's company, but by the end of the year Jack wrote that they had exhausted what they had to say to each other and often sat in silence, 'like an officers' mess in an Indian regiment, except there isn't as much booze.' Sometimes at weekends Martin or Jimmy Milligan came to stay from Glasgow, or Professor Ferguson and his wife would invite Jack for a meal. He had only a limited amount of contact with the student communist branch, having decided that 'they're all a bit cracked'. As a Popperian, and never a Marxist, the Communist Party dispirited him. He wrote, 'It's disagreeable to be connected to a political body which is a kind of religion for most of those associated with it, tied up with a lot of fusty metaphysics and out of date logic.'

I was surprised to find, re-reading Jack's letters – and he wrote to me every day when we were apart – what I had long forgotten, that during this year he read a great deal of Freud and Anna Freud and thought psychoanalysis 'a vast and splendid theoretical arc'. He wrote enthusiastically to suggest that after graduating I should have a psychoanalysis and become a child analyst. These attitudes must have changed quite quickly after he reached the Institute of Psychiatry. I was also surprised to see that he became an enthusiastic cook during that year. Food was mentioned in all his letters. I think it was hard for young men to get enough to eat when even bread was rationed. After he had used up his meat ration he cooked himself appalling meals, such as tinned spaghetti and tinned beetroot, but he often triumphantly reported that the butcher had given him more than his ration of meat. Generously, however, he was always offering to send me provisions – dried eggs, which he did not use, or oranges and grapefruit in a wooden box when there was a delivery of them to a local shop.

When I went up to St Andrews after our wedding I bought two cookery books. I hadn't cooked since I was thirteen, and enjoyed experimenting. This encouraged Jack to try harder, and after I left he wrote, 'I've decided to get interested in cooking just to see what can be done in a manly sort of way, i.e. without the niceties you put into it, and I find I can make a meal in half an hour.' Each day he told me in his letter what he had cooked. Sausages, chops, cabbage and potatoes were mentioned frequently, but he also reported cooking a lot of fish, which was not rationed, for example, 'poached haddock and tomatoes, with sliced potatoes and carrots cooked in the oven in milk', meat casseroles, liver and bacon, and 'Ambrose Heath's sardine recipe.' My children were astonished when I told them recently about this past history. After we set up house together in London I don't think Jack ever cooked again, although the children remember that on rare occasions when I was out and had not left a meal ready he would fry sausages for the family. That vacation, besides playing at housekeeping and entertaining Tony and Jack's professor and his wife, Jack and I would walk along the coast, which seemed always swathed in a damp mist.

Christmas, traditionally regarded as a Catholic festival in Scotland and as such not celebrated until the 1960s, was a normal working day. At the New Year John Uytman and his wife Camilla invited us to stay with them to celebrate Hogmanay, the descendant of a pagan midwinter festival. From midnight on December 31st through the small hours a long succession of visitors called at the house, 'first-footing'. Traditionally each should have brought a lump of coal for warmth, salt for wealth, cake for food and half a bottle of whisky, but most brought only the cake and whisky. In return they were regaled with cake and whisky before going on to 'first-foot' in another friend's house. The next two days were public holidays, required to recover from this ordeal, and much of New Year's Day we spent in the basement kitchen washing up the enormous amount of glass and china used, nursing terrible headaches. 'First-footing' is a custom I have never wished to take part in again.

Back in Oxford for the spring term I felt lonely. Having spent my first year doing medicine, I had to stay at Oxford for a fourth year. So I missed not only Jack, but most of my contemporaries, who had taken their degrees in the summer. I did have some friends left in college in the year below me, I went round to Christopher Hill's about once a week for a chat, and I met Henry Collins once or twice a week. Henry was not a student but a trade union historian who was lecturing on history to local adult education classes and a member of the communist historians' group. He used to take me out to dinner at an Indian restaurant, then a rarity in England, and, my letters to Jack record, I used to mend his socks. Later Henry shared a flat with Eric Hobsbawm in London, and, alas, died in early middle age.

I was very fond of him, we understood each other without any element of flirtation or sexual attraction. One evening he took me with him to a class he was teaching on trade union history and I was impressed not only by his handling of the class but by the quality of the students, who were very bright, politically involved local trade unionists. There was something of an air of mystery about Henry, I think only because he never gave any information about his personal life or his past. I occasionally wondered, quite absurdly and without foundation, and in the circumstances, disloyally, if he was a government informant. There were other such mysterious party members in Oxford, about whom I and others had the same passing thought, notably Peter Brinson, who had been a colonel in the army and later became a famous ballet critic. Subsequently, I realised that his air of mystery was probably because of his homosexuality at a time when this could lead to imprisonment. I still think it very likely that there was a government informant in the large and flourishing Oxford Communist Party, but this was surely not Henry.

Marriage had not solved my psychological problems. Only a reconciliation with my mother would have done that, and it did not occur. She had begun to write occasional cold, hostile letters to me, addressed to 'Miss B. Parker.' I continued to be plagued by insomnia, inability to eat, and more seriously, inability to work effectively. Whilst I had done a reasonable amount of work in my first two years, a much greater mastery of the subjects would need to be acquired in my final year if I was to get that first class degree which everyone expected of me. I received constant reassurance from my tutors that I did not need to worry, I was sure to get a first, but I knew this was not the case. Christopher Hill instructed Jack that I would do best if he could stop me working altogether, but of course I could not do this, although nothing I read seemed to sink in.

When it was time to take my finals, at the end of the summer term, I tried to cram in at the last minute knowledge that I had missed or forgotten. Kind Dr. Vaughan, the Principal of Somerville, who was keeping an eye on me, moved me into her house while I took the exams, but I'm not sure that the unfamiliar surroundings helped. Special 'sub fusc' clothing had to be worn for university exams, white shirts, black skirts or trousers, black socks or stockings, black shoes and ties, topped by a black mortarboard and black university gowns. These were the familiar gowns we had to wear every day, knee length and sleeved for scholars, short and sleeveless for commoners (those who did not hold scholarships). The crow-like appearance of a group of students in 'sub fusc' waiting to go into the examination hall disheartened anyone whose sense of humour was out of action.

Some weeks later I was summoned to a viva, an oral examination for students whose marks were on the borders of a second and first class degree. Questions were fired at you by a row of black-gowned dons sitting on the other side of a long, narrow table. Gone was the confidence which won me an entrance scholarship, yet to succeed in the viva you had to be very confident and either sparkling with ideas, or very learned. I didn't feel any of those things and knew that I could not succeed, and so it proved. I phoned my mother to tell her and was met with silence. A friend of mine at Somerville who applied to get married the following year, citing my marriage as a precedent, was refused permission, on the grounds that the college had confidently expected me to get a first, and instead I had got a second. They had no intention of repeating the experiment. Only those who were in Oxford or Cambridge at that time can appreciate the extraordinary significance given to getting a first class degree. These universities awarded a very small proportion of firsts and winning one was then seen as an accolade of a unique kind, unsurpassed by doctorates (which were at that time scorned by non-scientists) or even by subsequent publications. Failing the expectation that one would get a first often rankled with people for years, implanting a deep centre of low self-esteem.

Since marriage had not improved my health or ability to work and had caused a serious breach in my relations with my mother, I wonder now whether it would not have been better to have postponed marriage till the summer as she had wished. I left Oxford feeling unhappy because of my degree and the rejection of me by my mother to whom I had been so deeply attached throughout my childhood. But when I looked back later at my student days I mostly remember the beauty of the colleges, the intellectual interest of the course, the relative freedom to organise one's time and above all, the rich social life – never again is one likely to spend so much time with such a large circle of friends, so readily available. Disappointment over the degree soon faded and disappeared under preoccupations with work and children. It could not, in any case, altogether undermine the earlier intellectual confidence derived from having been a scholar of Somerville and St.Paul's. And within a few months I was reconciled with my mother.

Chapter 10

Married life, a death, and a birth 1948–1951

I left Oxford in the summer of 1948 quite uncertain about my future. My earlier, admittedly vague, ambition had been to make a contribution to a third world country as an economist, the only subject I had studied which seemed to have any useful application. This fantasy was never put to the test since Jack was clear that after wasting, as he saw it, five years in the army in North Africa and Europe, he wanted to settle down and pursue an academic career. Meanwhile, through Jack, I had become very interested in psychology, about which I had previously known almost nothing – it was not then taught at Oxford nor even mentioned at school. Jack, who had become an enthusiast for psychoanalysis, saw child psychotherapy as a future career for me. But since no training for this was possible in St Andrews he thought that I could easily find work teaching adult education classes in one of my degree subjects. Psychology departments were at that time starting up or expanding all over Britain and Jack was confident that after another year he would find a new university post in a city where I could find training.

However, early in 1948 he met Hans Eysenck at a meeting of the British Psychological Society and must have impressed him, since he immediately offered Jack a research job in the newly founded Institute of Psychiatry in London. This was sited at the Maudsley Hospital, and has no separate physical presence, so both are often loosely referred to as 'the Maudsley'. Aubrey Lewis, pioneer of evidence based psychiatry, had recently been appointed Professor of Psychiatry there, with Eysenck as head of the psychology department and Monte Shapiro as head of the first British training course in clinical psychology. But the offer was vague, the research topic undefined, and it was not until July that a definite written offer was made. For a long time Jack could not decide what to do. Unaware, of course, of the distinction that would later accrue to the Maudsley researchers on the whole he favoured remaining in St Andrews. This was because he thought that he would prefer to combine research with teaching, that it would be a mistake, career wise, to leave his present job after only a year and that it would be best if we stayed far away from my mother. At St Andrews his situation was improving. A second lecturer had recently been appointed to the department so that in future Jack need only teach the subjects he was interested in and would have time for some research, which he was already planning. True, my proposed training in psychotherapy would have to be postponed but I was less committed to this prospect than Jack, and wrote, 'it doesn't matter to me where we live, as long as it's within reach of a library. And don't let money enter into the decision, this is the time in our lives when we can be adventurous'. I think I was still dreaming about doing good works in Africa or India or at least a sojourn abroad but that was definitely not an option for Jack.

In the course of the summer term Jack and the St Andrews university authorities became disenchanted with each other. The head of the faculty objected to his plan to give lectures on psychoanalysis on the grounds that the students were insufficiently mature and, away from their parents' support, would find the topic disturbing. And, as the Cold War set in, Jack became aware that the university authorities were troubled by his membership of the Communist Party. When he received a definite offer from Aubrey Lewis in July his faculty head urged him to accept it, and told him that the university would waive the statutory notice requirement and pay his salary until he started his new job in September. So towards the end of August we moved to London.

We spent most of the summer in St Andrews apart from a week attending an international psychology conference in Edinburgh, where, somewhat awestruck, I met Eysenck and Shapiro, and another week spent with Jack's elderly Aunt Jenny, who lived with her daughter Janet near Burwash, in Sussex. Meantime my mother had gradually become more reconciled to our marriage and suggested that we stay with her in September until we could find a flat. She had two single beds moved from the top floor of her house in Blackheath into the rarely used ground floor dining room, pushed the table and chairs into a corner and there we started our life in London in some unease and discomfort.

During the summer Jack's future colleagues had persuaded us that if I wanted to be a psychologist I would need an academic qualification.

Fortunately, at that time University College offered a 'qualifying' course in psychology for graduates in other subjects. Students could be exempted from courses they had already studied – I was exempted from physiology and philosophy. At the end of the year we sat the normal psychology degree examinations. If we passed to a sufficient standard we were not awarded a degree but were entitled to take a higher degree in psychology. There was a full programme of lectures and workshops each day, somehow compressing the work of the three-year degree course into one year. This imposed timetabling was a rude shock after the independent approach to learning at Oxford but it still left a massive learning task to do on one's own. I tackled this in a very systematic way, buying past examination papers and selecting for study only those topics and questions that had come up most frequently. This procedure, although effective, left me subsequently with huge gaps in my knowledge of psychology.

Another shock was the contrast between the beauty of the Oxford colleges which had permeated my consciousness for four years and the ramshackle, dreary nature of the University College psychology department at that time, a warren of narrow passages and tiny offices with peeling paint and grubby, distempered walls. Fortunately the experience of the course was transformed by my friendship from the first day with a fellow student, Mary Tingle. She was the daughter of a Welsh Methodist minister, quite ordinary in appearance apart from her very expressive face. Unlike any other of my friends she had no intellectual or political interests but she was high-spirited, irreverent, and the funniest person I have ever known. She combined an eye for the absurdity of life with considerable dramatic powers – everything that happened to Mary she turned into an amusing story to add to her already vast stock. But I was always aware that she was also both kind-hearted and principled. We spent each day together, deriving much amusement from the performances of Sir Cyril Burt, then Professor of Psychology at University College. Short, plump and self important, he would declaim his lectures whilst strutting up and down the middle aisle of the lecture room. He wore, perhaps to assume the status of medical authority, a short white doctor's jacket from which his round stomach protruded, his thumbs sticking out of the jacket pockets.

Since Mary and I were both quite impractical we unashamedly used our charms to persuade some men students to set up for us the elaborate apparatus required in experiments on perception, then an essential part of the practical course. During the final exams we would have been at a loss without their surreptious help. Mary was living in digs for the year and knew few people in London, so as soon as Jack and I had our own flat she was delighted to come to lunch almost every weekend. The following year she took a course in educational psychology in Birmingham, later becoming senior educational psychologist there. She married a fellow Welshman, Bryn Thomas, a sports teacher, and had two children. We kept in touch and met from time to time until her death in 2007, but over the years life remorselessly eroded her high spirits and jokiness, though not her kindness.

At the Maudsley Jack found himself a member of the new Occupational Psychiatry Research Unit, soon renamed the Social Psychiatry Research Unit, funded by the Medical Research Council, and directed by Aubrey Lewis. Lewis proved to have a gift for selecting very bright junior researchers and giving them a free hand, whilst expecting that they worked hard. Jack and Neil O'Connor were assigned to work on occupational aspects of mental handicap, as it was then called. Neil was born in Kalgoorlie, an Australian mining town, but he had done a first degree in Oxford before the war and unlike Jack had acquired an Oxford accent and a very un-Australian reticence, discretion, elegance of manner and dry wit. He loved sports cars and expensive suits and later sported a monocle. They were about the same age, and Neil was, unexpectedly, a member of the Communist Party, and unlike Jack remained one for many years. Neil never talked about his background or his past and there was something deeply mysterious about him, which gave rise to very unlikely rumours that he was a government agent within the party. Neither Neil nor Jack initially knew anything at all about people with mental handicap, who at that time were assigned to one of three groups, according to their degree of handicap and their IQ – the feebleminded, imbeciles, and idiots. Most were certified and incarcerated with an almost indeterminate sentence in hospital 'colonies', of up to 2000 inmates, where the staff seemed to be similarly incarcerated for an indeterminate period. If the doctors did any research it was of the kind typified by Jack as 'counting the pubic hairs of Mongols,' as people with Downs syndrome were then called.

Jack and Neil decided to focus on the 'high grade' or 'feebleminded' patients in one very large hospital in Kent. They began by testing them, and discovered that many were of normal intelligence – the average IQ of the group was well above 70, then considered the borderline between normality and 'feeblemindedness'. Most came from poorly functioning working-class families and as disturbed, backward, and often delinquent children they had been sent to residential 'special schools' and, almost as a routine, moved on to 'mental deficiency' hospitals. There they worked as labourers around the hospital or were occupied by old-fashioned hand crafts, such as envelope making, needlework, or basket making. Jack and Neil set up workshops where they motivated the patients by paying them trade union rates and saw that they were trained in factory discipline, time keeping and the simple repetitive work which might be available to them outside the hospital. Many patients were then able to hold down jobs in neighbouring factories and eventually be discharged.

Although Jack and Neil's names were often linked, this was in fact the only project they did together and subsequently, whilst remaining friends, they pursued very different lines of research. Neil became a specialist in Soviet psychology, then scarcely known in Britain. He was primarily interested in theory, and used experimental techniques to study the psychological functioning of retarded and autistic people. Jack was rather impatient with theories and was primarily interested in attempting to improve people's lives through research into services and institutions for children and their families, and through influencing government policy.

Outside our work Jack and I were preoccupied with trying to find a flat to rent. The housing shortage in London was very acute – over two million houses had been destroyed or severely damaged in bombing raids and almost no new housing had been built during the war. We had no capital with which to pay the large deposit required for a house purchase. I was not earning any money and Jack's salary as a junior researcher did not go far in London. Rents were controlled, but housing was so scarce that landlords or anyone handing on a lease could ask for a large premium. Scams were frequent and Jack and I, innocently inexperienced, soon fell for one. We answered an advertisement for a flat in north London, borrowing the premium required. A man calling himself the son of the owner phoned, saying he would pick us up in a taxi, collect the keys of the flat from his father, and if we liked the flat and paid the premium we could have it right away. With great excitement we got in the taxi and our benefactor, an agreeable, talkative man, described the flat to us very enthusiastically. When we arrived at The White House, a large private estate of flats in central London where his father supposedly lived, he told us before he went off that his father would need £100 of the deposit before releasing the keys. We gave him the money and of course he did not return, leaving us feeling foolish and impoverished, but wiser, and the unpaid taxi driver irate.

My mother was exceptionally busy since, on top of all her usual commitments she had been appointed as one of two women on the newly set up Royal Commission on Gambling. It was a subject close to her heart because of the role of gambling in the failure of her marriage, but she also enjoyed getting to know and marvel at her fellow members, almost all representatives of the Great and the Good (and the Rich) who had very little knowledge of the lives of ordinary people. But in November came the terrible news that she had developed cancer. As soon as she discovered the lump in her breast she went to see her doctor and a radical mastectomy was quickly arranged at the local hospital. The tumour must have been very fast growing. After the operation the surgeon asked to see Michael and me and told us that our mother's illness would inevitably recur, since the cancer had spread well beyond the breast. But, he insisted, on no account should we spoil the time she had left by letting her know about this. Such advice was almost always given by doctors at the time and we did not query it. Whilst I now think it demeaning to people to withhold such information, in my mother's case it did result in her having twelve exceptionally happy months. And somehow, by not telling her, we ourselves managed to push the information from our minds and in a sense not to believe it, since she seemed to recover so quickly.

By the New Year she was back at work and at last we found not just a flat but one that we thought was perfect. A psychologist at the Maudsley was buying a house and offered his flat to us for a £200 premium. The rent was reasonable and we found the money. When later we came to leave the flat we passed it on to another psychologist, but we did not ask for a premium, since we thought this practice was wrong. Two years later we heard that he had transferred the flat to another couple, charging them an even larger premium than we had paid. Our flat was the first floor of a large, stylish early eighteenth-century house on the north side of Clapham Common. Graham Greene had owned the house next door and used it as the setting for the novel he published two years later, *The End of the Affair*. We had one bedroom, a large living room divided in two by folding doors, overlooking the trees on the common, a narrow bathroom and a very narrow galley kitchen. We bought a bed, two easy chairs, a table and chairs, and for the rest gradually bought furnishings from small advertisements outside local newspaper shops. I had again to tackle catering at a time when most food was still rationed – food rationing continued until 1954 – but this was a familiar experience and Jack and I both had lunch 'off the ration' in canteens.

By a strange and happy coincidence the tenants of the flat above us were two communists, the historian Eric Hobsbawm, then a lecturer at Birkbeck College, and his first wife Muriel, a senior civil servant, both ferociously intelligent. Both were tall and slim, Eric with a strikingly long, some would say ugly, but mobile and expressive face, Muriel attractive and smartly dressed. I thought my own powers of concentration were unusually good until I met Eric. In the summer he would take his typewriter and a small table into the front garden of the house, sit by the path and type for hours at a furious speed, never ever glancing up, however many residents, noisy workmen or strangers walked past. He and Muriel frequently invited us to have coffee and a drink with them in the evening, perhaps to get a break from the endless bitter and noisy quarrels which otherwise seemed to occupy their evenings, and which, since the sound insulation in the flats was poor, we were unavoidably witness to. They were in the final stage of a very unhappy marriage and even in our presence each savagely attacked whatever the other said. However, in other respects the evenings were always entertaining. Eric was a magnificent raconteur, weaving into his conversation anecdotes from the library of historical books and memoirs stored in his remarkable memory. He also entertained us by playing blues and jazz records, especially of Bessie Smith, whose singing seemed to mirror the hurt and anger in his own life.

By the end of my qualifying course in the summer of 1949 there was no further mention of my training as a child analyst, which had always been Jack's idea rather than mine. Both he and I had been exposed during the year to the devastating scepticism about psychoanalysis which prevailed amongst Maudsley psychologists and to a lesser extent at University College. In any case, by now I was clear that I wanted to do research rather than therapy, preferably in the area of education. From childhood I had heard endless discussions of the failure of the state system and the unmet educational needs of working-class children and I hoped that I could do research which would contribute towards solving these problems. But first I thought I needed first hand experience of state schools, so I decided that I would look locally for a teaching job in September – at that time graduates did not require a teaching qualification. My mother was very dispirited by this news. It seemed to her that after all my education I was abandoning her ambitions and hopes for me. There was some truth in her feeling, I was going through a very unambitious phase.

This may have been in part because I was learning a new role, that of a married woman with her own home and responsibilities for housekeeping and entertaining, but it was more due to a failure of confidence. I was very conscious of my youth and inexperience. My Oxford contemporaries had dispersed and I was now mainly in the company of older people. I was then twenty-two, Eric and his wife in their early thirties, Jack was twenty-nine and his colleagues were all about his age or older. They had spent years in the forces and now held responsible jobs, and I was a student and felt very young and inferior. In retrospect I think that the downside of marrying someone much older than myself whilst still at Oxford was that I never experienced life as an independent person. I never had to earn my own living, find myself a job and accommodation and generally manage life on my own. I had always lived with my mother, or at college and then in a sense I became a dependent of Jack's.

During the time we spent in London my mother gradually became reconciled to my marriage, and realised that Jack was a kind, trustworthy and reliable person. Perhaps knowing that we would not ourselves be able to afford a holiday, she suggested that in August we should accompany herself and Spikes as their guests on a driving trip through the Dordogne Valley. We were delighted at the prospect, knowing nothing of France apart from the week we had spent in Paris for my twenty-first birthday – which had also been a present from my mother. British government currency restrictions only allowed people to take £50 each abroad, but this was plenty for our purposes. We avoided Paris and large towns and stayed in small country *auberges*, where the accommodation was basic and not always clean, but the meals were superb and cheap. In the evenings we would dine outside, often in a garden, drinking wine until we were ready to go to bed. In 1949 there were still few foreign tourists in France and no attempt was made to cater specially for them, so the country felt very foreign, in the way that Paris had done two years earlier.

As well as visiting the beautiful chateaux and villages in the Dordogne valley we were among the first to visit the Palaeolithic Lascaux caves, discovered in 1940 by four teenage boys after a local landslide. They had only been opened in the previous year and we were lucky to see them. They were permanently closed to the public in 1963 because of damage caused by the carbon dioxide emitted by large numbers of visitors. The walls of the complex sequence of caves are covered with large, realistic and impressively beautiful painted images of animals, believed to be about 16,000 years old. I remember the holiday as very happy. We laughed a lot and the four of us got on well. My mother did all the driving – Spikes had never learnt to drive and it was nearly ten years before Jack and I could afford to buy a car – but she seemed her usual tireless self.

Less than two months later, early in October, she became ill and was told that her cancer had recurred. At that time chemotherapy was not available and a relapse was, in, effect, a death sentence. She survived for nearly four months. Now she suffered the shock that, rightly or wrongly, she had been spared a year before. She felt bitter and despairing, so sure had she been that her recovery was complete. She was fifty-two, at the height of her powers, the six terrible war years spent in the much bombed docklands, supervising her school and the next door Rest Centre and travelling round England for the N.U.T. in exhausting war time conditions, were at last over. Her life was now much easier and she no longer had any responsibility for Michael and me. She had begun for the first time to spend money on herself – she had recently bought her first ring, had started to buy her clothes from Oxford Street stores and was planning to travel to countries she had always wanted to see. She was outraged at the blow that fate had struck her and so was I. All my old devotion flooded back, together with guilt at the distress I had caused her. Without a moment's hesitation I abandoned my brief teaching career and decided to spend as much time as possible with her. Each weekday I took the tube to Charing Cross and then the Southern railway to Blackheath. After 5p.m. and at weekends I was not usually needed, Spikes was there and my brother, now a pupil in the chambers of Dudley Collard, a very left-wing barrister, visited at weekends. Later, Michael became a Q.C. and then a circuit judge. I accompanied my mother, in cars driven by volunteers, to hospital for radiotherapy treatment, which at that time left patients feeling very ill, and I did the shopping, washing, and prepared the meals.

Somehow my mother soon came to terms with her anger. Almost at once, in November, she had to cope with the death of her own mother to whom she was devoted. My grandmother, very distressed by her daughter's illness, became ill, took to her bed and died at home, according to her death certificate from pneumonia. Soon afterwards an old friend of my mother's, Aneuran Bevan, phoned, and despite as Minister of Health having recently launched the NHS, urged my mother to try alternative medicine. One of the least credulous of women, she was not tempted. After her initial despair she never complained of, or spoke of, her own death again. I think that she entered a state of denial, managing not even to think, let alone talk, about it. In this way she was able to immerse herself in as much work as she could manage and to remain always cheerful except when she felt very ill. She could not go to her school, since she was too weak to drive or use public transport, but she insisted on attending meetings at the headquarters of the National Union of Teachers and the Royal Commission and both organisations collected and returned her by car. These journeys were in themselves stressful, because of the inevitable jolts and bumps. But she managed to make such useful contributions, so forcefully, in her usual lively manner, that people did not appreciate how ill she was and that she would collapse as soon as she got home. Weeks before she died she took the chair of the N.U.T. Salaries Committee, and,

I was told later, guided it line by line through a long and intricate memorandum which was to be discussed at the forthcoming annual conference. She had many visitors and could for a short time be livelier than they were. Members of the Royal Commission sent her a crate of quarter bottles of champagne, which, whilst she was well enough, she drank with enjoyment.

My mother, three months before she died.

In the final weeks of her life her condition suddenly deteriorated rapidly and I stayed with her all the time. Her G.P. and close friend Harry Boyd drove over every afternoon from Custom House to spend time with her and inject her with morphine. One day, unable to come, he sent his woman partner, who attacked me angrily for expecting him to make the long and tedious journey through the Blackwall Tunnel each day. I felt that was a decision for him to make. Soon my mother was too weak to sit up or eat, hardly able to drink or talk and lumps appeared all over her body. She was catheterised, a district nurse called daily, but with hindsight I realise that we should have employed a full time nurse, though no one thought of this at the time. I was twenty-three, without experience of illness and was miserably aware that I did not know how to make her comfortable. In the last few days Michael came to stay and help but he was even more useless than I. It didn't occur to any of us that she should go into a hospital.

Her pain increased and was no longer controlled. Dr. Boyd had promised her that he would not let her suffer too long, and I think that eventually he gave her an overlarge injection of morphine, telling me when he left that day only that she would not last long. Two years later he himself died of stomach cancer and I hope that he was given the same loving care by his doctor that he gave to my mother. That night I told Michael he should go to bed, that I would sit up with her and would call him and Spikes if she seemed to be much worse. I think that in truth I was selfishly possessive of her and did not want anyone else to share the privilege of being with her. I must have assumed that I would know if she was dying and I certainly vaguely imagined that before this happened there would be a death-bed scene, in which we would comfort her and she would say farewell to us all. She talked ceaselessly for most of the night. At first I listened intently, thinking that she would be reviewing significant events in her life, but in fact her speech was incoherent and rambling, not making any sense and she was quite unaware of my presence. Towards dawn she stopped talking and her breathing became stertorous, which I didn't recognise as the usher of death. This was followed by terrible rattling sounds and then she died without ever regaining consciousness. It was early on Thursday, February 10th, 1950.

Somehow my grief was largely suspended whilst Michael and I carried out all the post death business, notifying various authorities, liasing with the N.U.T., making and answering phone calls, arranging the funeral, sending out invitations, seeing our mother's sister and friends. Since no one was supposed to know of Spikes' presence in the household he could do little to help. Probably because of my mother's membership of the Royal Commission, newspapers as well as educational journals published obituaries of her. Whilst most were laudatory and accurate, the one in 'Modern Education' provided me with wry amusement. This stated, correctly, that my mother 'lived for the common child, never losing faith in his (sic) potentialities.' It continued, 'Neither was she self seeking. It is perhaps not generally known that she declined an honour offered her for the New Year List.' So she did, but not for this reason. In November she had received letters, which I still have, from the Prime Minister offering her an OBE, and from Chuter Ede, then Minister of Education and an old friend. He wrote in reply to a letter from her, 'I am very bitterly disappointed (these words were underlined) that so small an offer should have been made to you, and I have seen the Chief Whip about it. His advice was that 'if you turn it down flatly it is unlikely that another offer would be made'. They both agreed that my mother should instead write a temporising letter, pleading that her membership of the Royal Commission made it inadvisable to accept at this juncture and that in the following year they would both use their influence to see she was offered a more appropriate award as Dame or at least CBE. Chuter Ede enclosed a draft letter to the Prime Minister that she copied and sent off. My mother had spent her life, directly and indirectly, in the cause of working-class children and she saw no reason why this should not be publicly recognised. The correspondence does suggest that even in December she preferred not to recognise that she was near to death.

After her funeral her will was read. My mother had very little to leave. The house was rented and the rugs and other furnishings that she had bought would obviously remain for Spikes. She also left her savings, of less than a thousand pounds, to be divided between Michael and me. She left her washing machine to her sister Ivy, who had never been able to afford one, her car to Michael – a valuable acquisition, since new cars were only very slowly coming on to the market – and her jewellery to me. In fact, her only real jewel was her new ring, which I still wear – it is my only ring. The N.U.T. announced an appeal for funds for a memorial to my mother. Michael and I were not consulted on the form that this should take and I was furious when it emerged that the large sum collected was to be spent on opening a new ward in the local hospital. My mother had always, rightly in that era, been sceptical of the effectiveness of most medical treatment and hated hospitals. She would, I knew, have much preferred the money to be spent on an educational project to help working-class children. I had to grit my teeth when attending the opening of the ward.

I rarely saw Spikes after my mother's death. Some years later he retired from his headship in West Ham and moved to Suffolk, to be near his oldest daughter, Diana, and taught physics in a girl's school. He spent his last years living with Diana and her family, taking my mother's prized rugs and furniture with him. His son-in-law, Peter Hewett, wrote a requiem for him when he died, aged 82, which ended:

'A difficult, stubborn, pigheaded, dishonest old man:
Yet the main flavour he leaves on the air
– The old sod –
Is one of invincible gallantry. Rest now'

I didn't recognise this description of a man who, though I disliked him, I thought had great dignity and authority.

When my mother's funeral and its aftermath were over I became distraught with sorrow and guilt at the unhappiness I had caused her. I sought out her closest women friends, trying to find whether she still harboured any resentment towards me during her illness. They assured me that she had not and had only spoken warmly of me but I bitterly regretted that I had never apologised to her for our earlier rift. I lost weight and my hair came out in large chunks. Jack became very anxious and suggested that we should go to the country for a holiday. We went to Alfriston, a pretty village in East Sussex, where we walked on the Downs and by the sea. When we returned I looked for another teaching job, one which would be less stressful than my earlier brief experience in a Brixton secondary school. Almost immediately I found one, teaching English (in which I had absolutely no qualifications, but an Oxford degree was considered sufficient) at Westminster Abbey Choir School. This boarding school in the Abbey precincts combined three functions, preparing boys (choristers were then always boys) for the public schools' entrance exam, training them in singing, and providing a choir for Abbey services. Of these, the third always took priority. So school holidays took place when no special services were timetabled, the terms continued through Christmas and Easter and school lessons often took place in the early evenings, fitted round services, choir practice, and music lessons, and cancelled or shifted if need be.

The boys who looked so angelic in their surplices were not of course little angels, they could be jealous of each other and unkind. But they were kept under a firm discipline and frequently reminded that they were very lucky to be attending the school. I felt sorry for them, never able to be with their families on festive occasions, their days so tightly scheduled that they were never able to mess around like other children. But they themselves did not complain and were usually very cheerful. They enjoyed singing, were proud of the important role they played in the services, where royalty and government ministers were sometimes present, they enjoyed the admiration they attracted and perhaps they appreciated the beauty of the Abbey. They took only a mild interest at best in school lessons, but most of them were bright and in classes of twelve or fifteen not difficult to teach. I simply followed the textbooks used by the previous teacher. As Jack had to commute to Kent and often worked late I didn't mind the irregular and lengthy hours. The Abbey was beautiful, I was not expected to attend services, though sometimes I went to hear the singing, and my work was very easy.

I don't think that in any event I would have stayed long in this job, which was providing an income but in other respects was absurdly far from what I wanted to do. In fact I only remained for a term since I had hardly started when I discovered, much to the annoyance of the headmaster, that I was pregnant. This was not a planned pregnancy, we wanted to have children, but not so soon. But after being initially disconcerted we were both happy about the prospective birth, which proved to be the best way of drawing a line under my mother's death. Pregnancy in 1950 was viewed rather differently from today. Visible pregnancy was still seen as in some way indecent and pregnant women in public positions, such as teachers, were expected to leave their jobs before the pregnancy 'showed'. Maternity clothes were designed to conceal, so like most women then I wore a smock and a loose coat. I had one 'best' outfit throughout three pregnancies – a skirt with a large cut out area from which the 'bump' protruded, concealed by a long, loose, swinging jacket. Hospitals, certainly King's College Hospital in Camberwell which I attended, took an assembly line approach to their patients. At the ante-natal clinic we sat on benches in the corridors for hours on end – everyone was told to come at the same time – and eventually were briefly and I am sure efficiently examined, but with no consideration of our psychological needs. There were no ante-natal classes, nor any discussion of, or information about, the momentous event that was approaching.

The baby was expected before Christmas, but didn't arrive until January 3rd. An acquaintance of Jack's newly arrived from New Zealand, Maurice Lee, whose wife and five children were to join him when he had found a job and a house, spent Christmas with us. He proved to be a useful distraction, talking almost incessantly, often amusingly. For the first time I cooked a goose, and vowed never to do so again, the huge amounts of strong flavoured fat lingered for days. In the absence of pre-natal classes and of friends who had had a baby I looked for a helpful book and found one called *Childbirth Without*

Fear by an English obstetrician, Grantley Dick Read. Ostracised by most of the medical establishment, he was an early advocate of non-medicalised natural childbirth. He argued that the pain women suffer is the consequence of their fear and accompanying tension and need not occur, nor need medical intervention, if women understood the process of childbirth and would relax. The advice seemed straightforward enough, so when my waters finally broke one night I got into the ambulance with a certain amount of confidence.

But when Jack left me at the hospital entrance – fathers were not then allowed into the labour ward – I suddenly felt very alone, deserted amongst strangers. And strange events followed. I was shaved and told to have a bath, although I'd had one at home a few hours before, dressed in a gown as for an operating theatre and then taken into the ward for women in the first stage of labour. My shock was extreme, so different was it from the scenario depicted by Grantley Dick Read. Fear possessed everyone in the room. The women were moaning and screaming, the nurses, grim-faced, seemed to fear they were not in control. One nurse was slapping the face of an admittedly very hysterical woman as I entered. My own labour proceeded without complications but was certainly not pain free, although alleviated by gas and air. At the end a medical student was called to perform an episiotomy. He was the first person to smile at me and talk in a relaxed, friendly way and I felt a wave of warmth towards him. With this exception from beginning to end the experience was horrendous. Not so much because of the birth itself, though no amount of reading could prepare you for the extraordinary processes that take over your body, but because of the inhumane hospital practices and procedures which infected the staff. I insisted on having my next two babies at home with visiting midwives and the experience could not have been more different. I was, in a sense, the hostess, and as such felt to an extent in control, easy in my own bed and familiar room. Jack could be present and the midwives were confident, warm and friendly.

As soon as he was born my first baby, a boy, was held up for me to see, then whisked away to another room. Exhilarated but exhausted I went to sleep, awestruck by the arrival of a new life. We had decided to name a boy William Michael, after Jack's great friend Bill Geddes and my brother Michael, and he was Bill from the start. A day after delivery if all went well mothers and babies were moved from Kings to a much smaller, less high powered hospital in East Dulwich and there we had to remain in bed for two weeks. The Nightingale ward I was taken to was very long with thirty-two beds, sixteen along each of the long walls, facing each other. The nurses' station was at one end so that they could oversee the whole ward. I didn't see much of Bill. The babies were kept in a separate ward where we couldn't hear them cry, and brought in to be fed at four hourly intervals, but not between 10pm and 6am, to allow us to sleep. After the 10a.m. feed the curtains were drawn and, like the babies, we were settled down again to sleep till lunch time. Visitors, although not children, were allowed from 3-4p.m., and husbands only from 7–8p.m. This system of fixed visiting times did have the advantage of protecting patients from the exhaustion of too many visitors, but the disadvantage was that patients without visitors at those times felt conspicuously neglected. At first those of us who were not fretting about younger children appreciated the imposed complete rest after the trauma of the hospital childbirth, but after a few days time dragged interminably.

The nurses' main aim seemed to be to try to establish breastfeeding. This must have been a thankless task since many women hardly tried, thinking it distasteful and knowing that after the babies were taken from our ward the nurses would give a bottle to any that appeared hungry. As was usual amongst working-class women at the time few intended to breastfeed when they got home. I myself had no problems with breastfeeding and breastfed all my three older children. The nurses were kind but impersonal, perhaps because they were dealing with any one of thirty-two patients – the system of assigning nurses to look after particular patients was not yet in use. The night sister was a bully who intimidated the ward, shouting angrily at any patient whom she considered out of order. No doctor or more senior nurse ever visited the ward at night so her bad temper was unrestrained.

The day before I was due to be discharged I was taken into a side room and allowed for the first time to watch a nurse bath my baby and change his nappy. With this as my sole education in baby care I set out for home the next day with Jack and our two-week-old son, excited but terrified. Neither of us had had any contact with babies before and none of our friends had yet had babies. We put him in his cot in our bedroom, and hovered over him anxiously. Soon we needed to change his nappy and had to check in a baby book how to do it. At that time disposable nappies had not been introduced. Babies wore two nappies, which had to be folded in a special way, put on separately and secured with safety pins – an inner, muslin nappy and an outer, very bulky towelling one, much too big for a small baby. Over this went a vest and a long nightdress worn during the day as well as at night, knitted 'bootees' and a knitted 'matinee jacket.'

Middle class mothers followed medical instructions not to enclose the nappies in rubber knickers, which caused a rash if used for long, so our babies' clothes tended to be constantly damp. We did not have a washing machine, which would not have fitted into our small kitchen or bathroom, and, extravagantly, we used a service which collected nappies and returned them clean and dry. We had bought the baby equipment – cot, pram and bath – second-hand, very cheaply. This was, I realised later, another class-linked choice. Working-class families were prepared to go heavily into debt to buy new equipment for their first child.

Fathers were only expected to take a day or two off for a baby's birth, so the next day Jack returned to work. I certainly didn't intend to be restricted to the role of mother and housewife for long, but I had no clear plans about when and how I would pursue my career. For some months I found motherhood more stressful than fulfilling. Left on my own I was very anxious. Bill showed no sign of having been trained by the nurses to feed at four hourly intervals. I was not at first thrown by this since I had a copy of the recently published *Baby and Child Care* by the U.S. paediatrician Benjamin Spock, who advocated treating children from birth flexibly and as individuals, feeding babies when they seemed hungry. Yes, but when, I wondered, should you feed them if they cried for a large part of the day? The doctor at the infant welfare clinic and the health visitor who called round offered no useful help, although they pointed out that Bill was healthy and growing well.

Driven to despair I would spend long hours pushing him in the pram, which almost always stopped him crying. In the end, the best advice was given to me, surprisingly, by Auntie Ivy, who occasionally made the long journey from Essex to allow me to go out for a few hours on my own. 'It's just because he has a very sensitive nature, dear,' she would say, 'you must just wait, he will grow out of crying'. And so he did, before he was six months old. Perhaps he had been anxious at being in the hands of such an anxious mother. So searing had the experience been that it is surprising that I had another baby in less than two years and then three more. None of them cried very much and I became increasingly addicted to small babies and able to take them in my stride.

My first experience of early motherhood was made more desolate by my social isolation. The busy social life of my student days seemed a distant dream. There were no mother and baby groups at that time, I had no friends with small children, and no relatives to call on except Ivy. Buggies for small babies that could be taken on buses were not then available, so without a car I was confined to the distance I could push a pram. Jack was away for long hours because of commuting to the hospital in Kent where he was working. Moreover, he had to spend Saturday mornings in the Maudsley – at that time everyone worked a five and a half day week. And Sunday afternoons, and most evenings, he spent writing his Ph.D. thesis. Sometimes the Maudsley Communist Party group met in the evenings in our flat, a big social event for me. If Bill was asleep I could attend. The members included, besides Neil O'Connor and Jack, Monte Shapiro, and Ann and Alan Clarke, who were then Ph.D. students of Eysenck, all psychologists, and one psychiatrist, Max Hamilton. Two or three psychologists from Oxford or elsewhere sometimes came. It was really a study group, which worked its way through volumes of Pavlov, as a more relevant and perhaps illuminating alternative to Marx. Politics or hospital issues were hardly ever discussed.

During the summer we decided that with the legacy from my mother we should get a mortgage on a house. Although the French couple in the ground floor flat seemed to have no problem bringing up their two little boys, everyone assured us that all right thinking British parents, if they possibly could, provided their children with a garden. We found a house with a long lease in Cavendish Road, leading off the south side of Clapham Common near Clapham South tube station. The road was noisy, on a busy bus route and since the front gardens were very small the houses were very near the road. Like millions of others built in London before the First World War our house was semi-detached, with a bay windowed front room and a back room opening on to a small garden. The kitchen and scullery were at the side, over looking and over shadowed by the adjoining house. We bought our first washing machine. Washing machines, still very cumbersome and only partially labour saving, were very much a middle class perquisite and the two elderly sisters who sold us the house were shocked at our extravagance in buying one.

We stayed there for seven years and I always found both the house and the neighbourhood ugly and depressing, and for a long while mourned our previous flat. As long as I can remember I have always been strongly affected by the aesthetic qualities, or lack of them, in my homes, especially the proportions of the rooms, their lightness, and whether they overlook trees and grass. This house failed on all counts, but we did get a lot of space for our money -three floors, with five bedrooms, and a cellar. This meant that we could supplement our income by taking lodgers.

An immediate and major benefit of the move was that I heard of and joined the local branch of the Communist Party, which had a women's section. This brought an end to my social isolation. The members were vocal, energetic working-class women from local housing estates, often with quite large families. Our activities and discussions were a world away from those of the Oxford student branch. There was no study of Marxism, about which the women knew little or nothing, nor of world affairs or even national politics. Instead we discussed and agitated on issues that concerned women on the estates, mainly to do with facilities for children, housing and local transport. Pushing our prams, we distributed leaflets, held small meetings in flats and organised delegations to the local MP and local Labour councillors. We almost always met with a very hostile reception from them – this was 1951 and the cold war was well under way – and as women, attempts were made to bully us.

Our spokeswoman was usually Doreen Hamilton, Max Hamilton's wife, a university graduate and the only other middle class member of the group. Doreen was a very articulate, energetic, assertive and strong-minded woman, well able to put down bullies. She was a natural leader, and despite her different social origin and education accepted as such by all the women in the group. She was short and stout, uninterested in her appearance or clothes, and seemed quite middle aged to me, though she was then only in her mid thirties. She had married late, which meant, by the standards of the time, over the age of 30, and had two young children. She came to play an important role in my life.

Jack had no contact with the local Communist Party, but he joined the Ex-Service Movement for Peace, which had recently been founded and was in some way affiliated to the Communist Party. Only five years after the end of the war it seemed, incredibly, that with the onset of the Korean war in 1950 we might be moving towards a third world war. What appeared to start as a civil war between North and South Korea rapidly became a proxy for a war between the U.S., which supplied the South with forces and arms, and the Soviet Union and China, which supplied the North. North Korean towns and villages were heavily bombed by U.S. forces and napalm was used for the first time. The U.S. Government openly discussed the possible use of atomic weapons. Jack, never before – or afterwards – an agitator, was so horrified that every Sunday for some time he took a soap box to Clapham Common and addressed the assembled crowd under the Ex-Service banner. The crowd, alas, was usually only half a dozen or so people, supported by myself with the pram. Several local members of the Ex-Service Movement came frequently to our house. They were all working-class men with whom Jack, an army private himself for years, got on very comfortably whilst I marvelled at the tedium, as I saw it, of their conversation. With the end of the Korean War in 1953 fears of a third world war temporarily abated.

Jack took no active part in politics thereafter, but he became involved in helping the work of the National Council for Civil Liberties (NCCL), now 'Liberty'. During the 1950s they focussed on the defence of people in asylums and mental hospital who were then effectively outside the law. Their campaign led to the setting up of a Royal Commission and eventually to the repeal of the Mental Deficiency Act of 1913, with its provisions for certifying and detaining 'mental defectives' and to the enactment of the Mental Health Act of 1959, which made the provision of community care a statutory duty. Jack worked closely with the NCCL in their campaign and also with government, supplying both with scientific evidence, and he was appointed as the only non-medical consultant advisor to the Department of Health.

In September my life abruptly changed when at the age of nine months Bill weaned himself. I had been giving him water to drink from a cup for some time, I never gave him a bottle, when one day he pushed my breast away and thereafter only wanted to drink from a cup. Suddenly I felt liberated. It was not just that he no longer needed me as a physical life support, but I felt no longer psychologically tied so closely to him as before. We could both have separate, more independent lives. I could now embark on training to become a researcher and establishing an identity beyond that of housewife and mother. Although I had not been consciously fretting that this identity was in abeyance, as soon as Bill had weaned himself I felt that I must at once start a new life. But first I would need to find a childminder whom I could trust. Wonderfully, Doreen Hamilton offered to look after Bill with her two children, a baby of Bill's age and a little girl of two, from 9–2p.m. on weekdays. She would use the money I gave her to employ a daily help so that she herself could give enough attention to the three very young children. I felt quite confident that Bill would be in good hands and that she would never neglect him for her own children.

At this juncture Monte Shapiro, head of the clinical psychology course at the Maudsley, and a member of the Communist Party group, said he would welcome me as a Ph.D. student to do an experimental test of his hypothesis about the effects of brain damage on psychological functioning. This was not at all the area in which I had hoped to research but the Maudsley was so close, Monte was so persuasive, and prepared to let me study part time, that I decided to accept the offer. I thought I would at the least learn how to do research. The arrangement with Doreen worked extremely well. I pushed Bill in the pram to her house, which was in the next road, each morning, and when I returned after lunch Doreen and I would take our prams to Clapham Common and spend the afternoon together. We became close friends.

When Bill was about fourteen months old I became pregnant again. For some reason I was quite unwell during this second, planned, pregnancy, and our decidedly old-fashioned G.P., calling at the house, said that I smelled strongly of acetone and must be starving. She recommended that I should go away to the country to rest and restore my appetite. The only person I knew who lived in the country was Lucy Munby, an old friend from the Oxford student Communist Party, who was living in a village near Cambridge with her husband and small son. She kindly offered to put me up for as long as I needed and I enjoyed strolling in the country lanes, which she rarely had the time for. After a week or two, though, it seemed to me a crazy arrangement, I should be living with my own husband and son, whom I was missing. Back home and feeling too weak to cope with Bill, I decided to find someone to look after him all day. Jack's New Zealand friend, Maurice Lee, a teacher, was living in Balham with his wife, Betty, and their five children. Betty was a Glaswegian, who belonged to the generation of working-class Scots who had all their teeth extracted and replaced by dentures as a twenty-first birthday present from their parents, to save subsequent dental charges. She had a very warm, humorous personality and a great love of children – before she had her own she would round up neighbouring children and take them out for walks. Now her youngest child had started school and she was working in a local shop, so we offered to pay her the same salary to look after Bill, collecting him in the morning and bringing him home at about 5p.m. She was delighted with the arrangement, and he seemed very happy with her. She was sad and disappointed when I reclaimed Bill after John was born.

In order to pay for childcare and a cleaner we took a lodger, sometimes two. Our first lodger was Eric Hobsbawm. Before Bill was born Eric and Muriel had finally separated. At about the same time Eric was appointed to a fellowship in King's College Cambridge and provided with rooms. As he was still lecturing at Birkbeck College and needed to stay in London for part of the week he was pleased to have a *pied à terre* with us in London and we were always happy to see him. After he acquired his own London flat Ajita Chakraborti, an Indian psychiatrist who was working in a nearby hospital, and who became a good friend, lived with us for several years – later I was to stay with her in Calcutta. But we were never short of lodgers whom we found by advertising in the windows of newspaper shops. At that time many, perhaps most, of the local landladies specified 'No coloured' sometimes 'No coloured or Irish'. By not making such stipulations we could always let our rooms, usually to Nigerian students or skilled workers from the Caribbean. Later, when we were particularly hard-up, we had three young Thai women, working in the Thai bank in London, living with us *en famille* to improve their English. It must have been a strange experience for them to live in our untidy household with two small, noisy boys -they themselves were so quiet, orderly, and delicate in all their ways. Their fine motor skills and mobility were extraordinary – they could bend their fingers back to touch the back of their hands and delighted in such occupations as peeling a large bunch of grapes, leaving it intact.

Between these diversions and the birth of a third baby I continued to work for my Ph.D. This had started as an experimental study with patients at Springfield hospital, Tooting, then an old style mental hospital, with locked wards. Patients remained there for decades, often for life, some standing in catatonic postures or sitting immobile for hours on end. It was a chilling place, only relieved for me by the absurdity of lunch in the medical dining room. The doctors and I sat round a long dining table, the physician superintendent at the head. Whilst we were brought, say, shepherd's pie, by one of the kitchen staff, he was served a superior meal, say, steak or chops, from a silver platter, by his personal man servant.

After finishing the first round of experiments I fell out with Monte Shapiro about the implications of the results and the experiments that should follow. Monte, often high spirited and enthusiastic, was also notorious for his explosive temper and inability to brook disagreement and I felt that I could not continue working with him. When I told Hans Eysenck, head of psychology, and no friend of Monte's, he shrugged (his most frequent and characteristic gesture) and said that there was no alternative supervisor. However if I wanted to work on my own he would be willing to be the nominal supervisor but he would not provide any supervision, the topic was not in his area of interest. My recollection is that he did not even read my thesis before I submitted it. So it was that the study became mainly an historical and theoretical discussion of the psychological effects of brain damage Now, it has occurred to me that these events echoed my exclusion from the German class at school and having to prepare for School Certificate German on my own. But Monte really was a very difficult man to work with unless you were prepared to accept his dictates and I was quite happy researching and writing on my own.

Chapter 11

Postscript 1950–2010

I had initially intended to end this memoir with the completion of my doctorate, but I decided that the story of my subsequent experiences as a woman academic with children throws some light on the history of women in the second half of the twentieth century. This is not a family memoir, I have written little about my husband and children, but it will be clear that they played a vital role in my life. I have entitled this section Postscript, not only because it was an afterthought, but also because it is selective, and is not a detailed chronological account.

A researcher and a working mother

After working intermittently on my Ph.D. thesis for nearly five years I finished it in July 1956. Bill was then five, John three, Jenny seven months and I was thirty. I at once set about looking for a job that would both be satisfying and increase our income. At the time very few women with young children worked, but I felt a need for intellectual stimulus and I came, after all, from a line of working mothers. In this Jack entirely supported me. But there was no question of his sharing domestic responsibilities and work time equally with me. Before the women's movement of the sixties this arrangement was virtually unknown, and in any case it would definitely not have appealed to Jack. But he had always encouraged me to study despite the cost of childcare and he was now happy for me to get a job. For some years we had been chronically hard up by middle class standards. Jack's salary was quite small and the childcare I'd needed to study for my Ph.D. had been expensive. We could not afford to buy a car or to go away for holidays, other than to stay with friends, we had a meal in a restaurant once a year and we bought most things, including furniture and the children's clothes, second- hand.

Jack would have been willing for me to work full-time but I did not consider doing so. This was partly because I remembered how desperately I had missed my own mother and partly because I enjoyed being with my children – though not all day, every day. And we could hardly have managed a family if I had been as committed to work as Jack. He was already a rather absent father. He worked in his study most evenings and weekends and often travelled abroad as a consultant for the World Health Organisation (WHO). His first, six week, assignment had taken place when John was only a few weeks old and Bill barely two. Both children woke frequently in the night and I stumbled around, hardly knowing day from night. But I knew that Jack was doing important work, influencing WHO policy and establishing his reputation. Almost my only visitor was Neil O'Connor who called round for a chat. It was one of those small, kindly acts, which the donor quickly forgets and the recipient long remembers.

Although I would have liked a research job none was available, so I applied for the post of part-time clinical psychologist at the (then) London Hospital, Whitechapel. I had no clinical experience or training, but courses in clinical psychology had only recently been started and the fact that I had a Ph.D. from the Institute of Psychiatry was considered an acceptable qualification. My job was to attend case conferences and do IQ and projective tests, which I had hurriedly to practice on friends and relatives. For a time the work was interesting. I learned to be a proficient tester and became familiar with a great range of psychological problems. Someone else might well have made more of the job, but for me it was primarily a stop-gap until I could do paid research. And it was wonderful to be able at last to buy the children clothes and toys from sources other than jumble sales. The journey to and from Whitechapel was time consuming, but Jenny was looked after by an au pair girl whilst I was out, whilst Jack, on his bike, took Bill to the local infant school and John to a local authority nursery school. We were lucky to get a place there. Nursery schools and classes were then very scarce and the playgroup movement was still in the future.

By 1959 Jack had moved up the salary scale and with my part-time salary we were financially much better off. We were now able to buy a car and leave the house and street I had always hated in Clapham for a quiet, tree lined street, Burbage Road, just off Dulwich village and less than two miles from the Maudsley Hospital where Jack worked. The house was similar to our previous one, but with much larger, better proportioned rooms, well set back from the road. For the first time we had central heating installed. Before this, we had accepted as given that in the winter you would feel cold if you left the kitchen or in the evenings the sitting room, and that you had to brace yourself to get out of bed in the mornings. When John was born at home in December 1952 there was ice on the inside of our bedroom window. The garden of our new house was big enough for the children to practise long jumps, and it backed on to a sports ground. In many ways Dulwich was an ideal environment for a family. The owners of the small local shops were friendly to children, especially Mr. Bartley, the greengrocer, who always smiled at young children and gave them a few grapes or cherries. The boys could cycle to school, there were other children next door and opposite and they all roamed freely together round Dulwich Village. They could play in the sports ground behind our house and in a large stretch of unbuilt-on ground behind the houses opposite, difficult to access unless you knew the secret. The panic about paedophilia had not then set in and it didn't occur to us to curb the children's freedom.

While at the London Hospital I wrote three articles arising from my Ph.D. thesis on the psychological effects of brain damage. Desmond Pond, a senior psychiatrist in the Maudsley Hospital Children's Department who specialised in epilepsy, read my articles and suggested that I apply for a post-doctoral grant from the Medical Research Council (MRC) to work in his group. I was awarded a three-year part-time grant and in 1960 I moved to the Maudsley. Desmond was a kind and generous patron. He gave me a small room to myself in the Children's Department and a free hand to develop the research as I wished. The Maudsley, besides being wonderfully near my new home, was a very exciting place. Aubrey Lewis, the Director, was very confrontational, whilst Hans Eysenck, Head of Psychology, was very laid back, but both could be terrifying figures. Any comment you made to them was likely to be dissected and shown to be foolish. Aubrey Lewis expected the staff to work very hard, be productive, think sceptically and achieve exacting methodological standards in their research. Psychology had a high profile and unlike its position in many hospitals was not seen as subservient to psychiatry. The atmosphere was competitive and pervasively critical – someone suggested that the Institute's motto at that time should have been 'Thou fool'. But it was also always stimulating. At coffee and lunch times people would cluster together to argue about the latest journal articles.

Not everyone could flourish in this atmosphere but those who did were stamped for life with the imprint of Aubrey Lewis. Despite the competitive atmosphere friendships were made in the coffee room and I soon became friends with Lorna Wing. She was a passionate animal lover, who crusaded against the over feeding of pets and advised us on the best kind of dog for our children – a female labrador. She is more widely known as an expert on autism. She and her husband John, both psychiatrists, had a severely retarded autistic daughter. At that time most psychiatrists believed that autism was caused by a 'refrigerator' mother. Lorna, herself a warm-hearted, affectionate woman, was infuriated by this cruel theory and played an important role in demolishing its credibility.

I decided that the best use of the time available to me would be to analyse existing evidence about some aspect of epilepsy. Epilepsy was at that time a very stigmatised condition and those suffering from it tended to be seen as having specific and undesirable psychological characteristics. In an article entitled, 'The personality of epileptics: a discussion of the evidence' I analysed all the available evidence for this belief. I showed that there was some, though inconclusive, evidence that psychological disorders are more prevalent amongst epileptics than the general population. There was also evidence that different types of epilepsy or locations of epileptic focus may be associated with different types of psychopathology. But the studies showed that the personalities and psychological disturbances of epileptics vary widely – they did not support the belief in a characteristic 'epileptic personality'. I pointed out that in any case most studies had included only epileptics who attend hospital clinics, and had used very inadequate measures. I think that this article did have an impact on the stereotypes then held about epileptics, although they have still not gone away.

Amongst the friends I made in the coffee room was Jim Margerison, a doctor who specialised in epilepsy and electro-encephalography and was very interested in psychology. An ex-bomber pilot, with the broken nose of an amateur boxer, he had trained as a doctor after the war. He was a classical extravert, always needing responsive company, an inveterate flirt, high spirited and drawn to dangerous situations. He loved to drive his car into skids on the icy roads that were then frequent in the winter. He smoked and drank heavily. A generous man, he had the habit of every time he wanted a cigarette – which was very often – taking out two and offering one to me. But I never smoked more than four or five cigarettes a day and soon stopped altogether, despite the fact that Jack was also a heavy smoker, lighting a cigarette, or later his pipe, before he got out of bed in the morning. It was only in the mid-fifties that the relationship between smoking and lung cancer had been firmly established and it took a long time for the message to be widely acted on, even by doctors and scientists.

Jim persuaded me – he was very persuasive – that we should work together on experimental studies of the extent to which abnormal EEG discharges affect ongoing psychological functions. On one occasion we commandeered the TV set from the medical staff common room, to the fury of the hospital secretary, to try the effect of different types of TV programme on EEG discharges. When my MRC grant ended in 1963 I was appointed to a part-time lectureship in the department of Experimental Neurophysiology – their first psychologist. I spent four years in this position, mostly working with Jim. Doing experimental work was great fun and in a clinic with helpful technicians and a plentiful supply of patients we could be very productive. We would discuss a problem, throw up ideas, devise a way of testing one of them, quickly carry it out and immediately analyse the results. The publications and conference papers, so important for success at the Maudsley, took rather longer, especially because Jim was extremely obsessional in his approach to writing. I wrote eight articles during this time, most of them jointly with Jim, and was elected a member of the elitist Experimental Psychology Society. Soon after I left the Maudsley Jim, in early middle-age, had a massive heart attack and died.

In 1964, with funds from the (then) Spastics Society, the Institute of Education established a chair in Child Development and offered it to Jack. We now felt positively affluent and decided to buy a holiday cottage within easy reach of London. Everyone in the family loved walking in the country – the children had been on treks with the Forest School camps – and remembering my visits to the Ryles I hoped to find a house in the South Downs. After much searching, in 1966 the landlady of a pub in the village of East Dean, in West Sussex, told us there were some derelict cottages at the end of her lane. They were built of fine flint but had been abandoned for many decades, the roofs fallen in and most of the interior rotted away. They had never had sanitation or an electricity supply and water came from a well at the rear. But they looked over a field of cows at the front and the South Downs, only minutes away, at the back. We bought them at once, very cheaply, and discovered that they had originally, in 1797, been built as one house, converted in the nineteenth century into four back-to-back cottages for workers on the Goodwood Estate. We took out a mortgage with my salary and had the building gutted and restored. The house turned out to be much bigger than we had expected, light and spacious with five bedrooms and a table tennis room. But we soon had five children to fill it, having adopted two babies, Martin and Lucy, from care.

We kept this house for more than twenty-five years, much longer than anywhere else I have ever lived. I loved it, and the surrounding country, deeply, as did the children. We spent half terms and part of the school holidays there and when the older children had left school we went every other weekend. After I eventually, reluctantly, sold it, I kept dreaming of it. I knew all the walks from the house and all those a shortish drive away. We would leave London after the Friday evening rush hour and two hours later breathe the intoxicatingly fresh air at East Dean and gaze at the brilliant stars, absorbing the complete darkness and the silence which can never be found in London. On Saturdays we would walk for about ten miles, taking a picnic, and on Sundays return to London mid-afternoon before the rush hour. During longer stays we often visited Chichester, six miles to the south, and further south, West Wittering, a sprawling undeveloped beach. In the summer we sometimes went there late after almost everyone had left and made a fire in the sand dunes and cooked supper.

East Dean was then a very small but ancient village, listed in the Domesday book, with about 250 inhabitants, two buses a day, a post office, one shop, a garage, a church, a cricket team and one pub, the Star and Garter. This was the village centre, presided over by Mrs. Ruffles, a warm, generous but firm landlady. After closing the pub in the afternoon, instead of turning her customers out she made tea for them all in a huge pot. Like most publicans at the time she didn't serve meals but during the interim period after we had moved in, and as yet had no oven, she cooked a roast lunch for us, alongside of her own, to take home on Sundays.

The village then had several working farms on its outskirts and many of the residents belonged to the three families whose names predominated in the churchyard. We soon discovered that there were long standing tensions between the villagers. 'Incomers', such as the tractor driver and his wife who had lived there for fifteen years, were regarded with suspicion, and anyone whose morals were deemed questionable was ostracised. There were a few middle class residents, including the writers Christopher Fry and Robert Gittings, and some retired couples, but we were the first weekenders. We tried to avoid being drawn into the middle class social network, though we got to know a number of people in the village and I used to visit regularly some elderly, increasingly eccentric widows. Now, East Dean is no longer a working village. It has only one farm, with huge fields and very few workers, there are no buses, the post office, shop and cricket team have gone, and the Star and Garter under new management is a gastro pub, with play equipment in the garden for children and bed and breakfast on offer. Middle class people, working in Chichester or retired, have bought many of the old cottages so the village looks much smarter. The countryside is still lovely.

After seven years at the Maudsley I decided on a drastic change of research direction. This was partly because although I had attained reasonable EEG expertise I realised that someone as completely impractical as myself, with no real interest in or deep knowledge of electro-physiology, could not make an independent contribution to this field of study. It was also because I was now clear that I wanted to focus my research on issues in child development which would have socially useful implications. At forty I at last knew what I really wanted to do and set about making it happen, rather than, as before, responding to opportunities that presented themselves.

The Maudsley was no place to site this kind of research so in the autumn of 1967 I resigned my lectureship and moved to the Institute of Education. This was a considerable culture shock. Gone was the intellectual cut-and-thrust and the pressure to work and publish of the

Maudsley. Coffee time discussions tended to centre on TV programmes rather than journal articles. On one of my first visits to the senior common room one academic was telling another, 'In an interview, I always look first at a man's shoes – if they're not well polished I write him off'. Jack's department was of course different and later the ethos of the whole Institute, which always had a few brilliant professors, became transformed. Many universities then did not allow married couples to work in the same department. Jack was always uneasy that he would be suspected of nepotism and did not want me to apply for a senior research fellowship in the Institute, but I did so and was appointed, I believe on my own merits. But I kept a low profile in our research Unit as well as the main Institute, and I didn't attend policy meetings. I thought that if Jack and I disagreed this would cause talk, and if we agreed we might seem too much of a united front. We never in fact worked together although Jack strongly influenced my ideas about residential institutions.

I very much admired his work, but our research strategies were quite different. Jack wrote very thoughtfully on such issues as the relationship between academic and applied psychology but his research was mainly concerned with improving services. He emphasised the importance of epidemiological studies, that is, first studying the size, the characteristics, and the needs of the people that a service is intended for. Although this may seem an obvious step in fact most new services and extensions to services are hastily set up following a media scandal or political crisis. His other main strategy was to make very bold experimental interventions, setting up new model institutions and services. Over the years he had acquired the kind of charisma and authority needed to secure the very large scale funding that such projects require. My own preference was for challenging widely held beliefs or theories bearing on childcare or education which I thought were held dogmatically, without adequate evidence, and my preferred method was to test these beliefs where possible by direct observation, and also interviews.

The first study I did after moving to the Institute of Education arose from my scepticism about the then very widely believed theories of John Bowlby. He asserted that young children deprived of maternal care in the first two years of life grow up to be 'affectionless psychopaths' and that 'good mothering is almost useless if delayed beyond the age of two and a half.' He was opposed to all nursery or school care for children under three, and insisted that from three to five years it should only be part-time. Historically, this did not make sense. Women in the north had always worked in the mills and used childminders, but Lancashire people were not 'affectionless psychopaths'. Later Bowlby came increasingly to modify this theory, but it was the original assertion that was very influential for many years. Whilst it led to the more humane treatment of children in hospitals, its implications were felt by many women as oppressive.

I thought that residential nurseries run by voluntary bodies would be the ideal setting in which to test Bowlby's theory. I applied for funds to Dr. Barnardo's Society and began by spending a lot of time reading their files, finding out why and when children entered and left their nurseries. I found that they were usually placed soon after birth by single mothers and that a sizeable number stayed for at least two years before they returned to their mothers or were adopted. A natural experiment seemed possible. By assessing the children when they were just two and then following the development of both those who were adopted and those who were not, comparing them with children reared at home, Bowlby's theory, and more generally the belief in the long term influence of an unusual early social experience, could be tested.

I then spent a good deal of time preparing for the research by visiting residential nurseries all over the country, pondering on the differences between nursery and home life. Sometimes I got up very early to arrive before the children were woken up, other days I stayed until they had been put to bed at night. The care was in many ways excellent. The children lived in groups of six with two staff, they were well fed and clothed and plentifully supplied with toys and books. But adult-child relationships were markedly different from those in a family. The nurses were constantly moved between groups. I discovered from staff books that by the age of two a child had on average been looked after for at least a week by twenty-four different nurses. Although usually kind, the nurses were encouraged to be detached, not intimate with the children. They tended to watch over them rather than becoming involved or playing with them. Getting up time in the morning was as brisk as an army turnout and bedtime was a perfunctory affair, the staff anxious to get off duty. Often a child would become attached to a particular nurse, who would, however, soon move on. The children certainly lacked both continuity in care and affection. At two, few had major behaviour problems, but they tended to be very aggressive to each other and clinging to any adult who came along.

As well as devising ways of assessing staff-child relationships we had to test the two-year-old children. Neither my research officer, Ann Joseph, nor myself had much experience of testing two-year-olds, which can be a challenging encounter. So before starting the project we went round a large Southwark housing estate and some Peabody buildings, knocking on the doors and asking if there were any toddlers we could test. We were almost always welcomed and we saw some unusual childcare practices. One woman in cramped quarters with a noisy, active two-year-old kept him in a pushchair and when she wanted him to be quiet put up the hood and turned him to face the wall. Like a canary, he was instantly silenced.

Grants from Dr. Barnardo's and the Rowntree Trust enabled me, with Jill Hodges and other research officers, to follow the children until they were sixteen. The study did have implications for child development theory. We found that contrary to Bowlby's theory, spending their first two years in a nursery with little or no parental contact did not usually result in the children growing up 'affectionless' or even disturbed. The sequalae to nursery care depended very much on the amount of attention and affection that they received after leaving the nurseries. Most adopted children did develop a strong affectionate relationship with their new parents, it was with their peers that about half of them still had difficulties at sixteen. Those children who returned to their mothers, who often by then had a new partner, other children, little spare time and few resources, were less likely to become attached to them and more often had behaviour problems.

The findings of the study did influence policy on adoption. They also had a dramatic effect on nursery care. Quite soon after receiving our findings first Dr. Barnardo's, then other bodies, closed their residential nurseries. This was an astonishing volte-face. Dr. Barnardo's governing council had until recently been dominated by bishops who believed that the main aim of their Homes should be to produce good Christians. (A similar aim was taken very seriously in a Catholic boys' home I visited, where after school the boys were kept busy in a workshop making coffins, to keep their minds on the reality of death, I was told.) I would have preferred Dr. Barnardo's to consider changing the way children were cared for in nurseries and finding out what problems might be involved in alternative forms of care, such as long term fostering. I suspect that the decision to close the nurseries was as strongly influenced by their high cost, at a time when the society wanted funds to develop other ways of helping families, as by my research.

In a parallel study, influenced by Jack, I showed that the different ways in which residential nurseries were organised affected staff language and behaviour and, as a consequence, the children's language development. In hierarchical nurseries where the matron made every decision, including when the children could be taken into the garden or the TV could be turned on, the nurse in charge of a group was really just minding the children, and up to seventy-five per cent of their talk consisted of commands or 'routine' remarks such as 'Good boy'. In the most autonomous groups, separately housed in a flat or cottage, the nurses were more like foster mothers and their activities and their talk with the children was more varied and interesting. I predicted, and found, that in these nurseries the children's language development was more advanced than in the hierarchical nurseries. I also found that in all the nurseries, whenever two nurses were looking after a group of six children, the more senior would always be in charge. Irrespective of her training the nurse not in charge would interact and talk much less to the children than the nurse in charge, so that the effect of having an extra nurse present was quite small. It would have been much more productive to put each nurse in charge of three children.

I thought the findings had important implications for other kinds of institution, such as old people's homes, but there was then, and still is, little general interest in the way in which institutions function. Moreover I didn't put enough effort into generating public discussion about this issue to make an impact. It took me a long time to realise that social science research findings usually only influence policy makers if they are widely discussed in the quality press and media. But also, research findings only influence policy if they resonate with the ideology and/or the financial or political needs of policy makers, so that, as in the case of my residential nurseries study, they have reason to welcome the findings.

With both Jack and I working in Bloomsbury it seemed sensible for us to move north of the Thames and avoid the lengthy journey along the congested Walworth Road. We looked first at houses in Islington and Camden Town, both within walking distance of the Institute of Education, but then by chance we were sent particulars of a house in the Vale of Health in Hampstead. The Vale of Health, we discovered, is a small hamlet built in the late eighteenth and nineteenth century and entirely surrounded by the Heath except for its access road. Amongst former residents were Leigh Hunt, who was visited there by all the Romantic poets and a century later, Lytton Strachey, Stanley Spencer, and D.H. Lawrence. One sunny day I went to see the house in my lunch hour. It was in The Gables, a terrace built in 1883 at the far end of the Vale, separated from the heath only by a footpath, which ended in a large pond. As I stood outside it was very quiet. Nothing moved except the squirrels on the grass slope opposite and I felt that I was in the country. Without even going into the house I decided we must buy it. Later we discovered that at weekends streams of people pass by, peering into our windows, but during the week we had that part of the heath to ourselves.

Because the house had been divided into bed sitting rooms, lacked a kitchen, was very damp and needed a lot of work, the price was £17,500. This was just before the house price boom of 1970. Even so we could only afford it because Jack and Neil O'Connor had recently received an award from the Kennedy International Scientific Trust. The house was on four floors, quite narrow, with two rooms on each floor. We moved in on January 1st 1970 – New Year's Day was not made a bank holiday until 1974. I stayed there for sixteen years until I was alone in the house, Jack had died, and all the children had left home. After school I used to take the children on the heath and Lucy, the youngest, claims she still knows every inch of it. Soon after we arrived a neighbouring house was bought by the Prasads, an Irish-Indian couple with four young children, whom our two youngest children grew up with, playing together on the heath outside our houses. When we arrived The Gables was a dilapidated terrace, most houses divided into flats or bed sitting rooms. Now, the Gables, like the whole of the

Vale, is very smart, and four bedroom terraced houses, smaller than ours, sell for two million pounds.

In 1971 Jack resigned his chair and with a large grant from the then Department of Health set up the Thomas Coram Research Unit within the Institute of Education. This involved him giving up his tenured university post for a seven-year contract, but we did not see that as a problem. I worked in the Unit as a Senior Research Officer in the Institute and then Reader until Jack's death in 1979, when I became the next Unit Director, and a professor. Of the most significant research projects I directed after the residential nursery/adoption projects, the first was a comparison of the conversations of four-year-old girls with their teachers at morning nursery school and with their mothers at home in the afternoon. This was prompted by my unease, in an earlier study of children's play in nursery schools, at the very artificial way that the teachers talked to the children. The generally received wisdom at the time was that working-class mothers fail to stimulate their children, some teachers insisting that they never talk to them. It was believed that the children's language could best be helped by teachers asking them 'educational' questions. Hence they spent most of their time moving around the children asking them a series of 'cognitive demands' about their ongoing play, e.g. 'what happens when you roll the dough?' These questions were prompted not, of course, by curiosity, but with the aim of introducing the child to concepts, in this case of shape. Often the questions were left unanswered, because, the teachers believed, the children were unable to answer but I suspected it was because they were uninterested in the questions or uncertain how they were supposed to respond to them.

In fact, our recordings of the same children talking at home (we sewed tiny radio microphones into their clothes) showed them spontaneously using the very concepts and verbal skills the teachers thought they lacked. There were social class differences in the mothers' language – middle class mothers tended to be more explicit and to place much more stress on giving their children a wide range of general knowledge and vocabulary. But in both middle and working-class homes a vast amount of talk was going on. The children, by talking to their mothers, arguing, and endlessly asking rather than answering, questions, provided their own varied and effective contexts for language learning. We were not observing hand picked families – all the mothers who met our criteria agreed to take part, though we missed the very dysfunctional families who did not send their children to a morning nursery class. In contrast the much less frequent, much briefer, adult initiated conversations with the staff at school failed to engage the children's interest. Moreover, the teachers' talk was narrowly focussed on play. At home the children's persistent curiosity as well as their numerous wrangles with their mothers meant that conversation ranged over the past and future, the worlds of work, money and relationships.

We did not dispute the importance of nursery schools. They socialise children into a wider world, accustom them to different authority figures and provide them with valuable play experiences and companions, often not available at home. And we certainly didn't believe that children need to spend all day with their mothers. Our intention was to point to the power of the home, including working-class homes, in stimulating language development, and to challenge the general acceptance of the 'play curriculum' of the nursery school. We wanted to start a discussion about whether children's interests and curiosity about all aspects of the world – what Susan Isaacs called their 'thirst for understanding' – can be fostered more in nursery schools.

The book about this study that I published with Martin Hughes in 1984 caused a good deal of controversy. Some teachers felt threatened, some women felt, wrongly, that we were arguing that women should stay at home. Two feminists wrote a book *Democracy in the Kitchen*, which was an attack on our study on the grounds that we had argued that working-class mothers should be more like middle class mothers and that we ignored the fact that both groups of mothers are oppressed. However, our book sold very well at home and abroad, and is still being sold and is still on the reading list of many primary teachers' courses. But the changes that have since occurred in nursery schools are not those we had hoped for. Instead they resulted from government pressure to introduce literacy and numeracy at an ever earlier age.

The other projects I directed in the eighties addressed issues to do with race, of personal concern to me because we had adopted two mixed race children. In the seventies it was often argued that the IQ difference then found between black and white groups was genetically determined. I was able to show, and published the result in *Nature*, that in children aged two to five who had been in residential nurseries since infancy there was no difference between the average IQ of white and black children. By the eighties the question debated was why black children of African-Caribbean origin were consistently found to have lower school attainments than white children. I decided to attempt to answer this question in a very large scale project. To see at what age a difference emerges we assessed white and black (African Caribbean and mixed race) children shortly before they started at infant school and followed them until they moved to junior school. To avoid the possibility that black children did badly because they attended 'worse' schools we chose equal numbers of black and white boys and girls who were attending the same classes in thirty-three multiracial schools, mainly in very materially disadvantaged areas. Each year we observed them and their teachers in the classroom, assessed their progress, interviewed their class teachers and parents and at age seven, the children as well.

We found that within our largely working-class sample there was a huge difference in their knowledge of the 'three Rs' before they started school. A few could read some words and write their first name but many could produce only an unformed scribble. More than half did not know that print goes from left to right or that one reads the print, not the pictures, in a book. Their attainments were related both to the level of their mother's education and to the children's own verbal ability, but there was no average difference between black and white children, although there was a gender difference. Girls, both black and white, tended to have better early writing skills than boys. By the end of infant school there was still no overall difference between black and white children in attainment but the black girls were ahead of all other groups in reading and writing, whilst the black boys were doing the worst. Ian Plewis later found that these differences remained when the children were eleven.

We also found that the black boys were the group most often said by their teachers, and observed by us, to be aggressive, disobedient and to fool around in class. But this cannot be the only explanation for their lower attainments since the black girls, who also had more behaviour problems than the white children, though fewer than the black boys, were doing much better at school. We couldn't find any factors in the home, either, that were responsible, although the children of single parents, both black and white, tended to have more behaviour problems. We were looking for, but did not observe, overt or covert racism from teachers, though we observed plenty of racism between children in the playground. And although the teachers' expectations of all the children tended to be low, they were not especially low in the case of black boys. In short, we were unable to account for the poor performance of the black boys, which is probably caused by a complex interaction of factors.

The study had many interesting incidental findings. In the top infants year at age seven we found that children on average only spent eight minutes a day at school reading, a proportion that must have increased later with the introduction of the 'literacy hour'. Half of the seven year olds said they disliked reading at home either because they didn't know a lot of the words or because it was a solitary activity which they resorted to only when there was nothing more interesting to do. Many women will not be surprised to learn that at the age of seven the boys, both black and white, tended to overestimate their attainments, rating themselves as above average. Sadly, unbeknownst to themselves or to their parents, their attainments were well below the national norms. The majority of children enjoyed school but said they didn't find the lessons interesting, it was the social life they enjoyed. And whilst many thought that playtimes were the best part of the school day, for some, especially white girls, rough behaviour and teasing made it the worst part.

The study made relatively little impact. This was partly because those on the left were unwilling to believe that the teachers showed no racism. Teacher racism, conscious or not, is the easiest way to explain the failure of black boys. But our observers, who included a black teacher, did spend a lot of time in each class, alert to this possibility. The lack of impact may also have been because we produced so many findings, of which I have listed only a few, which interacted in such complex ways that they were difficult to describe. With hindsight it would have been better to try to get across just two or three simple key findings, including the fact that an ethnic difference was not present at the start of infant school. The National Curriculum, introduced after our project had ended, has succeeded in raising overall reading standards but it did not address issues of social inequality, which remain.

The last project I directed in the Unit also arose directly from my personal concern about race, as well as from my long-term interest in children in care. For some time in the Unit we had discussed the insistence by social workers on the 'same race placement' of children in care. Black (including mixed race) children placed in a white family would, they argued, suffer from 'identity confusion', fail to develop a 'positive black identity' and would not be taught the strategies they need to cope in a racist society. They also believed that mixed race children would have a particularly poor and confused self image and that their only hope was to be assimilated as 'black' into a black family. This policy resulted in the removal of many black and mixed race children from white foster homes where they had happily spent some years, whilst others lingered in children's homes because of the shortage of black foster and adoptive parents. But the policy was based on assumptions about the identities of children living in their own homes which were without any evidential basis. So I decided with Ann Phoenix, a very able young African Caribbean researcher – she is now co-Director of the Unit – to study, with a team of black and white interviewers, the racialised identities of black, mixed race and white fourteen to eighteen year olds living with their own parents in the London area, and attending local authority or fee paying schools. About half were living with both parents, most of the rest with a single white mother.

We found that the majority of the fifty-eight mixed white and African Caribbean young people living at home whom we interviewed regarded themselves as 'mixed' or 'brown', and not 'black'. The majority also felt positive about their racialised identity, seeing mixed parentage as an advantage, because they felt comfortable with both black and white people. Girls often said that their appearance was admired by both black and white girls. Those young people who felt positive about their colour tended to live in multiracial areas and attend multiracial schools, many of which had effective anti-racist policies. But whether or not they were living with a black parent had no influence on whether they felt 'black' or spoke positively about their mixed parentage.

This was also the case with their cultural loyalties. Those who lived in white neighbourhoods and attended predominantly white schools, whether or not they lived with a black parent tended to have close white friends and to be involved in white culture (clothes, music etc.), whilst those in multiracial areas and schools were more likely to have close black friends and to be enthusiasts for some form of contemporary black youth culture. However, a substantial proportion of these mixed race young people had no strong sense that there were distinct black and white cultures. Two thirds of them identified themselves as 'Londoners', in preference to 'English', and said they felt most comfortable in their multiracial city.

All of them, except a small number who looked white, had at some time experienced racism. The form of racism they had found most wounding was the name calling which had been rife in their primary schools. How much racism they experienced was influenced by their social class and gender. Mixed race working-class boys suffered the most racial abuse and discrimination, middle class girls the least. But whatever their social class, black and mixed race boys in predominantly white schools where the peer culture was racist, as in some independent boys' schools, often suffered greatly. All the young people said they had strategies to deal with racism, of which the commonest was simply to ignore it or discount it as stupid. This was also the advice most often given by their parents, whether black or white, anxious to keep them out of trouble. But only half the parents, black or white, had given them any advice or discussed racist experiences with them or had told them to be proud of their colour or told them about black role models.

Some young people did share the characteristics which social workers thought mixed race young people should have, i.e. they thought of themselves as black, rather than mixed, they said that racism was much discussed in their family, they adhered to a black culture and thought that there were great differences between black and white people and their cultures. But these were not necessarily young people who lived with a black parent. They were those who lived with a strongly politicised parent, who was as often white as black.

Mixed race and black children in care should certainly not be placed in white families who harbour any racism. But our finding that the main influence on the racialised and cultural identities of young people living with their parents was the ethnic mix of their school and neighbourhood, not the colour of their parents, raised serious doubts about the policy of 'same race placement'. We probably contributed to the slight moderating of this policy that has since occurred, but it has certainly not disappeared. Our study also highlighted the legitimacy of 'mixed' as an ethnic category. At the time of the study, in the late eighties, it was 'politically correct' to refer to mixed race people as 'black' and many of the young people told us that they were often upset, when filling out forms, to be forced to categorise themselves as either black or white. Partly because of the increasing numbers of ethnically mixed children and perhaps with some influence from our study, this is no longer the case – official forms now almost always offer at least one, often several, ethically mixed categories.

We also in some sense legitimised research on people of mixed race, which up till then had hardly begun in the U.K. Our book *Black, White or Mixed Race?* went into a second edition.

All my research grew out of my own experience and values. As a life long rebel it was natural for me to challenge received ideas. As a graduate of Aubrey Lewis' regime at the Maudsley I had learnt to be sceptical of received academic theories and to appreciate the importance of methodological rigour. And as an egalitarian the projects that I undertook did not arise 'from the literature', the traditional point of origin of academic research, but from what Jack described as a wish 'to make science work for human betterment.' All my research was concerned with children who were in some respects socially underprivileged – children in care, working-class and black children. I was known to have left-wing and avowedly anti-racist views and my research has been accused of political bias, but the data have always been mainly collected and statistically analysed by a team of others. My bias lay in selecting the questions, not in influencing the answers.

Looking back, I am amazed at the amount I undertook in the eighties, whilst bringing up, or perhaps just living with, my youngest child Lucy through her teenage years. Besides the political activities and consultancies abroad which I describe later, I was directing three of the research projects described above, supervising doctoral students, publishing two books and twenty-eight articles or chapters in books, and directing a multidisciplinary research unit. This had a staff of between twenty-two to thirty psychologists, sociologists, statisticians and anthropologists. There were few women directors of research units at the time, and in most research units women tended to be in the minority and to occupy the more junior posts. Whilst I was Director, the new Deputy Director and a number of the senior staff were women, and in all between two thirds and three quarters of our academic staff were women. One of the main rationales of a Unit is that it can train and retain researchers. Our researchers tended to stay in our Unit for at least five years and a large proportion later became professors. Unlike a university department we had to provide our own funds, apart from the salaries of the three most senior staff whom by that time had tenured university posts. There was therefore constant pressure on us to secure grants. We had a 'rolling contract' with the Department of Health, which gave a measure of continuity and in 1981 we acquired the status of an SSRC 'Designated Research Centre', which gave seven researchers contracts for eight years. We thus had immensely more security than is currently the case but we still needed to get funds for a number of projects.

Our staff had less autonomy in their research than university lecturers do, because they had to fit within the overall programme of the Unit, which was to study the social, educational and health needs of young children and their families and the services provided for them. In addition, the Director was ultimately responsible for the quality of the Unit research. I shared this responsibility with the deputy Director, but for more senior researchers joining the Unit the constraints on their autonomy could be a problem. This did at times result in conflicts and strains, which I was eventually glad to escape.

Until Jack died I had been very much a back room researcher, having very little contact with the Institute of Education and no administrative or management experience beyond my own projects. It would have been helpful to receive management training after my appointment. My assets were that I had some reputation as a psychologist – I was elected a Fellow of the British Psychological Society in 1977 – and I had very high research standards, acquired at the Maudsley. I was determined that the Unit should continue to be a centre for high quality, policy relevant research. As Director I had to sit on committees of the Institute of Education, of which the Unit was a part, and which I had never before attended, and I had to defend the Unit's corner within the Institute.

I was immensely helped by Basil Bernstein, a brilliant and famous Professor of Sociology in the Institute, who always supported the Unit's interests. He was an old family friend, whose iconoclasm and high spirits had won over even my teenage children, who tended to scorn our friends. He was an equal success with the younger children, on one occasion entertaining them by impersonating a sheep, with his sheepskin jacket turned inside out, crawling round the sitting room, baa-ing. Basil charmed and flattered his allies, and was cuttingly rude and hostile to his enemies, never fearing, and often succeeding in, making enemies. Whilst I intensely disliked committee meetings and found them terminally boring, Basil positively enjoyed them, regarding them as stimulating occasions for battle. He manipulated the proceedings to obtain the decisions he wanted and block those he didn't. He made careful plans in advance, formed allies before the meeting and employed tactics to delay or expedite particular items on the agenda. At the end of a meeting he would be elated by his success or furious if he had failed.

These were skills I was never going to, or indeed wanted to, acquire, but I did learn the importance of having a social network within a large institution of people who would support each other. I also set up what Jack had refused to have, an Advisory Group from outside the Institute of distinguished academics and senior administrators, including some of my friends, to consult with and to offer support to the Unit. This they did, without in anyway infringing on our autonomy. I took the issue of support very seriously, since the large scale research funding our Unit needed was beginning to get much harder to find. I even considered trying to get a royal patron, but the staff (wrongly, in my opinion) thought that would be a step too far. Social science researchers are now in a difficult position. Funds are much less readily available, and funders, especially government, tend to want specific, immediate issues addressed, rather than problems of greater generality, which may require following through over a long period of time. Government now prefers to commission one-off projects rather than support Units. But in a Unit staff can be retained and will acquire the depth of knowledge required for good research, and the wide perspective needed to assist government planning.

The position of women academics, however, has in many ways improved. There were very few women professors at the Institute of Education in my time, but now there are virtually as many women professors as men. (This is not the case, though, in most university departments). Some women academics at the Institute in the past complained of encountering sexism at work, but I don't think that I did, except perhaps in respect of my salary. The salary paid to individual professors in the Institute of Education varied, and was not revealed, but I knew that I was paid less than Jack, and I successfully argued for a (limited) increase. Working mothers now receive much less public disapproval than in the past, and women themselves are now more confident in pursuing their career ambitions. In my own case, before Jack's death I saw my own career as definitely subordinate to his. I very much admired his research, he had an international reputation, and I did not question that I should work part-time, and take the major responsibility for the children and home. There was probably an element of sexism in this decision, which would have disappointed my mother. Now, many couples aim at a greater equality in their lives. But taking second place did mean that I could work part-time, which I did until I was fifty. Professional women with children now often work fulltime, but unless their husbands share responsibilities at home more or less equally with them they are often torn between their roles as mother and worker, conflicted and exhausted.

Women are also more fortunate now in the childcare resources available to them – registered, inspected childminders, many nursery classes and private nurseries, and, crucially, in cities there are after-school and holiday play centres. I had to rely on two sources of childcare. The first source was working-class women who wanted to work, but because they had a young child and there were hardly any preschool facilities available could not do so. Mrs. Truscott who worked for me for some years, had been a bus conductor during the war, a job she reluctantly gave up when the men came back from the forces. She was determined to keep working and it suited her to spend the morning in my house, bringing her small son Ronny with her, combining housework with looking after the children. She was a very energetic, capable woman. Typically, she arrived one morning announcing that she had decided to clear out and reorganise my cellar. When Ronny started school she got a job in a shop and soon became its manager.

The other major source of childcare in the past was *au pair* girls. European girls who had just left school at eighteen were then flooding into the U.K. to improve their English by helping in a middle class family. They were often exploited, but we tried not to do this, and we encouraged them to go to classes and have a social life outside our family. A succession of seven domesticated and good-natured Danish girls, who already spoke English quite well, each stayed with us for a year and usually found their successor for us. Two of them are still in touch, fifty years later. They worked only in the mornings, doing light housework and looking after our young children. Their big advantage was that they would look after a child who was unwell, as child minders and nurseries often will not, and they could be paid extra to occasionally work all day or to baby sit. The disadvantages were that they only remained for a year, and a good deal of time and emotional energy had to be spent in making them feel comfortable, and not homesick or lonely.

When we could afford it we switched to employing a daily nanny, Linda, who had her own life outside work. Linda was not a trained nanny but she had previously looked after the four children of two musicians who were often on tour. She was attracted to our family because her boy friend was Jamaican. They often spent the evening in Ronny Scott's Soho jazz club, but he always drove her to work punctually next morning in his aged Jaguar. Linda stayed with us until the youngest children had started school, when I managed with only a cleaner. But then school holidays became a major problem, more so than is the case now. For years Linda, married and with her own children, had my two youngest children to stay for a week during each holiday. For the rest, I would take some time off and juggle where possible with other mothers to take it in turn to look after both sets of children for half the day. Today in London, at least, there are a great variety of holiday centres which cater for the children of working mothers.

The social lives of mothers with young children have immensely improved. The terrible social isolation that I felt at first can now be avoided by joining mother and baby groups, playgroups and blogging. Collapsible buggies, car ownership, together with increased prosperity make it possible for women with babies and young children to travel beyond pram-pushing distance, and cafés, art galleries and museums now welcome or tolerate young children. Primary schools, which when my children were young had signs saying, 'No parents beyond this point', now encourage them to visit and become involved in the school. And fathers are more likely to assume some responsibility for looking after their children.

Political activity and the peace movement

Politically, I was rather inactive in the early 1950s. I was preoccupied with my two very young children and the research for my Ph.D., and I had less contact with my local Communist Party branch after Doreen Hamilton, my close friend and fellow member of the branch, moved to Leeds in 1953. This was a great blow – we had met with our children almost every day for two years and her departure left a huge hole in my life. Her husband, Max, later became Professor of Psychiatry in Leeds and much later Doreen became chair of the Leeds Labour party. In 1956 came the devastating news that Khrushchev had denounced Stalin for bringing about a reign of terror, to be followed some months later by news of the Soviet crushing of the Hungarian revolution. Jack and I, with almost all of our communist friends, left the party, as did a quarter of the party's membership, including most of its intellectuals.

It is hard to convey the shock and deep disillusionment we felt on discovering that the tales of fake trials and mass murders, which we had dismissed as right-wing propaganda, were in fact true, and that our own leaders had deliberately deceived us and that our belief that a socialist society was being built had been an illusion. The communists I knew had joined the party for what were basically moral reasons, believing it was deeply committed to bringing about an egalitarian, just society. We had believed that the Soviet Union, despite its poverty, embodied these values and was evidence that socialism could be a reality. Whilst some people like Doreen Hamilton promptly transferred their energies to the Labour Party, and others, like myself, to CND, probably most, disillusioned and shocked, became politically inactive.

Jack was one of these. He had never been active in the Communist Party, having always been unenthusiastic about Marxism, and hostile to its 'democratic centralism', which meant that policy was virtually dictated by the leadership. The main legacy of his party membership was that each time he visited the U.S. his sponsors (usually universities) had to negotiate a special dispensation without which he would have been refused a visa. Characteristically he made no attempt to conceal his past membership of the party. Thereafter Jack supported, though he did not join, the Labour Party. He remained passionately committed to social justice but he believed that he could most effectively help to achieve this through his research. He also engaged in two psychological controversies with egalitarian implications – the issue of whether the lower average IQ of black and also of working-class children was largely genetic in origin, and the related controversy of the 'Burt affair'. Sir Cyril Burt, a distinguished psychologist, had collected a great deal of data from studies of twins which he argued proved that the lower average IQ of working-class children was largely genetic in origin. After his death a number of leading psychologists, including Jack, discovered that there were grounds for suspecting that he had falsified this data. Jack questioned whether he had not also invented his supposed assistants, who were joint authors of some of his papers, and of whom no other trace could be found. Jack greatly enjoyed taking part in the controversy. He had for a long time regarded Burt's work with suspicion and used to refer to him as 'the old delinquent' (one of Burt's best known books was called *The Young Delinquent*).

With my family background I have always felt a moral obligation to be directly involved at some level in political activity. From 1958, when the Aldermaston marches started, this mainly took the form of involvement in the peace movement. The children were too young to be taken on marches but I took them to some of the CND rallies in Trafalgar Square. Nuclear war was at that time a serious and immanent threat. This was brought home during the Cuban crisis of October 1962 when the U.S. discovered that the Soviet Union was installing nuclear missiles in Cuba and both countries were unquestionably poised to use nuclear weapons. For about a week everyone I knew was seriously and realistically very afraid, to an extent I have not seen before or since, though few so pathetically as one staff psychologist in the Maudsley, who told me, almost in tears, he was too young to die.

My support for CND, like that of many others, waxed and waned with the severity of the nuclear threat. During the seventies there were many other important issues. I joined demonstrations against the Falklands war, and I joined the picket line of Asian women at the Grunwick film processing factory. They struck for over a year in an attempt to improve their conditions and the right to join a union and I thought it important to show support for these remarkable women. Even though their struggle was in the end largely unsuccessful, they broke the stereotype that Asian women are always docile and exploitable. Jack tended to disapprove of these activities, which I think he thought inappropriate for me, and probably pointless.

In 1979, the year that Jack died, the decision to deploy U.S. cruise missiles in Britain led to renewed support for CND, and the following year I became a very active member of the Hampstead CND branch. There were perhaps thirty of us who regularly attended branch meetings, all with professional jobs, and perhaps ten who were very committed and active. Most of us were middle aged or older, probably a number were ex-members of the Communist Party, but we didn't discuss party politics, what united us was a sense of moral outrage. We ran a stall and collected money in the high street every Saturday, leafleted, organised local marches and usually met with friendly responses and cash contributions – in 1984 CND had 100,000 members. Some of us went from time to time to visit one of our branch members who was living in the women's peace camp set up in 1982 by the gates of the Greenham Common U.S. Air Force base, where Cruise missiles were based. Only women could visit – the campers had a fanatical objection to the presence of men, whatever their views or sympathies. A nucleus of women lived there for long periods of time in great discomfort, joined on occasion by up to 50,000 women who linked hands round the nine mile perimeter fence, pulling some sections down.

Whilst the camps almost certainly made no impact on policy they were inspirational for many women, showing that they could work together daringly and effectively without men – the Greenham song began, 'We are women, We are women, We are strong, We are strong'.

They dispensed with the hierarchical structures and committees which they associated with male dominated organisations, though I thought a little more structure would have improved life. Responsibilities, for example for washing up and keeping the camps clean, were not allocated and I noticed that the older women quietly did all the chores. I made my own contribution to the camp when for a short period I acted as a night guard. At one gate the women had recently been disturbed by visits in the middle of the night from a group of young men, intent on disruption. I volunteered to take a turn once a week, sitting up all night, to give the alarm if unwelcome visitors approached. I was always slightly irritated by the fact that the women took this contribution for granted, without thanks or even conversation. But it must have seemed a very small contribution to them in comparison with the disruption they had accepted in their own lives. I found it an eerie and beautiful solitary experience, watching the dawn slowly arrive through the trees, but after a month or so I gave it up as too dangerous. No men, young or old, arrived, but driving home for a bath, and then on to my office, I could not keep my eyes from constantly shutting.

A few of us in the Hampstead group were willing to be involved in the kind of direct action taken by the Greenham women, that is, peaceful but illegal activities. This most often involved refusing to move from the entrance to air bases or the like when instructed to do so by police, who then, usually carefully, carried us away and arrested us. Our object was to demonstrate the depth of our feelings in a way that would gain media coverage, which was especially likely if our cases came to court, even more so if we were sent to prison. I was arrested three times, once spending the night in a small police cell with my closest CND friend, Hilary Embling. This was a slightly alarming experience, which drew us together – no one knew where we were, we had not been allowed to make a phone call and we felt at the mercy of the police. I was only twice brought to court, when I made my statement, paid my fine, and drove to work. I worried that refusing to pay the fine and being sent to prison might exceed the tolerance of the Department of Health, on whose funds our Unit depended. But Hilary refused to pay and was sent to Holloway prison, an experience, she said, that anyone who had been to a girls' boarding school would not have found difficult. Later she and her husband moved to mid Wales to plant trees, and I periodically visit her there.

My only seriously alarming experience in the peace movement came after I suggested that the members of our CND group should take it in turn, as a gesture of solidarity, to each spend a night camping with an international peace group which had set up camp in Jubilee Gardens, by the old LCC building. I volunteered to go first. It was Saturday evening, I introduced myself, chatted, and set up camp quite near the entrance to the gardens. Soon everyone retreated to their tents for the night, but it was very cold and I couldn't get to sleep. After what seemed a long time I heard a group of men shouting that they were going to 'get the peace campers', attacking our parked cars as they approached. I realised that they were very near and that my tent would be one of the first they would encounter. Perhaps I should have tried to warn the others but I suppose I assumed that everyone could hear them, they were making an enormous noise. I was surprised to find myself quite calmly considering how I could protect myself and deciding that my best bet was to try to make the tent look empty, by tying it up and lying under my sleeping bag, with the blankets on top. Perhaps it did look empty, at any rate they just slashed through the tent with knives and pulled it up, not noticing me underneath. My poor neighbour, a young Dutchman, was asleep with his tent not tied up, his head near the opening. They kicked him savagely in the face and went on to attack the next tent.

Obstructing a U.S. air base, 1984.

Very soon the police siren could be heard – in that pre-mobile phone era someone outside must have phoned them. The men ran off and the police called an ambulance and started to interview people. I had nothing to tell them, I had seen nothing, but I knew that when the police had gone the campers would be sure to organise a 'sharing time' for everyone to talk the experience through. Probably wrongly, this prospect did not appeal to me. I felt a desperate need to get back to normal life, warm myself with a hot bath and go to bed. Normal life was Lucy, at eighteen preparing to go out 'clubbing', concerned for me but looking forward to the night ahead, happily living in a different world.

During the eighties I joined an international peace group of child psychologists and psychiatrists. At an initial meeting near Helsinki I met, and immediately became friends with, a Finnish child psychiatrist, Tytti Solantaus and later an American activist, Diane Levin, and we have remained in touch, and good friends, ever since, meeting most years. The group subsequently met in Holland and West Germany, committed to publicising the psychological damage to children of living with the nuclear threat. With my Maudsley-trained scepticism, I had to conclude after studying the available research that there was little evidence of this damage. The major sources of anxiety to young people were still their relations with their parents and with other young people, exams, and job prospects. The real danger to them, I concluded, was that there would be a nuclear war, not their anxiety about this possibility.

Adventures abroad

During the 1970s I began to travel outside Europe, as I had long hoped to do. Before Jack's death in 1979 we went together to meetings in the U.S., and to Israel, where we disliked the palpable hostility to Arabs and the militarism of Israeli society. We stayed in a *kibbutz*, just under the Golan Heights, at a time when the policy of rearing children together, away from their parents, was beginning to be modified. I found the practice of collective eating in a very large British restaurant type cafeteria unpleasantly reminiscent of school. Some couples were moderating this practice at the edges, having tea and cakes in their own quarters. It was noticeable that the leaders and those who had the prestige jobs, e.g. as tractor drivers, were all men, whilst women predominated in the laundry, kitchens and childcare.

We spent three weeks in Jamaica working on a study of the effects on later functioning of severe malnutrition in infancy. Getting off the plane felt like walking into an oven and I found day after day of blue skies and intense heat, varied only by occasional deluges of rain, very wearing. But at weekends we would drive from the university campus in Kingston over the mountains, through the remote villages where many of the children in the study lived, to the wonderful unspoilt tropical beaches on the west coast – the tourist industry had then hardly begun to develop The study came up with interesting findings. A serious long-term impact of early severe malnutrition was not inevitable, it was very much less in those children who were subsequently better fed and better educated. But we were frustratingly always looking at Jamaican culture from the outside and we did not get to know any Jamaicans, since the researchers were all American and British.

Another long trip was to New Zealand. Jack made several return visits to see his relatives but, beautiful, socially egalitarian, relaxed and easygoing though New Zealand is, he never wanted to remain, or to live anywhere except in London. Really, he would have liked to live in a penthouse in Soho. This trip was paid for by the New Zealand Association of Parents of Mentally Handicapped Children and involved us in visiting all the main towns in both the North and South Islands. Although, like most New Zealanders then, these parents thought that more important and interesting work must be going on elsewhere in the world, this was not the case. The parents' association jointly with the government ran all the institutions and services, which were the best Jack had seen anywhere.

On my way home – I returned before Jack – I stayed in Calcutta with our friend Ajita Chakraborti, and was stunned by the intense sensory impact of India, the noise, the smells, the bright colours, the endless crowds – even when we drove to Ajita's family bungalow in 'the country' there seemed to be nearly as many people throughout the journey as in the city. And, of course, the extreme poverty was very disturbing – the countless beggars, the maimed, hitching themselves along the pavements and the throngs of people living, washing their clothes and sleeping on the street, amongst the wandering cows. Ajita lived by herself in a small top floor flat, with a cook and a driver, who both slept on the roof under an awning, and an eleven-year-old boy who ran errands for her. She kept him busy, going to local shops, bringing her a drink from the kitchen, or her bag from her bedroom or a book from the other side of the room. Ajita pointed out that she was helping the boy, by teaching him English, but I thought at a cost to herself – over the years the physical lethargy that he, with the other servants, facilitated, must surely have helped to increase her weight and damage her health.

At that time the Naxalites, a violent Maoist group, given to assassinating the wealthy, were active in Calcutta. Most airlines had stopped using the airport – I had to travel there by a Thai airline – and middle class people stayed home at night. My plane left about midnight and Ajita arranged for her driver, who didn't speak English, to take me to the airport. She thought it too risky to accompany me. He dropped me outside and I discovered almost at once that something was very wrong. The large hall I entered was full of Indians asleep on benches, with no sign of anybody else, or of any of the trappings of an airport – shops, cafés, checking-in desks. I wandered around, increasingly worried, until at last I found an official who spoke a little English. He explained to me that this was the local airport, the international airport was some way off. He pointed out the direction and as I set off with my luggage along the unlit, deserted road, from nowhere, it seemed, the ubiquitous beggars appeared. Several of them accompanied me all the way, never ceasing to ask for money, while I tried not to think about assassins. It was the only occasion when I have ever felt relief at reaching an airport.

In August 1983 I met my older daughter, Jenny, in Australia. She had just spent six months working in New Zealand, living with some of Jack's relatives. We stayed briefly outside Sydney with Jack's old friend, Bill Geddes and his Maori wife, Nyaere. Their house was on the edge of the beach where they kept their yacht. The entire wall facing the beach was made of glass, and the front garden was full of avocado, banana, and mango trees. We moved on to Adelaide, to stay with Maud Mcbriar, sister of Alan, from whose house I had got married.

Maud, who had often stayed with us in London, was a botanist, a committed environmentalist and peace campaigner. We went on a peace march with her before flying the 1500 kms. to Alice Springs. Distances are so vast in Australia that to see much of it in a three week holiday, flying is unavoidable. Alice is in the exact middle of Australia, surrounded by desert. Despite its pretty name it seemed a dreary town, with large numbers of aborigines drifting around, bedraggled, beaten and resigned, clutching bottles of wine. We stayed in the Y.W.C.A. and visited Catherine, the daughter of a former student of Jack's. Catherine had come through a wild youth and was now a welfare worker. We thought she was still pretty wild. One day she drove us very fast along pot-holed roads and across creeks, the water coming up to the windscreen, to our destination. This was a near vertical cliff, covered with aboriginal carvings, which women were not supposed to see, let alone climb. Later she told us that her handbrake wasn't working, and her foot brake was faulty.

Alice Springs is the centre from which tourists visit Ayers Rock. Catherine urged us instead to go in the opposite direction, 'out bush', and lent us groundsheets and two blankets – no tent was required for what proved to be the ultimate in 'camping sauvage'. We hired a mini- Moke, which we loaded with petrol, water and food, and drove through the desert to a sandy, dried-up river bed. At night we gathered wood fallen from the gum trees, and dried grass, lit a fire, and cooked inexpertly, burning the food, the ashes blowing in our faces. We went to sleep by the fire, looking up at the stars. Dawn began from a grey sky at about 6.45a.m., with parrots and many other brightly coloured birds singing all around us. We were a very long way from anyone else and it was an extraordinary, unforgettable experience. We saw dingoes, and wallabies running in and out of rock caves, and an injured snake. We were probably a bit reckless to ignore the possibility of visits in the night from dangerous animals or men, but, under Catherine's influence, we didn't think about such risks.

In the early morning we walked but during most of the day the heat was so intense that we resorted to driving around just to get some breeze. We had to wear wide brimmed hats, our faces completely covered with veils to ward off the ceaseless insect attacks. After three days it was a great relief to fly on to Cairns, a tropical city on the north west coast, luxuriant with bougainvilleas and palm trees, surrounded by mangrove swamps. We consulted the Tourist Office about another camping trip. They told us that there were boat trips to Fitzroy Island, forty five minutes away, stopping for a couple of hours. It would be possible instead of returning with the boat to camp 'sauvage ' there. It was not so hot as in the desert and would probably rain, so we went to Woolworths, and bought a small tent, sleeping bags and firelighters, as well as snorkels and masks and tinned food.

Fitzroy Island, so named by Captain Cook, is a small mountainous island covered in lush woodlands, surrounded by coral beaches and reefs. There was a lighthouse, but no other building except a bar. Every day the boat from Cairns brought trippers, who could buy drinks and snacks at the bar, which had showers and toilets. It belonged to the boat's owner, who locked it up when the boat left. A friendly kangaroo appeared at that time to eat the leftovers. We felt tremendous elation when the boat departed and we could pitch our tent wherever we liked under the palm trees at the edge of the tropical beach and explore the island on our own. Snorkelling amongst the brilliantly coloured tropical fish was spectacular. Each day when the boat trip arrived we could replenish our water supply and have a shower at the bar. It rained at times, but there was plenty of rather damp wood to make a fire for cooking. Inevitably, the island is now a 'luxury resort' with restaurants, bistros, gift shops and an expensive hotel. Back in Cairns we travelled north, through sugar cane country, visiting a sugar mill. We made forays into the tropical rain forest with its enormous trees, where the house plants I have to nurse assiduously at home were growing exuberantly in their natural environment. Finally, our time ran out and we flew home from Sydney.

In 1989 I had another adventurous holiday with Jenny. We walked across the Norwegian Hardangervidda, an unpopulated mountain plateau surrounded by peaks. There were no roads or buildings, other than mountain huts for walkers. It was early July and snow still covered much of the terrain. We had anticipated the snow, but not the strength of the sun and we soon got sunburnt. Each day we trudged through deep snow, scrambled over rocks and forded icy streams in our boots. The mountain huts, which are like superior youth hostels, are spaced at six hourly intervals but (I was after all, sixty-three) it more often took us eight hours to go from one to another. They had comfortable bunks and some had piped cold water, but in the more remote huts you fetched water from a nearby lake with a bucket. Some huts had staff who cooked meals, the food brought in by backpack or helicopter, but in the remote, unstaffed huts tinned and packaged food was left on shelves, walkers being trusted to leave the payment. The misery of cold wet feet and sunburn was outweighed by the extraordinary wild beauty of the landscape and the exhilarating mountain air.

From 1983 I made a number of visits to India, Indonesia and Ethiopia as a consultant on early education and childcare for WHO and Save the Children. I travelled round on my own, met by local academics or doctors, who often arrived hours, or, once, days, late, and took me to remote villages and city slums to visit preschool services. Sometimes I was put up in a hotel but more often I stayed in a university guest house, where the rooms at that time usually contained no more than a bed with mosquito netting, hooks to hang clothes on and a central low watt electric light bulb. This accommodation had the merit of not arousing the resentment of Indian academics, whose salaries were then very low and who could be understandably bitter if foreign consultants lived in luxury.

Later I visited India and Nepal several times on holiday, but during my consultancies I was working a long way from the tourist trail. I was shocked by the extreme poverty I saw and the frequency of depression amongst the women. In India I was told that village women, instead of offering sympathy and comfort to a depressed woman, were harsh and critical, believing that she must be hardened if she was to survive. Many did not, and jumped into the village well. I became sceptical about the usefulness of my role. Whilst foreigners could offer valuable information and advice about medicine and scientific issues, childcare and education are strongly influenced by social and cultural values. Apart from a few academics most people in these countries saw no value in play facilities and toy libraries. I thought it would have been more important to resource primary schools better and support attempts to get more children, and especially more girls, to attend them. In remote Indian villages even the teachers tended to appear sporadically because of the long journey from the towns where they lived and the low status of the job, whilst girls were only reluctantly released by their parents from the childcare and domestic roles assigned to them at an early age. The north-south difference in attitudes to children in all social classes was brought home to me when a well-to-do Ethiopian woman with two children told me that she was going to give her next baby to her brother. He was unmarried, working in an embassy abroad, and she thought that he would be less lonely with a child to bring up.

Ethiopia also taught me the spuriousness of the impressions a visiting foreigner may receive. With some other European child development specialists I was invited in 1986 to spend a week in a very large, walled children's 'colony', comprising numbers of different houses, catering for more than a thousand 'orphans' (often one parent survived) from infancy to eighteen. It was only a year since the terrible famine of 1984-5, when a million people were believed to have died from starvation. During an initial stay in Addis Ababa I was naively surprised to see that most people looked well fed and I was told that there had been no serious food shortages in the capital. The famine had been regional and those who starved were poor peasants.

The colony was a long distance from Addis Ababa, in a potentially hostile tribal area, and the grounds were patrolled by armed guards. It was the Ethiopian 'show' children's home, a kind of non-fee paying Eton. The standard of living of the children was far higher than that of most of the population, they were well dressed, well fed and well educated, and when they left they were likely to get a place in the university or army officer training unit. The Maoist government insisted that as the children grew older they should also work on the land for part of the day. Contacts with relatives, even a parent, were severely discouraged, perhaps prohibited, and children were arbitrarily moved between houses, away from friends. We visited all the houses and schools and were impressed by the amenities, though I was troubled by the colony's isolation and the enormous difference between the children's lives and those of almost all other Ethiopian children. We were, of course, always with an official interpreter. We were there to discuss recent Western developments in childcare with some senior government officials and we stressed the need for continuity in relationships and for personalised care. What happened in the following year made this psychological approach seem pathetically inadequate There was a 'rebellion' by senior children, protesting against an increase in their hours of manual labour, during which several of them were shot by the guards.

Before that, in August 1985 I went to stay with my niece, Melissa Parker, in northern Sudan. She was researching for a D.Phil. in anthropology, living in a Muslim village, and she thought a visit from an older woman relative would improve her status. I was fifty-nine, and after camping in the Australian desert and roughing it in India thought myself able to cope with the rigours that might be involved. Melissa met me at Khartoum airport and we spent a day sightseeing. It was blindingly hot, and in the shade-less camel market I fainted. Melissa took me by taxi to the air-conditioned Meridian hotel, where an iced coke revived me. She must have thought this a very unpromising start. Next morning we got a bus south and after travelling for hours through the desert, I saw, incredulously, what I realised must be a mirage ahead, an oasis of trees, which disappeared as we got closer.

At last we reached El Duem, a road junction on the White Nile, busy with stalls selling nuts, tea and coca cola to lorry and camel drivers, and men who were hiring out camels. No other women could be seen. Melissa, whose Arabic was fluent, found and bargained with a lorry driver, who was going in approximately the right direction, to take us to El Goroshi, our next stop. This is a largish market town where we were to spend the night with a public health officer, Mr. Khidier. There were other passengers, travelling on the roof, but Melissa negotiated seats for us next to the driver. She promptly fell asleep but I stayed awake, unwilling to miss the extraordinary experience of driving quite fast through the barren desert, alongside a canal. It was very late when we got to El Goroshi and the home of the Khidier family. I got a vague impression that there were a large number of people, adults and children, all asleep on the floor of the main room, the mattresses more or less touching each other. Although desperately tired I felt uneasy as we joined them, and had a strange hallucinogenic experience in the night. It seemed that a man crept up to my mattress, and stole the purse I had put under the blanket. This experience was so vivid, so unlike a dream, that in the morning I immediately told Melissa what had happened. But then I checked, and found that my purse had not been moved.

In daylight I saw that we were in a one storey concrete house, surrounded by a barren mud yard, with a hole-in -the-ground outside toilet. Our hostess made delicious Arabic meals, usually cooking on a little oil stove in the yard. Breakfast consisted of sliced hardboiled eggs, meat stew, chickpea fritters, and tomato and cucumber salad. We sat on low stools at a low round table and ate with our fingers from communal dishes, whilst the children ate in the kitchen. The thirteen-year-old daughter, still at school, washed the dishes and the floors and prepared vegetables. Her parents had decided not to subject her to female circumcision, then the fate of almost all Sudanese village girls.

Mr.Khidier drove us in his van to our destination, Omndaman, a village with about 1200 inhabitants, of whom at least half were under the age of fifteen. It was an unforgettably dreary looking collection of mud huts, framed with wooden poles, with mud floors, set in a vast flat area of cracked dry mud, almost without plant life. The women and children lived in separate huts from the men, who paid them formal visits, and I was never clear when and where they had sex. Unlike the anthropologists whose books I had read, Melissa had no quarters of her own, but in every respect shared the lives of the village women, apart from surreptitiously swallowing vitamin pills. She lived with an older woman, her married daughters and their children. The only items of furniture were very low beds with wooden frames and string bases, used for sleeping and for sitting on during the day, and a low round table. We women and the children in the family all slept together in a separate hut at night, together with the goats. Cooking was done outside on wood fires, and water was brought by the children from the canal, about fifteen minutes walk away. There were no hygienic arrangements, people simply walked away from the buildings. The villagers kept goats, a few chickens and some very scrawny donkeys. There were no wheeled vehicles and only one radio, which belonged to the recently appointed school teacher. He supplemented the scarce writing equipment by teaching children to write in the dried mud with sticks.

The villagers were desperately poor, even by African standards. In the morning they boiled up goat's milk with tea and a lot of sugar and during the day drank black tea or sometimes small cups of delicious coffee, flavoured with cardamom pods, always heavily sugared. The staple food was *kissera*, a flat bread made from sorghum and cooked in a pan over an open fire, which I thought tasted very unpleasant, supplemented by a little dried goat meat, and an occasional chicken. They had very few vegetables. I helped Melissa weigh every adult in the village for a Blue Nile project and found just how thin they were. No one approached being overweight. The older people weighed only five or six stone, probably because they were given less to eat. In both rural India and the Sudan I saw no evidence to support the belief that old people are better respected and cared for in non-Western countries. It is true that they remained in the family but they continued to do a day's work, on less demanding jobs, and were noticeably even thinner than their children. Most people in Omnadan were not only thin but unhealthy. Meningitis struck some of the children and bilharzia was particularly rife from drinking the only source of water, from the canal. But the family welcomed me very warmly, generously sharing whatever they had, pleased with the food we brought. The girls were delighted with the cheap jewellery I had brought them and the picture post cards of London.

As I spoke only a few words of Arabic and Melissa didn't want to talk to me much in English, I had to try to work out what was going on all day from people's behaviour and expressions, an interesting exercise. One five-year-old girl in the family, nursemaid to a toddler, seemed unaccountably sad, neglected, and unkempt, her clothes ragged. She was immensely pleased when I did her hair and put it into bunches. Later I discovered that she had been adopted into the family on the death of her parents, perhaps reluctantly, as an extra person to feed. On the other hand later her marriage would bring the family her bride price. Children were expected to contribute to the work of the family from the age of four or five and not expected to ask questions or address adults unnecessarily, nor of course were they given toys. Nonetheless, they grew up with the same basic intellectual skills as our carefully cultivated children.

The villagers were Muslims, but not very devout. There was no mosque or imam and though some of them aspired to make the pilgrimage to Mecca, people did not pray five times a day. But the women and older girls wore headscarves and dressed modestly, the teenage girls were circumcised, as a matter of honour, and unmarried girls were not supposed even to go around the village on their own. They were shocked that Melissa would journey to Khartoum alone. In market towns like El Goroshi there was barely a woman to be seen in the streets – the buying and selling was done by men. To me, it seemed strange to see young men walking around with their friends, holding hands, and never, of course, with a woman.

Back in Khartoum, where we stayed briefly with an ex-pat. British academic, and even more so back in Hampstead, I felt overwhelmed, confused, by the huge change in lifestyle. The experience had also, uncomfortably, brought home to me the limits of my adaptability. I was enormously relieved to leave the village. I had no problem sleeping in a hut with goats, but I had great problems eating the villagers' food and drinking their tea. I felt an immense admiration for Melissa who had established friendly relations with the women and adolescent girls, and drank their water and shared their meals and their life, with all its serious health hazards. Melissa is now Director of the Centre for Research in International Medical Anthropology at Brunel University. She works in sub Saharan Africa each summer, taking her family with her, but Omnadam is too unhealthy a place for her to visit with her children.

As a child, I spent hours looking through my school atlas. England, which was my whole world, looked small and insignificant and I longed to be able to visit far off countries. As an adult, mainly through my work, sometimes on holiday, I have visited Turkey, Israel, Russia, Uzbekistan, China, India, Nepal, Indonesia, Australia and New Zealand, Egypt, Morocco, Sudan, Jamaica and the United States, as well as almost every country in Europe. As a child, I had imagined that travel was about seeing different ways of life, beautiful scenery, ancient buildings and people in picturesque clothes. So it is, but the reality often includes observing the suffering of many of these people and their extreme poverty, and feeling the discomfort of being relatively rich amongst very poor people – typified by the WHO headquarters in Delhi, adjacent to a shanty town. Reality may also encompass the discomfort of great heat or cold, and the exhaustion and anxiety of travel, especially, as was often the case with me, if you are on your own. Yet it was the uncomfortable journeys that were the most rewarding and have remained most strongly with me. The tourist industry protects people from the reality of travel, but by living in its safe, comfortable bubble you don't experience the life of the country you have come to see. I consider myself very fortunate to have been able to travel as I did.

Retirement and old age

In 1990 I was sixty-four, and had been Director of the Unit for ten years. The idea of retiring a year early and shedding all my responsibilities was very attractive. I certainly did not regret taking on the job, which had opened out my life in new ways. I was proud of the Unit, and of having helped to maintain, perhaps in some ways to improve it. I had enjoyed encouraging and helping the more junior staff and doctoral students to publish, to study for Ph.Ds, and to develop their careers, although I think I had a reputation for assessing their work rather sternly. I also enjoyed getting to know a much wider range of academics than I had known as a 'backroom' researcher. But I found it frustrating that I had to give up, as too time-consuming, a hands-on role in research. I had always enormously enjoyed collecting data, visiting schools or nurseries and especially making observations. Now, although I could and did listen to tape recorded interviews, I missed the 'feel' of the schools, the staff and the children. Jack had made the same complaint, eventually ruefully (and wrongly) describing his role in the Unit as 'simply that of a superior clerk, signing papers for others.'

The most difficult aspect of the job for me was coping with hostility. When I mentioned this after I'd retired to a senior member of the Unit she told me that no one had sensed this, quite the contrary, they thought of me as very resilient and independent. But although I did what I thought was necessary, whether or not it created hostility, I didn't enjoy doing so. And I found the role of Director alienating. It contrasted markedly with the warmth and comradeship of my other working role at that time, in the women's peace movement. I felt that I couldn't form friendships with particular members of the staff because I might be accused of favouritism. Probably this situation would have been improved if I had spent more time socialising with staff. After Jack's death in 1979 Lucy and I lived alone. She had just started at secondary school, and until she felt more confident she would come to the Unit after school and do her homework in the next room. Both then and subsequently I would make it a priority to hurry home by 5p.m., and because of my shorter working day I tended to eat a sandwich lunch as I worked. For my role as Director of the Unit this routine was a disadvantage. Jack used to chat in an unhurried way with members of the staff over a drink at the end of the day, as well as attend meetings, rarely returning home before 7.30.

I wasn't, of course, planning a life of leisure for my retirement. I would first write a book with Ann Phoenix about our mixed race project and then start a completely new life. In fact, after writing the book I did embark on another project, working with Ian Sinclair, Professor of Social Work at York University, to produce a report for the Department of Health on the future of residential care homes for children. Ian is a tolerant, relaxed man, with the perfect manners, but none of the pretensions, of an old Etonian, and deeply committed to children's welfare. But whilst we got on very well our opinions ultimately diverged, Ian seeing residential care for children in a much more positive light than I. Perhaps at some level we were influenced by our very different experiences at boarding school. In the end I thought it better if he wrote the report on his own, whilst I concentrated on my new interest. This was the history of art, which I studied by doing a diploma, part-time, in the extra-mural department of London University. I had for some time nursed this ambition – in my last year at work I often went to the lunch hour lectures at the National Gallery. In these, the lecturer would stand in front of two or three pictures in the Gallery, discussing them in immense detail so that one looked at a painting for perhaps twenty minutes, which on my own I would have passed after a few minutes.

At that time to sit for the diploma you studied five courses from any periods of your choice, which could be done over a number of years. You had to write essays each term and take a final written examination, now abolished, which reduced many of the women students, middle aged and elderly, to tears or nausea. I had a very strong feminist for my main tutor who spent rather more time than I would have wished talking about Lacan and Foucault, and interpreting paintings, not always convincingly, from a feminist standpoint. Still, I very much enjoyed the course. It left me feeling at home in the main London art galleries and able to look at the work in visiting art exhibitions in some sort of historical context. Subsequently, for six months each year, I attended, and still attend, extra-mural courses on my first love, literature, especially poetry. Studying in this way is for me a very enjoyable way of continuing to think and learn.

In 1997 I was elected a fellow of the British Academy, the humanities and social science equivalent of the Royal Society, founded in 1902 for 'the promotion of historical, philosophical, and philological (an archaic term for the study of literature) studies.' This was a great honour, especially as only ten per cent of the Fellows at the time were women. The proportion has since risen to fifteen per cent. The Academy is located in a very grand house in Carlton House Terrace, a few doors from the Royal Society, and aims to promote and help communicate British research and scholarship in arts and social sciences, in the U.K. and abroad. It is organised in disciplinary sections, psychology being the most recently established, with a larger proportion of women and of middle aged, rather than elderly, academics than the other sections. The sections meet twice a year and are involved in arranging public lectures in their disciplines, and allocating research funds, although it sometimes seems that, like the rest of the living world, our main function is to perpetuate ourselves, by electing new Fellows.

All the psychologists who attended meetings were actively engaged in research and perhaps this influenced my decision to start another research project. I had been intrigued for some time by the differing attitudes of my colleagues to retirement. Jack, for instance, had been appalled by the prospect, despite assurances that he would find plenty to do and that he would be in demand all over the world as a consultant. I think that his work had been so central to his life, almost all embracing, for over thirty years, that he could not believe that there was any acceptable alternative. Each summer we took the children camping in France or Italy for three weeks and I thought him a wonderful father during these holidays, taking the children in turn for a special outing with him, full of ideas for each day's activities. But sometimes he would look at his watch and mutter to me, 'Oh God, it's not midday yet.' Every year, on the day after Boxing Day he would return to his study.

He became increasingly addicted to work, so that when we went for weekends in East Dean with the two youngest children he began to spend most of the time preparing papers for committees or conferences. He read novels at times and he very much enjoyed watching sport, especially tennis, on the TV, but he had no interests that began to rival his interest in his work. He was not a scholar who would be happy in retirement with his books. I think what he feared missing was the social and intellectual stimulus of working with like-minded colleagues, the knowledge that he was influencing policy, and perhaps the status. In the event, he died at 60. Happily retired now myself – I never for a moment regretted retiring – I wondered how many academics felt as Jack had and whether in fact they got the resources to go on with their work if they wanted to.

I decided on a project that I could manage on my own, except for the computing, for which I got a grant from the Nuffield Trust. I sent a questionnaire to all academics who had retired from English universities, other than for reasons of health, in 1993-5, that is, three to five years previously. Lucy and her partner and several of my friends rallied round one Saturday to help with the massive task of addressing all the envelopes and inserting the questionnaires. Nearly three quarters of the academics returned them, and many wrote extensively about their experiences on the final blank page provided. I found that two thirds had retired early, before they were sixty-five, most often because of disliking the excessive bureaucratic demands made on them. But nearly half of those who remained at work until sixty-five, who were mostly professors, would, like Jack, have preferred not to retire at all. Over half of all the academics were still employed, mostly part-time, mostly in universities or in adult education teaching or with consultancies. Only three per cent of the sample had made a complete change of occupation, e.g. one become a sports journalist, another an antiques dealer. Two thirds of those who had been professors or readers had published, and attended an academic conference, in the past year.

Although some academics had found the first year of retirement difficult the majority said that they were now more contented, and enjoyed their greater leisure time – most often spent travelling, or gardening or listening to or playing music. However, those who had stayed at work till they were sixty-five were less likely to say that they were now contented. But, apart from the high flyers with international reputations and large grants, many of those who had continued in academic work complained of a loss of status and of any acknowledged role in the university and of being given very inadequate resources. Half were not provided with a share in a room, or even access to academic email and one in ten did not have the free use of their university library.

I decided to see if by working through the British Academy I could help to improve the position of retired academics. They are not a very needy group, I know, but relative to my own favoured situation – I still had a room and access to any resources I needed – many were deprived. And they were, after all, in a sense my own tribe. I got permission to invite Fellows to a meeting on the subject, as a result of which we set up a working group of six, all of us retired. We decided, using the resources of the Academy, to write to the senior administrators and heads of department in seventeen universities and twenty-eight Oxford and Cambridge colleges, asking them whether they had a policy of supporting the work of retired academics and what facilities they offered. We found that very few had an explicit policy and the facilities they offered varied enormously, with, unsurprisingly, the wealthiest Oxford and Cambridge colleges being the most generous. But the variability was not only a matter of wealth, since low or no cost facilities, such as access to academic email and libraries, were not always provided. Part of the problem was a widespread folklore belief that retired staff would be a bore or a nuisance if they were allowed to hang around their departments. But given the increasing pressure on university staff it seemed strange that their help was not enlisted, unpaid, on a *quid pro quo* basis. A few universities had done so, offering facilities to retired academics for renewable periods of time in return for research publications or student supervision.

Our working group drew up a proposed Code of Practice for universities. Amongst the proposals we made were that retired staff who continue academic work should be given titular recognition, e.g. as Senior Fellow, and that the policies and the facilities offered should be open and explicit. In March 2002 we held a one day conference at the Academy, attended by senior academics, representatives from universities, the AUT (Association of University Teachers) and the vice-president of the Royal Society. The proposed code was discussed in groups, and it was agreed that the next step was to ask the Council of the British Academy to launch it.

Perhaps I should have predicted the rest of the story, since I already knew that the Academy then was dominated by Fellows with conservative attitudes, opposed to change. The Royal Society had said that they were happy to act jointly with the British Academy Council, which, however, decided at the end of May that it was not appropriate to send universities a Code of Practice. We suggested that the Code could be renamed 'Guidelines', but at the end of July Council restated that it was not our place to tell universities how to conduct their affairs and that the document must be further revised. Eventually we came up with a list of points universities 'might like to consider' and Council agreed in the autumn to send it to all universities. The following year a friend in Sheffield told me that his university had not received this letter. I wrote to the British Academy and was told that the letter had inadvertently got to the bottom of a pile of correspondence and had not been sent out. I gave up at that point.

Subsequently, I made several attempts to get the Academy to consider the ethnic mix of its Fellows – they are almost entirely white. The Council had recently responded to outside criticism by acknowledging the desirability of electing more women and more academics beyond the 'golden triangle' (Oxford, Cambridge and London universities) if this could be done without lowering standards – the presumption seemed to be that this might be a problem. Some headway has been made in these respects, but there is still a complete unwillingness by many Fellows to even recognise ethnicity as an issue. However, in the past two years the Academy has begun to engage with public policy issues, and this may lead in the future to changes in its membership policy.

I still feel that I should be involved in the community. I do continue to join peace marches and demonstrations, though now I cheat somewhat by having coffee in a café on the route, falling in with the marchers when they reach me. I joined, and still work for, Amnesty International's Urgent Action group, and I became a trustee of a local charity, which later closed from lack of funds. This provided services for the elderly which are beyond the remit of the local authority, e.g. a telephone information and help line, regular visitors to isolated people, tea parties and tea dances in estates which brought together their elderly residents. I also became active in the residents' association of the estate where now I live. After nearly seventeen years in our house in the Vale of Health I had moved in November 1986, when all my children had left home, to a flat in Hampstead Hill Gardens. It was the lower ground floor of a very large Victorian house, which had been cleverly redesigned into interesting spaces, and my flat came with possession of the large rear garden. I stayed there for nearly ten years, eventually moving because every spring I became depressed when the large copper beech tree just outside my windows came into leaf, immensely darkening the flat for the summer, and also because Hampstead had become increasingly the resort of the rich and 'chichi', the ordinary shops replaced by restaurants and boutiques.

I moved to a much more socially mixed, not to say down at heel, area, Camden Town. It had buses and tubes to every part of London, so I gave Lucy my car and never bought another. My terrace, in Camden Mews, had been converted in the 1970s from the stables of large houses in Camden Road. The houses were very narrow, on three floors, cleverly designed with an open plan to give a feeling of a large space. They had tiny yards with a pond, which formed part of a toad route – every spring a long succession of toads passed through – and my house had a beautiful roof garden, shaded by a prolific vine, with a morning glory covering one wall, and a profusion of flowers in pots.

But after three and a half years I was driven to move again. Once out of my mews Camden Town proved to be a very noisy, dirty, crime ridden, treeless place in which to live, and my next door neighbour held extremely noisy parties, starting around 11p.m. And after what proved to be a temporary hip problem, which made climbing stairs agony, I had to acknowledge that at seventy-four it would make more sense to live in a flat. So in 2000 I moved into my present home, where I hope to spend the rest of my life. Like my Hampstead flat it is one floor of a large late Victorian house, but it is the first floor, with large, very light rooms overlooking trees. It backs on to the Highgate side of Hampstead Heath, where I walk most days, and at the front is a row of little shops and cafés and a bus stop. In the summer I badly miss having a garden or even a balcony, but perfection is never on offer, and I can admire the front gardens in the quiet suburban streets around.

My friends Philip and Nori Graham live very near, as does Lucy, with her always interesting, affectionate, beautiful and exhausting children, with whom I give her some help. My neighbours in the house are very friendly and until recently I represented them on the committee of the residents' association – this house is one block in an estate – and I became involved in local environmental campaigns. Joining a small book group of five to six women, fourteen years ago, became an important part of my life. We are a very stable, committed group, and most years we have spent a weekend away together.

Old Age

So now I find myself, unexpectedly, at the age of eighty-three. At forty, I thought sixty-five was about as old as anyone would wish to live, and even ten years ago I did not expect, or think that I would want, to reach eighty. When my first grandchild was born I was fifty-five, and initially I found the idea of being a grandmother hard to come to terms with. It seemed as though I had suddenly been put on a par with my own grandmother, sitting over the fire in her old age uniform of long black skirts and shawls, although I felt quite different, youthful and energetic, with a teenaged daughter. But I loved my grandchildren – I now have five – and soon worked out that being a grandparent has become to an extent dissociated from being old. Old age has retreated and retirement, which used to precede death by only a few years, now provides many of us with the bonus of getting some sort of income with which to pursue our academic or leisure interests, generally for at least a decade, whilst we are still fit and healthy. Being old was certainly no part of my identity in my sixties and I had very few role models of what it was like to grow old. My grandmother died at seventy-five, working as hard as ever, but she seemed to me to have been old as long as I had known her. My mother died at fifty-two, and I cannot imagine her at my age. My husband, who was seven years older than me, died at sixty. Neither of them got old. Full of energy – Jack used to cycle from Hampstead to work every day – they were both unexpectedly killed by cancer.

Some time in my mid-seventies my self-image abruptly altered. I was talking to a railway clerk when he picked up the phone, and said 'Hallo, I've got an elderly lady here, and…' I looked round the room, puzzled, I hadn't noticed there was another woman present. Then suddenly for the first time I realised how I appeared to others and that I had to take this on board. But after years of yoga and fast walking I was still very mobile and energetic and felt a kind of surprise as well as sadness when my brother, most of my men friends and some of my women friends died in their seventies. It wasn't until a long period of illness this year that I understood the reality of feeling seriously old – the stiffening joints, the aching back, the disturbed nights, the cruel loss of energy, the slow climbing of stairs, the weakening vision and hearing, the deepening wrinkles and the maddening lapses of memory, bringing anxieties about Alzheimer's disease, which lies in wait for nearly one in five of us if we live beyond eighty. Now I understand what lay behind Yeats' bitter cry, "this caricature/ Decrepit age, that has been tied to me/ As to a dog's tail".

But it is also true that if not too disabled or too impoverished or ill most of the pleasures of life remain for those of us in our eighties, if in a modified form. I never expected to enjoy life at eighty-three, but most of the time I do. I still find the world is intensely interesting, even if there are aspects of contemporary culture that I strongly dislike, and even though I sometimes feel an outsider, a survivor from a long past era. Helping with my grandchildren is a source of interest and gives me a satisfying sense of being useful. The familiar pleasures of walking, though more slowly and less far, of reading, writing, listening to music, watching DVDs, going to art galleries and the theatre, eating good food, drinking coffee and wine, watching one's children and grandchildren develop, all remain. 'A thing of beauty' is still a joy, perhaps for ever. I worry less and I am more accepting, less critical of myself and of others. And perhaps because I realise that the time for enjoyment may be short, I think I appreciate more than I did when younger the simple pleasures of watching the seasons change, sitting in the sun, the kindness of strangers and the consolations of friendship.

Friends are particularly important in old age, when you are less likely to have the social contacts that come from work or other activities in the community and may well live on your own. I have three much loved and loving children and five affectionate grandchildren but for their sakes as well as mine I would not like to depend on them for my social life. Friends, as well as enjoying each other's company, give each other affection and respect, sympathy, advice, and support. A lot of people also look to friends for a shoulder to weep on when they are upset, and to confide in, but perhaps because I learnt very early to manage unhappiness on my own I have never felt that I needed or wanted a confidant. Developing and sustaining friendships takes time, and when I had children at home, a husband, and a demanding job, there were periods when I somewhat neglected my friends. But I always knew they were important, and I remember fantasising when we lived in Dulwich and had a good American friend staying with us for several months, how wonderful it would be if all my friends could come to live in my street. I think it's important to keep in touch with, and meet, friends, if only occasionally over the years – it is much more difficult to pick up a friendship after a lengthy and complete separation, when both of you may have changed considerably.

At times I feel with Lamb, 'All, all are gone, the old familiar faces'. Many of my friends, especially the men, have died and others no longer live in London. But I still at times meet friends from each period of my life, from school days onwards. Some have moved as far away as west Wales and Scotland, others who lived for a while in London have returned to their own countries, but almost all of them occasionally visit London. I have some friends living in or around London, and a group of five of us, all psychologists, who first met over fifty years ago, meet regularly for lunch in each other's houses. And I am lucky to have some younger friends in their fifties and sixties, notably Ann Phoenix, whom I worked with, as well as the present and past members of my book group.

I fear that I may seem smug. There is inevitably a great deal in my life that I haven't written about. There must be much that I have forgotten and there is much that is too intimate or doesn't seem important or relevant enough to include. I have written very little about my children and grandchildren because I think it would be intrusive to do so. And there is little or nothing here about some of the terrible events of the last thirty years or so of my life, including the death of two of my sons, the harrowing terminal illness and death of my husband, and much later, my abandonment by a lover. I picked myself up after all of these experiences and somehow continued on my way, but they are too painful to write about. Yet writing this memoir has brought home to me that my life has also been in many ways both fortunate and privileged.

Appendix

List of Publications

Books

Tizard, B., and Phoenix, A., 1993. *Black, White, or Mixed Race?* London and New York: Routledge, 1993. Revised edition 2002.

Tizard, B., Farquar, C., Blatchford P., Burke, J., and Plewis, I., *Young Children at School in the Inner City*, Hove and London: Lawrence Erlbaum, 1988.

Tizard, B., and Hughes, M., *Young Children Learning*. London: Fontana Paperbacks, 1984. 2nd edition 2002.

Tizard, B., Burchell, B., and Mortimore, J., *Involving Parents in Nursery and Infant Schools*, London: Grant McIntyre, 1978.

Tizard, B., *Adoption: A Second Chance*, London: Open Books, 1977.

Tizard, B., *Early Education*, Windsor: NFER Publishing Co., 1974.

Edited Books.

Tizard, B., and Varma, V., *Vulnerability and Resilience in Development*. London: Jessica Kingsley, 1992.

Tizard, B., and Harvey, D., *The Biology of Play*. London: Spastics International Publications, 1977.

Barbara Tizard has also written about a hundred articles and chapters in books. A list can be obtained as a downloadable pdf from the Institute of Education, London.

Index

air raid 132–3, 141–3, 156, 170, 191–3
Art history diploma 297

Bernstein, Basil 277
Bevin Boys 216
Boyd, Harry 179, 243
British Academy 298, 300–1
British Restaurants 153, 217

C.E.W.C. conference 171–3
Chakraborti, Ajita 255, 286–7
childcare 257, 278–9, 290–1
Christmas 14–15, 58, 65, 101–3, 105, 230, 247
cinema in thirties 50, 84–5, 178
Clarion Movement 67, 70, 99
Clarke, Ann and Alan 251
class awareness 52–3
Clynes, J.R. (my great uncle) 2, 17–21, 60–4
CND 281–4
Collins, Henry 226, 230–1
Communist Party
    attraction of 130–2, 213–5
    my involvement with at
        Clapham 252–5
    at High Wycombe 128–132, 144
    at Oxford 199–201, 204, 206–8
        216, 221–4, 230–1
    resigned from 280–2
    my family hostile to 62, 70, 175, 184
    policy during war 148–150
Cove, W.G. 100, 178

Cowan, Nancy 127–8, 137, 163–4
Cowan, Pauline 199, 208
Cuban crisis 281
Czech Student Festival 218–220

diet, working-class 15, 103–7

East Dean 262–3
Elkins, Tom 174, 186, 188, 194–5
Embling, Hilary 283–4
Eysenck, Hans 233, 256, 259

Finer, Sammy 211
fog holidays 119
food rations 148, 153–5, 176–7, 229, 239
Forest School 40–2
Forest School Camps 93–6
Frost, Angela 164–5, 166, 168, 171, 173

Geddes, Bill 221, 227, 248, 287
general election 1945 207–8
Giles, G.T.C. 129, 144–153, 168–9, 207, 215, 226
Ginsburg, Jean 176, 182, 198
Godson, Rufus 216
Graham, Philip and Nori 303
Greenham Common 282–3
Grunwick Stike 282

Hall, Margaret 210
Hamilton, Doreen 252, 254, 280
Hamilton, Max 251, 280

Hewett, Peter and Diana 179–180, 245
High Wycombe billet 126–8, 181
Hill, Christopher 210–12, 225, 227, 230–1
hitchhiking 95, 167, 208–9
Hobsbawn, Eric 124, 200, 215, 239–40, 255
Hodges, Jill 266
Hodgkin, Dorothy 204
Hogmanay 230
Horesh, Lilian 121–2, 127, 143, 163–5, 186
Hughes, John 213
Hughes, Martin 270
Hutchinson, Pat 176, 198

Independent Labour Party 18, 61
Institute of Education 261, 263–4, 269, 276–8, 307
Institute of Psychiatry
    see Maudsley Hospital
Inter Schools Committee 172, 174, 181, 185–6, 194, 196, 202

Kirk, Edith (my grandmother)
    death 242
    early life 66
    political and religious beliefs and personality 67, 70–5
    relations with husband 75–6
Kirk, Tom (my grandfather)
    career 60–4
    death 66
    drunkeness 59, 65
    political, union activities 59, 63

Levin, Diane 285
Lewis, Aubrey 233–4, 236, 259–60, 275
Lloyd, Tony 228
lodgers 71, 252, 255

London Hospital 79, 258–9
Lyons Corner House 150, 222

Mcbriar, Alan and Maud 227, 287
Mankowitz, Wolf 172
Manning, Leah 30, 57
Margerison, Jim 260–1
Mason, Pamela 171, 188, 205
Maudsley Hospital 229, 233, 236, 240, 251, 254, 258–9, 261–4, 275–6, 285
meals
    at boarding school 33–4, 46
    at my grandmother's 104–7
    at my mother's 176–7
    at St Paul's 116–7
Menon, Krishna 172
Milligan, Jimmy 208, 228
Milligan, Martin 199–201, 208
Munby, Lucy 255

National Council for Civil Liberties (Liberty) 253
National Union of Teachers (N.U.T.) conference 96, 99–100

O'Connor, Neil 236, 251, 258, 268

Parker, Elsie Vera (my mother)
    ambitions 5–6, 13, 29, 110, 207, 224
    characteristics 35, 76, 78–81, 112
    declines honour 244
    education 80
    educational beliefs 97–8
    illness and death 241–5
    N.U.T. president 96
    political beliefs 2, 56–8, 70, 113, 143
    war work 140, 152
Parker, Herbert (my father) 2–5, 8, 13–6, 19–24
Parker, Melissa (my niece) 292–5

Parker, Michael (my brother)
  at boarding school 39–41
  at Cambridge 175, 222
  career 242
  at City of London school 112,
    125, 171–2
  early childhood 4–14, 16, 21–5
  our mother's death 242–8
  in R.A.F. 184
  relations with me 7, 83–5, 100,
    226

Paul, George 210
Paul, Margaret 223
Pedgrift, Francie (my great aunt)
  and family 9–11, 90, 139–40
Phoenix, Ann 273, 305
Pines, Malcolm 173–5
Pond, Desmond 259
Popper, Karl 221
PPE course 206–7, 209–12

Rayment, Ivy (my aunt) 7, 24–8, 90
Rayment, Kathleen (my cousin) 10,
    24–8
Rayment, Will (my uncle) 26
Reisz, Karel 172–3, 188, 191
Ryle, Anthony and family 186–94,
    204–7

Shapiro, Monte 233–4, 251, 254,
    256
Sinclair, Ian 297
Socialist Sunday Schools 67–70
Solantaus, Tytti 285
Somerville interview 187–8
Spikes, W. H. 91–2, 134–6, 150–2,
    177–80, 193, 225, 240–5
Springfield Hospital 256
St Andrews University 227–9,
    233–4
Staynes, Gillian 164–5

Strudwick, Miss 116, 157–9, 183
Symons, Teresa 119–29, 162, 164,
    187

Tanner, Vivienne 164–7
Taylor, A.J.P. 211
teenage culture 174
Thatcher, Margaret 199
Thomas Coram Research Unit 269,
    276–7
Tingle, Mary 235–6
Tizard, Jack (my husband)
  death 303
  at Institute of Education 261
  marries me 226
  at Maudsley Hospital 236–7, 251
  new father 249–50
  at Oxford 217–8, 221
  passion for work 258, 298–9
  research strategy 264
  at St Andrews University 223,
    227–9, 234
  starts T.C.R.U. 269
tutorial system, Oxford 203

Uytman, John 228, 230

V1s, V2s 191–2, 196

Waley, Isabel and family 121,
    123–4, 127–8, 162–3
Westminster Abbey Choir
  School 246
Wigg, Martin 174, 186, 188
Williams-Ashman, Guy 173–5
Wing, Lorna 260
Wycombe Abbey School 125–6

youth hostels 166, 209

Zaiman, Elisabeth 182–3, 188, 198